COPYRIGHT LAW

IN A NUTSHELL

By

MARY LaFRANCE
William S. Boyd Professor of Law
William S. Boyd School of Law
University of Nevada, Las Vegas

THOMSON

WEST

Mat #40497514

© 2008 Thomson/West
     610 Opperman Drive
     St. Paul, MN 55123
     1–800–313–9378

Printed in the United States of America

ISBN: 978–0–314–16928–0

TEXT IS PRINTED ON 10% POST CONSUMER RECYCLED PAPER

To Gail

*

PREFACE

This book is for anyone who needs a concise but thorough introduction to copyright law. It is aimed at lawyers, students, artists, authors, and businesspersons, as well as intelligent consumers who just want to know more about the copyright issues reported by the media.

Copyright law has grown increasingly complex over the years. Also, there are many misconceptions that are surprisingly persistent, and new misconceptions arising all the time. A better understanding of copyright law will prevent costly mistakes, avoid unnecessary litigation, encourage consumers to take an active interest in legislative proposals, and enable authors and artists to focus on their creative work without the distraction of legal entanglements.

The book assumes that the reader has no prior knowledge of copyright law, but it does not shy away from addressing aspects of the law which are ambiguous, in a state of flux, or the subject of conflicting opinions from courts and commentators. Where the law is still evolving, the text identifies the areas of uncertainty and the most recent authorities that have attempted a resolution. The text also notes areas where further legislation is needed or is currently under consideration.

Because federal copyright law is a creature of statute, every aspect of copyright law addressed in the book is accompanied by references to the pertinent statutes and, where appropriate, their legislative histories. The most important aspects of each statute are discussed in the text, so that the reader can derive a good understanding of the material from the text alone. However, all of the relevant statutory citations are included in the text for those who wish to develop their understanding further.

OUTLINE

XI

TABLE OF CASES

References are to Pages

XVII

TABLE OF CASES

COPYRIGHT LAW

IN A NUTSHELL

*

CHAPTER 1

INTRODUCTION

The Patent and Copyright Clause of the United States Constitution grants Congress the power "to Promote the Progress of Science and useful Arts, by securing for limited Times to Authors and Inventors the exclusive right to their respective Writings and Discoveries." U.S. CONST., art. 1, sec. 8, cl. 8. The first federal copyright statute was enacted in 1790. Since then, the legislative scheme has been revised many times.

The most recent comprehensive revision of the federal copyright laws culminated in the Copyright Act of 1976 (the "1976 Act"), which took effect on January 1, 1978, and which is codified, with amendments, in Title 17 of the United States Code. Perhaps the most significant change introduced by the 1976 Act was the elimination of common law copyright protection for fixed works of authorship. Under the Copyright Act of 1909 (the "1909 Act") and earlier federal statutes, unpublished works of authorship enjoyed perpetual common law copyright protection, a doctrine carried over from English law. For most works, federal copyright law did not apply until publication. In contrast, under the 1976 Act, federal copyright attached to an original work of authorship from the moment it was fixed in a tangible medium of expression. Thus, as of January 1, 1978, common law copyright was virtually eliminated. Moreover, any attempt by a state to provide its own equivalent of copyright protection to fixed works, published or not, was expressly preempted by federal law. Thereafter, only unfixed works could be protected by state copyright law.

Essential to federal (as opposed to common law) copyright is the concept of the limited term, which is required by the "limited Times" language of the Patent and Copyright Clause. Any work published before 1923 has now entered the public domain in the United States, due to expiration of its term of protection. However, many works published as early as 1923 are still protected by copyright. Indeed, the last works published under the 1909 Act will not enter the public domain until 2072.

Because copyright in works created or published prior to January 1, 1978, is governed in many respects by the 1909 Copyright Act, a copyright lawyer must be familiar with both the 1976 Act and the 1909 Act in order to accurately assess the current copyright status and ownership of these pre–1978 works. For that reason, although this text focuses on the 1976 Act, it also addresses those provisions of the 1909 Act that are essential to modern copyright practice. Except where otherwise indicated, all statutory references in this text refer to Title 17.

CHAPTER 2

COPYRIGHTABLE SUBJECT MATTER

§ 2.1 Original Works of Authorship

Subject to limited exceptions in § 104 (foreign works) and § 105 (United States government works), the fundamental rules regarding copyrightable subject matter are established by § 102.

Under current law, compliance with formalities is not a prerequisite to copyright protection. Thus, a work that satisfies § 102 is protected by federal copyright from the moment it is fixed in a tangible medium of expression, without regard to whether it bears a copyright notice or has been registered. However, as discussed in Chapter 9, in order to *enforce* his or her exclusive rights through an infringement proceeding, the copyright owner is typically required to register the copyright, and as discussed in Chapter 4, copyright notice and registration offer additional benefits.

Section 102(a) sets forth the standard for determining whether a work is eligible for copyright protection. It provides that copyright subsists "in original works of authorship fixed in any tangible medium of expression, now known or later developed, from which they can be perceived, reproduced, or otherwise communicated, either directly or with the aid of a machine or device." The legislative history sums this up by saying: "Two essential elements—original work and tangible object—must merge through fixation in order to produce subject matter copyrightable under the statute." H.R. Rep. No. 94–1476, 94th Cong., 2d Sess. 53 (1976).

If a work satisfies these requirements, it is automatically protected by copyright until the copyright expires. Thus, copyright subsists in any work that satisfies § 102(a), unless excluded by § 104 or § 105, until the term of copyright has been exhausted. This is true regardless of whether the author registers the copyright, includes a notice of copyright on the work, or undertakes any other formal steps to "protect" the copyright.

The key concepts in § 102(a) are originality, works of authorship, and fixation.

A. Originality

A work must be original in order to be copyrightable. As discussed below, "original" means (1) not copied, and (2) at least minimally creative.

Although the Copyright Clause of the Constitution does not use the word "original," the Supreme Court has repeatedly held that originality is constitutionally required for copyright protection. In the *Trade-Mark Cases,* 100 U.S. (10 Otto) 82 (1879), the Court struck down one of Congress's early attempts at trademark legislation, holding, *inter alia*, that Congress could not rely on the Copyright Clause for its authority to protect trademarks. Trademarks are often unoriginal, and in the Court's view, the framers' use of the terms "authors" and "writings" in the Copyright Clause indicated their intent to limit copyright (and patent) protection to works that are original:

> In this, as in regard to inventions, originality is required. And while the word writings may be liberally construed, as it has been to include original designs for engravings, prints, & c., it is only such as are original, and are founded in the creative powers of the mind. The writings which are to be protected are the fruits of intellectual labor, embodied in the form of books, prints, engravings, and the like.

100 U.S. at 94.

In *Burrow-Giles Lithographic Co. v. Sarony*, 111 U.S. 53 (1884), the Court upheld Congress's grant of copyright protection to photographs, holding that even a mechanical reproduction of a real-life subject can be original enough to constitute a "writing." The Court held that copyright can extend to any works that are "original intellectual conceptions of the author," and that any person claiming copyright protection must prove "the existence of these facts of originality, of intellectual production, of thought, and conception." *Id.* at 58.

Even mundane works, works used primarily for advertising, and works that accurately depict real-life subject matter can satisfy the originality requirement. In *Bleistein v. Donaldson Lithographing*

Co., 188 U.S. 239 (1903), the Court upheld copyright protection in circus posters:

> [E]ven if they had been drawn from the life, that fact would not deprive them of protection. The opposite proposition would mean that a portrait by Velasquez or Whistler was common property because others might try their hand on the same face. Others are free to copy the original. They are not free to copy the copy. The copy is the personal reaction of an individual upon nature. Personality always contains something unique. It expresses its singularity even in handwriting, and a very modest grade of art has in it something irreducible, which is one man's alone. That something he may copyright unless there is a restriction in the words of the act.

Id. at 249–50.

Nor is copyright denied to works of dubious artistic merit or works depicting controversial subject matter, as long as they contain original expression: "It would be a dangerous undertaking for persons trained only to the law to constitute themselves final judges of the worth of pictorial illustrations, outside of the narrowest and most obvious limits." *Id.* at 251. On this basis, courts have upheld copyright protection for "obscene" films. *Mitchell Bros. Film Group v. Cinema Adult Theater,* 604 F.2d 852 (5th Cir. 1979).

In *Feist Publications v. Rural Telephone Service,* 499 U.S. 340 (1991), the Supreme Court held that a work must meet two requirements to satisfy the constitutional standard of originality: (1) the work must be independently created by the author (that is, not simply copied from another work), and (2) it must possess at least a minimal degree of creativity. The *Feist* Court stressed that only a modicum of creativity is required:

> To be sure, the requisite level of creativity is extremely low; even a slight amount will suffice. The vast majority of works make the grade quite easily, as they possess some creative spark, "no matter how crude, humble, or obvious it might be."

Feist, 499 U.S. at 345. The Court also distinguished originality from novelty:

> [A] work may be original even though it closely resembles other works so long as the similarity is fortuitous, not the result of copying. To illustrate, assume that two poets, each ignorant of the other, compose identical poems. Neither work is novel, yet both are original and, hence, copyrightable.

Id. at 345–46.

Although the Copyright Clause of the Constitution uses the term "writings," § 102(a) uses the term "original works of authorship" instead. The legislative history indicates that Congress deliberately left the latter term undefined, but intended "to incorporate without change the standard of originality established by the courts" under the 1909 Act, a standard that "does not include requirements of novelty, ingenuity, or esthetic merit." H.R. Rep. No. 94–1476, 94th Cong., 2d Sess. 51 (1976).

B. Works of Authorship

The copyright statutes do not define works of authorship. Congress used the term "original works of authorship" in § 102, rather than the broader term "writings," in order to avoid exhausting its constitutional power to define copyrightable expression, and to eliminate the uncertainties that had arisen due to the use of the term "writings" in the 1909 Act, which defined copyrightable subject matter as "all the writings of an author."

Although § 102(a) lists eight specific categories of copyrightable expression, this list is illustrative rather than exhaustive. The legislative indicates that Congress did not intend "to freeze the scope of copyright of copyrightable subject matter" into those forms of expression that were known in 1976, but rather intended to create a flexible standard that would encompass new and unforeseen forms of expression.

Despite the broad scope of "works of authorship," it is generally understood that copyright does not extend to expressive content that is truly *de minimis*. *Feist Publications v. Rural Telephone Service*, 499 U.S. 340, 359 (1991) (noting "a narrow category of works in which the creative spark is utterly lacking or so trivial as to be virtually nonexistent"). For example, Copyright Office Regulations state that "words and short phrases such as names, titles, and slogans; familiar symbols or designs; mere variations of typographical ornamentation, lettering or coloring; mere listing of ingredients or contents" are not copyrightable. 37 C.F.R. § 202.1(a). In general, courts have upheld these regulatory exclusions.

As discussed in greater detail in § 2.3 below, § 102(b) makes clear that works of authorship do not include abstract ideas or the utilitarian aspects of useful articles.

C. Fixation

Under § 102(a), original works of authorship are copyrightable if they are "fixed in any tangible medium of expression, now known or later developed, from which they can be perceived, reproduced, or otherwise communicated, either directly or with the aid of a machine or device."

As this language makes clear, copyright does not extend to unrecorded performances or conversations. (These can be protected by state law, although little authority exists.) The concept of fixation is implicit in the term "writings" in the Copyright Clause, and fixation is therefore constitutionally required. Section 102(a) simply makes this requirement explicit.

Fixation is important not only because it determines *whether* a work is copyrightable, but also because, under the 1976 Act, it determines *when* copyright protection begins. Under the 1909 Act, common law copyright protected a fixed work until publication, at which point the work either entered the public domain or began its term of federal copyright protection. Under the 1976 Act, federal copyright protection begins at the moment of fixation, thus leaving no scope for common law protection of fixed works.

Fixation may be in any tangible medium of expression. The medium need not make the copyrightable work directly perceptible by humans; it is enough that it can be made perceptible by a machine. For example, the copyrightable content of phonorecords, whether in the form of records, audio tapes, CDs, or mp3 files, cannot be perceived by humans without the use of a machine. The same is true of any digitized works. The reference to "any method now known or later developed" reflects Congress's recognition in 1976 that changes in technology would lead to new media of expression, and its intent not to foreclose copyright protection for works embodied in those later-developed media.

The fixation need not be permanent. As defined in § 101, a work is "fixed" when its tangible embodiment is "sufficiently permanent or stable to permit it to be perceived, reproduced, or otherwise communicated for a period of more than transitory duration." Accordingly, all of the following works are fixed: an ice sculpture, a drawing on a paper napkin, a design on the icing of a cake, and material stored in a computer hard drive.

The phrase "more than transitory duration" raises the question whether material stored only in a computer's short-term memory, or RAM, satisfies the fixation requirement. In contrast to the hard drive, storage in RAM is temporary, and ends when the computer is turned off. In theory, at least, an infringement claim could arise if an observer photographed or otherwise copied material that was temporarily visible on the computer's screen. The 1976 House Report states that the concept of fixation excludes "purely evanescent or transient reproductions such as those projected briefly on a screen, shown electronically on a television or other cathode ray tube, or captured momentarily in the 'memory' of a computer." H.R. Rep. No. 94–1476, 94th Cong., 2d Sess. 51 (1976). Although this implies that material stored only in RAM is not fixed, in 1978 a Congressionally-authorized commission of experts disagreed with this conclusion. Because this question arises most often in the context of determining whether unauthorized RAM storage can give rise to infringement liability for copying, this topic is addressed more fully in § 7.2 below.

As a result of the fixation requirement, an unscripted live event, such as a football game, is ordinarily not eligible for copyright protection. In contrast, a recording of that event is copyrightable. This means that federal copyright law would not prevent a spectator from recording a football game as it happened, but if the football team authorized someone to record the event, then the recording itself would be copyrighted.

Because of the fixation requirement, a live unrecorded broadcast is not protected by copyright. Nonetheless, there is a way in which broadcasters can obtain copyright protection for their live transmissions, such as sporting events. The last sentence of the definition of "fixation" provides: "A work consisting of sounds, images, or both, that are being transmitted, is 'fixed' for purposes of this title if a fixation of the work is being made simultaneously with its transmission." Congress included this language at the urging of broadcasters. Under this rule, a live broadcast is eligible for copyright protection if it is simultaneously recorded by or under the authority of the copyright owner. This means that if a person viewing the live broadcast makes an unauthorized recording of that broadcast, he or she is copying a copyrighted work, and is potentially liable for infringement.

It should also be noted that copying a live event may run afoul of copyright laws if the event involves the performance of a copyrighted work. If a person records a live concert or stage play, for example, he or she is creating a copy not only of the live, uncopyrighted performance, but also of the underlying musical or dramatic work that is being performed. Thus, it would be an overstatement to say that live performances have no copyright protection at all.

Certain live performances are eligible for protection under § 1101 of Title 17, which is not a copyright provision. See § 7.9 below.

In addition to be being tangible and more than transitory, in order for a fixation to qualify for copyright protection, it must be made "by or under the authority of the author." Most authors do their own fixations—for example, a writer may write by hand or on a computer or typewriter, a painter paints, a sculpture sculpts, and a composer may write out sheet music by hand or else compose on the piano while capturing the sounds on a tape recorder. However, the fixation may also be made under the author's authority—a writer may dictate, a bedridden sculptor may give detailed instructions to able-bodied assistants, or a musician may ask someone else to record his or her live performance. In contrast, a recording of a live performance that is made without the author's consent does not give rise to a copyrightable work. It is possible, however, that a court might give effect to an author's subsequent ratification of an unauthorized recording.

The tangible embodiment in which a copyrighted work is fixed is either a "copy" or a "phonorecord." The term "phonorecord" refers *only* to fixations of sound recordings; all other copyrightable fixations are "copies." Both terms apply not only to the original tangible embodiment of the work (for example, an original painting is a "copy" in copyright parlance), but also to tangible reproductions of the work (such as posters or lithographs of the painting). Except for the fact that phonorecords are limited to sound recordings, "copies" and "phonorecords" have identical definitions in § 101. These definitions closely track the language of § 102(a):

"Copies" are material objects, other than phonorecords, in which a work is fixed by any method now known or later developed, and from which the work can be perceived, reproduced, or otherwise communicated, either directly or with the aid of a machine or device.

§ 2.2   Categories of Copyrightable Works

As discussed above, § 102(a) states the general rule that any original work of authorship fixed in a tangible medium of expression is copyrightable, starting at the moment of fixation. However, to determine the exclusive rights of the copyright owner, it is often necessary to determine which type of copyrightable work has been created. For that reason, copyright law recognizes various categories of copyrightable works.

Copyrightable works are categorized in several ways—by subject matter (addressed here), by the type of authorship entity that produced the work (Chapter 3), and by the type of process through which the author(s) created the work (§ 2.8 and § 2.9 below).

Subject Matter Categories

Section 102(a) of the 1976 Act provides a non-exhaustive list of eight types of works that are copyrightable:

(1) literary works;

(2) musical works, including any accompanying words;

(3) dramatic works, including any accompanying music;

(4) pantomimes and choreographic works;

(5) pictorial, graphic, and sculptural works;

(6) motion pictures and other audiovisual works;

(7) sound recordings; and

(8) architectural works.

Because the list of categories is illustrative rather than comprehensive, a work that satisfies the general definition in section 102(a) will be copyrightable even if does not appear to fit into one of these categories. However, the list serves two purposes: (1) By including a particular type of work on the list, Congress eliminated any ambiguity about whether works of that type are eligible for copyright protection, and (2) by creating subject matter categories, Congress has been able, elsewhere in the copyright statutes, to assign different levels of copyright protection to different types of subject matter. In other words, in copyright law, one size does not fit all—the exclusive rights of the owner of copyright in a sound recording, for example, are different from the exclusive rights of the owner of the copyright in a novel.

Some of these categories are statutorily defined in § 101, while others have meanings that are based on common usage and/or judicial interpretation.

Literary works

Section 101 defines literary works as "works, other than audiovisual works, expressed in words, numbers, or other verbal or numerical symbols or indicia, regardless of the nature of the material objects, such as books, periodicals, manuscripts, phonorecords, films, tapes, disks, or cards, in which they are embodied."

This category includes all types of computer software—operating system software and applications software. It includes underlying code of video games, but it does not include the resulting screen displays, which are categorized as audiovisual works. Copyright applies to both object code and source code.

Musical works

The statutes do not define musical works, but it is well settled that this category includes instrumental works as well as works that combine music and lyrics. Musical works become "fixed" for copyright purposes when they are either written down in musical notations or recorded on audible media (analog or digital).

However, musical works are copyrightable separately from the actual audio recordings of those works, which fall into the category of sound recordings. As discussed in Chapters 7 and 8, the copyright laws applicable to sound recordings differ significantly from those which apply to musical works. When the first tangible fixation of a musical work takes the form of an audio recording, two copyrightable works—the musical work and the sound recording—are created simultaneously.

Although the term "nondramatic musical works" is used extensively in the copyright statutes (in §§ 110, 112, 115, 116, and 118), it has no statutory definition. This is not altogether surprising, since the statutes also do not define "musical works" or "dramatic works." It is trivial to say that a nondramatic musical work is any musical work *other than* a dramatic musical work. However, neither the statutes nor the case law provide a clear understanding of what constitutes a *dramatic* musical work.

In general, dramatic musical works are considered to be any musical works that were created as part of a dramatic work, such as an opera or musical play. The exact contours of this definition are unclear, however. For example, it remains uncertain whether a dramatic musical work must be fully integrated with the story-telling aspect of the dramatic work it accompanies (as in a typical opera) or whether it is enough that it serves as a musical interlude in a dramatic work (as in some musical plays) or as background music in a motion picture. It is also unclear whether a dramatic musical work might become a nondramatic musical work once it has been exploited separately from its dramatic context (for example, once an individual song has been released on a phonorecord).

Dramatic works

As noted above, dramatic works do not have a statutory definition, but this category includes stage plays, radio scripts, screenplays and teleplays. When a dramatic work is recorded, the recording is separately copyrightable, either as a sound recording (if there is no visual component) or as an audiovisual work.

Pantomimes and choreographic works

This category also lacks a statutory definition, but the terms are given their commonplace meaning. Works of this nature can be "fixed" for copyright purposes either by written notations or by visual recording media.

Pictorial, graphic, and sculptural works

Section 101 provides an elaborate statutory definition for this class of works:

"Pictorial, graphic, and sculptural works" include two-dimensional and three-dimensional works of fine, graphic, and applied art, photographs, prints and art reproductions, maps, globes, charts, diagrams, models, and technical drawings, including architectural plans. Such works shall include works of artistic craftsmanship insofar as their form but not their mechanical or utilitarian aspects are concerned; the design of a useful article, as defined in this section, shall be considered a pictorial, graphic, or sculptural work only if, and only to the extent that, such design incorporates pictorial, graphic, or sculptural features that can be identified separately from, and are capable of existing independently of, the utilitarian aspects of the article.

The second sentence of this definition, referring to works of artistic craftsmanship, draws a distinction between design elements that are dictated by artistic considerations, which are copyrightable, and those that are utilitarian features of an article, which are not copyrightable. This distinction is examined in § 2.4 below.

Motion pictures and other audiovisual works

Both of these related categories of works have statutory definitions. As the definitions make clear, audiovisual works are the broader of the two categories. Specifically, audiovisual works are the genus of which motion pictures are one species.

Section 101 defines audiovisual works as "works that consist of a series of related images which are intrinsically intended to be shown by the use of machines or devices such as projectors, viewers, or electronic equipment, together with accompanying sounds, if any, regardless of the nature of the material objects, such as films or tapes, in which the works are embodied."

Motion pictures are a subcategory of audiovisual works, "consisting of series of related images which, when shown in succession, impart an impression of motion, together with accompanying sounds, if any." Motion pictures include theatrical films and television shows (whether on film, video, digital, or other media), music videos, television commercials, audiovisual recordings of live events such as news or sporting events, and video game screen displays. Although the term motion pictures includes all of the audio aspects of a motion picture, it does not encompass aural recordings that have no visual component; these are instead classified as sound recordings.

As these definitions indicate, the only difference between motion pictures and other audiovisual works is that the series of related images that make up a motion picture are shown in a way that conveys an impression of motion. In contrast, an audiovisual work can consist of a series of static images displayed in succession, such as a slide show or PowerPoint presentation.

A motion picture or other audiovisual work need not have an aural component. Thus, a silent film qualifies as an audiovisual work and, specifically, as a motion picture.

Note that, with respect to the "series of related images" that comprise motion pictures and other audiovisual works, a single image, separated from the others in the series, constitutes a pictorial work. Thus, for example, a still image from a motion picture, a static PowerPoint image, or a single animation "gel," would each be a pictorial work.

Sound recordings

Section 101 defines sound recordings as "works that result from the fixation of a series of musical, spoken, or other sounds, but not including the sounds accompanying a motion picture or other audiovisual work, regardless of the nature of the material objects, such as disks, tapes, or other phonorecords, in which they are embodied."

Although musical recordings (whether on vinyl, tapes, or CDs) are the most familiar category of sound recordings, any audio recording that does not have a visual component is a sound recording. Thus, this category includes such works as books-on-tape, foreign language educational tapes, and recordings of natural sounds such as bird calls or ocean waves.

In the case of musical recordings, it is important to distinguish the copyright in the sound recording from the copyright in the underlying musical work. A sound recording captures a specific performance of a musical work. Typically, the copyright in the musical work and the copyright in a sound recording of that work are owned by separate persons. The copyright in a sound recording is normally owned by the record company that produced the recording. The copyright in the underlying musical composition may be owned by the author(s) of the music and lyrics, or by an assignee of the author(s)—typically a music publisher. A single copyrighted musical work may be recorded many times, resulting in many copyrighted sound recordings.

For example, in 1973 Dolly Parton wrote the music and lyrics for the song "I Will Always Love You." She is therefore the author of the musical work, and she either owns the copyright or has assigned it to a music publisher. She made the first sound recording of that song in 1973, and a second one in 1982. The copyright in each of these recordings is owned by the record company that produced it. Several other artists have made their own recordings of the song as well. The best known of these "cover" versions is Whitney Houston's 1992 recording. Each of these sound recordings enjoys a separate copyright. Thus, in this example, there is just one copyrighted musical work, but many copyrighted sound recordings of that work. Each of these copyrights has a separate owner and a separate expiration date. The rights of the copyright owners are somewhat different as well, because copyright law grants different rights to the owners of musical works than to the owners of sound recordings.

Congress first extended copyright protection to sound recordings in the Sound Recording Act of 1971. However, protection was not retroactive. Therefore, sound recordings fixed prior to February 15, 1972, are not protected by federal copyright law, although they may be protected by state law. As discussed in § 5.8 below, state courts and legislatures have recently begun clarifying the scope of state law protection for these older sound recordings.

Architectural Works

An architectural work is "the design of a building as embodied in any tangible medium of expression, including a building, architectural plans, or drawings." Copyright extends to the "overall form as well as the arrangement and composition of spaces and elements in the design," but not to "individual standard features."

The category of architectural works was added to § 102 by the Architectural Works Protection Act of

1990. Prior to 1990, architectural works were protected as "pictorial, graphic, and sculptural works," and even today that category encompasses "diagrams, models, and technical drawings, including architectural plans." Thus, as a result of the 1990 amendments, architectural works now enjoy protection under both categories. The 1990 legislation was necessary to comply with the Berne Convention, which required signatory countries to provide copyright protection for architectural designs as embodied in the buildings themselves, distinct from drawings, sketches, or models. In addition, prior to 1990 it was not clear whether copying a design from the building itself (rather than from drawings or plans) was copyright infringement. The addition of architectural works as a separate category makes clear that the building itself is a fixation that gives rise to copyright protection. Furthermore, when an architectural work is embodied in plans or drawings, it is protected both as an architectural work and as a pictorial, graphic, and sculptural work.

The legislative history of the 1990 legislation indicates that, in creating a separate category for architectural works, Congress intended to make the problematic "useful articles" analysis (see § 2.4 below) inapplicable to architectural works. In place of the "physical or conceptual separability" test that applies to useful articles, the copyrightability of architectural works is determined through a two-step analysis: First, the work must have original design elements, including the overall shape and interior architecture. Second, if such original elements are present, it must be determined whether they are functionally required. If they are not functionally required, then the architectural design is protected, and may be registered, without regard to physical or conceptual separability. The legislative history notes that, in contrast to useful articles, the "aesthetically pleasing overall shape of an architectural work" may be protected by copyright.

Copyright in an architectural work does extend to any elements that are functionally required. According to the legislative history, "[e]vidence that there is more than one method of obtaining a given functional result may be considered" in determining whether a particular element is functionally required.

The definition of "architectural works" refers specifically to the design of a "building." Congress chose this word instead of the broader term "three-dimensional structure" in order to make clear that architectural works do not include such structures as bridges, cloverleafs, canals, dams, and pedestrian walkways, because the Berne Convention did not mandate protection for non-habitable structures. According to the legislative history, the term "building" includes habitable structures such as houses and office buildings, as well as structures that are used but not inhabited by humans, such as churches, pergolas, gazebos, and garden pavilions.

§ 2.3   The Idea/Expression Dichotomy

Section 102(b) provides that copyright does not extend "to any idea, procedure, process, system, method of operation, concept, principle, or discovery, regardless of the form in which it is described, explained, illustrated, or embodied in such work." The rule that copyright does not protect ideas is often referred to as the "idea/expression dichotomy." This principle is derived from the Supreme Court's decision in *Baker v. Selden*, 101 U.S. (11 Otto) 99 (1879), which held that, under copyright law, the copyright owner of a book explaining a system of accounting could prohibit others from copying the original expression contained in the book, but could not prohibit them from copying the accounting system itself. *See also Mazer v. Stein*, 347 U.S. 201, 217 (1954) ("Unlike a patent, a copyright gives no exclusive right to the art disclosed; protection is given only to the expression of the idea—not the idea itself.").

The idea/expression dichotomy is important in determining the extent of copyright protection in the *nonliteral* elements of a work. It is clear, for example, that one who copies the exact words of a copyrighted novel is copying protected expression. It is less clear, however, whether copyright also extends to the plot and characters of that novel. At a high level of abstraction, elements like plot and character are simply abstract ideas. For example, the idea of a group of criminals stealing money from the vault of a Las Vegas casino is highly abstract. Similarly, the idea of a superhero who can fly is also quite abstract. But elements such as plot and character are not totally ineligible for copyright protection. The difference lies in the level of detail which the accused infringer has copied. If the story line of the film *Oceans 11* (the original or the remake) is copied at a high level of detail, a court is likely to conclude that the accused infringer copied protected expression rather than abstract ideas. Likewise, if the appearance and characteristics of the Superman character are reproduced in great detail, that, too, is likely to be treated as copying of protected expression. The difference is simply one of degree. The more details that are copied, the more likely it is that the copying involves copyrightable expression rather than uncopyrightable ideas. Although the general concept of this distinction is easy to understand, determining where to draw the line on a particular set of facts can be difficult.

The idea/expression dichotomy is also important in the protection of nonfiction works, such as the accounting text in *Baker v. Selden*. If a historian writes a book which purports to solve the mystery of the Hindenburg explosion or the disappearance of Jimmy Hoffa, both the historical facts and the historian's original theory explaining them are unprotected by copyright; even though the theory is original, it is considered an idea rather than expression.

Computer software can present particularly difficult problems in distinguishing idea from expression. Copyright in computer software extends not only to the literal code, but also to any creative choices that the programmer makes in determining the structure, sequence, and organization of each section of code; however, courts have had great difficulty distinguishing a program's abstract ideas from its copyrightable expression. One court went so far as to hold that a menu command hierarchy was ineligible for copyright protection under § 102(b), because it constituted a "method of operation." *Lotus Development Corp. v. Borland Int'l, Inc.,* 49 F.3d 807 (1st Cir. 1995), *aff'd by an equally divided court,* 516 U.S. 233 (1996). At the highest level of abstraction, of course, all computer programs are methods of operation. The same can be said of any set of instructions—like an accounting textbook—but there may still be elements of copyrightable expression within those instructions. The decision in *Lotus* has been criticized for failing to recognize that a computer program is a particularized *expression* of a method of operation, just as the accounting text in *Baker v. Selden* was a particularized expression of a method of accounting.

As discussed below, other specific applications of the idea/expression dichotomy can be found in the "useful articles" analysis and the merger doctrine.

§ 2.4   Useful Articles

When copyright was first extended to three-dimensional works of art in 1870, protection was limited to works of fine art. The 1909 Act, however, replaced the term "works of fine art" with the broader term "works of art," to make clear that copyright extended not only to the traditional fine arts but also to works of applied art. Starting in 1948, Copyright Office regulations allowed registration of "works of artistic craftsmanship insofar as their form but not their utilitarian aspects are concerned."

In *Mazer v. Stein*, 347 U.S. 201 (1954), the Supreme Court upheld these Copyright Office regulations, holding that artistic works embodied or reproduced in articles of manufacture did not lose their eligibility for copyright protection. *Mazer* involved male and female statuettes intended for use as lamp bases, with electric wiring, sockets, and lamp shades attached. Although it appeared that the statuettes might also be eligible for design patent protection, the Court held that neither design patent eligibility nor the intended or actual use of an artistic work in an article of manufacture foreclosed copyright protection for the artistic aspects of the work. The Copyright Office regulations were revised in 1954 to specify that, in the case of a utilitarian article, the only features eligible for copyright registration were those that could be "identified separately" and were "capable of existing independently as a work of art."

In the Copyright Act of 1976, Congress codified the principles of *Mazer* and the Copyright Office regulations by introducing the concept of a "useful article" in the § 101 definition of "pictorial, graphic, and sculptural works."

Generally speaking, useful articles are objects which have a utilitarian function. In some cases, these articles have an artistic component as well. Determining whether a useful article is copyrightable can be difficult because, under the idea/expression dichotomy as codified in 102(b), copyright does not extend to ideas or methods of operation; thus, while the purely artistic elements of a useful article are copyrightable, the purely utilitarian aspects are not.

By articulating a specific standard for copyright in useful articles in the 1976 Act, Congress was attempting to draw as clear a line as possible between copyrightable works of applied art (such as the statuettes used as lamp bases in *Mazer*) and uncopyrightable products of industrial design. As discussed below, however, the hoped-for clarity has not been achieved.

Useful articles are a subset of pictorial, graphic, and sculptural works. Section 101 defines a useful article as "an article having an intrinsic utilitarian function that is not merely to portray the appearance of the article or to convey information." Thus, a globe or map is not a useful article. Examples of items identified as useful articles in case law or the legislative history of § 101 include a bicycle rack, a belt buckle, eyeglass display cases, automobile wire wheel covers, automobiles, airplanes, dresses, food processors, television sets, and bedroom slippers made to look like bear paws. Courts routinely hold that clothing items are useful articles. Although the Second Circuit held that a clothing display mannequin shaped like a human torso was a useful article in *Carol Barnhart, Inc. v. Economy Cover Corp.*, 773 F.2d 411 (2d Cir. 1985), it reached the opposite conclusion with respect to fish mannequins used by taxidermists to mount fish skins in *Hart v. Dan*

Chase Taxidermy Supply Co., Inc., 86 F.3d 320 (2d Cir. 1996) (distinguishing *Carol Barnhart*), as did the Fourth Circuit with respect to taxidermists' animal mannequins in *Superior Form Builders, Inc. v. Dan Chase Taxidermy Supply Co., Inc.*, 74 F.3d 488 (4th Cir. 1996) (also distinguishing *Carol Barnhart*). According to the latter decisions, the utilitarian function of the fish and animal mannequins was to portray the appearance of the animal, and this placed them outside of the "useful articles" category, like a globe or a map.

The statutory test for determining whether a useful article is copyrightable is set forth in the § 101, where the definition of pictorial, graphic, and sculptural works provides that:

> Such works shall include works of artistic craftsmanship insofar as their form but not their mechanical or utilitarian aspects are concerned; the design of a useful article, as defined in this section, shall be considered a pictorial, graphic, or sculptural work only if, and only to the extent that, such design incorporates pictorial, graphic, or sculptural features that can be identified separately from, and are capable of existing independently of, the utilitarian aspects of the article.

The 1976 legislative history expands on this "separability" test, denying copyright to the shape of an industrial product unless that shape "contains some element that, physically or conceptually, can be identified as separable from the utilitarian aspects of that article;" it is not sufficient that the overall shape of the industrial product is aesthetically pleasing and valuable. If the product contains aesthetic elements that can be identified separately from its utilitarian features, copyright applies, but only to the aesthetic elements.

Most courts, including the influential Second Circuit, place great emphasis on the requirement of physical or conceptual separability in evaluating the copyrightability of useful articles Although physical separability has not been difficult to assess, courts continue to have difficulty defining and applying conceptual separability.

Separately identifiable aesthetic elements have been found in decorative belt buckles, *Kieselstein-Cord v. Accessories by Pearl, Inc.,* 632 F.2d 989, 993 (2d Cir. 1980), bedroom slippers shaped like bear paws, *Animal Fair, Inc. v. AMFESCO Indus., Inc.,* 620 F.Supp. 175 (D. Minn. 1985), female face mannequins (with the "hungry look" of a runway model) used in training hair and make-up stylists, *Pivot Point Intern., Inc. v. Charlene Prods., Inc.,* 372 F.3d 913 (7th Cir. 2004), and animal mannequins used by taxidermists to mount animal skins, *Superior Form Builders, supra* (alternative holding). Separately identifiable aesthetic elements were found to be lacking in life-sized human torso forms for displaying clothing, *Carol Barnhart, supra,* a curved bicycle rack, *Brandir International, Inc. v. Cascade Pacific Lumber Co.,* 834 F.2d 1142 (2d Cir. 1987), and an outdoor lighting fixture, *Esquire, Inc. v. Ringer,* 591 F.2d 796 (D.C. Cir. 1978).

All of these cases except *Esquire* relied specifically on the conceptual separability test. Few courts, however, have adopted a precise formulation of that test. Recent decisions of the Second Circuit, after considering and rejecting several formulations, have held that conceptual separability should be found where "design elements can be identified as reflecting the designer's artistic judgment exercised independently of functional influences." *Brandir,* 834 F.2d at 1145. Under this approach, courts examine the creative process, and determine which creative decisions were motivated by aesthetic concerns, and which by utilitarian concerns. The curved bicycle rack in *Brandir,* for example, was held to be uncopyrightable because, while it had its genesis in a wire sculpture, the designer then altered the overall shape of the design to make it usable as a bicycle rack. The Second Circuit's approach was endorsed by the Seventh Circuit in *Pivot Point, supra.*

§ 2.5   Merger

The merger doctrine is a judicially-developed application of the idea/expression dichotomy. Courts apply merger when idea and expression are so intertwined that extending copyright to the expression will have the impermissible effect of extending copyright to the idea itself. In such cases, courts will invoke the merger doctrine to withhold copyright protection from the expression. Courts invoke merger when there are so few ways to express a particular idea that protecting one such expression would make it difficult for others to express the same idea.

Although the merger doctrine is said to have originated in a case that rejected a claim of copyright in a jeweled bee pin, *Herbert Rosenthal Jewelry Corp. v. Kalpakian*, 446 F.2d 738 (9th Cir. 1971), better examples of the doctrine can be found in *Baker v. Selden,* 101 U.S. 99 (1879) (denying copyright protection to ruled ledger pages necessary to practice a particular method of accounting), *Kern River Gas Transmission Co. v. Coastal Corp.*, 899 F.2d 1458 (5th Cir. 1990) (denying copyright protection to portion of a map depicting the only government-approved location for a proposed pipeline), and *Veeck v. Southern Bldg. Code Congress Int'l, Inc.*, 293 F.3d 791 (5th Cir. 2002) (en banc) (denying copyright protection to model codes enacted as laws).

The more utilitarian the expression, the more likely it is that merger will apply. Merger often applies to recipes, simple instructions, contest rules, and simple legal or business forms. Merger is frequently invoked in determining the scope of copyright protection for portions of computer software, where there may be only one or very few ways to achieve the programmer's goal—the efficient expression of a particular instruction. *See, e.g., Computer Associates Int'l, Inc. v. Altai, Inc.*, 982 F.2d 693 (2d Cir. 1992).

The question whether merger applies in a given situation often depends on how broadly a court defines the "idea" underlying the expression. The more broadly the idea is defined, the less likely it is that merger will apply, because there are likely to be multiple ways to express such a broad idea. For example, the Third Circuit found merger inapplicable to a computer program where the idea of the program was, in the court's view, "the efficient management of a dental laboratory," and there were many ways to express the instructions necessary for a computer to achieve this broad result. *Whelan Assocs., Inc. v. Jaslow Dental Lab., Inc.*, 797 F.2d 1222, 1236 n.28 (3d Cir. 1986). If indeed there is only one idea underlying any computer program, merger will almost never apply to software. In contrast, the court in *Computer Associates, supra*, declined to identify one idea for an entire computer program, and instead instructed the district court to break the program into its component parts and to determine whether there were multiple ways to express the idea underlying each component part. Under this approach, the "idea" behind each portion of the software is likely to be more narrowly defined, and thus there is a greater likelihood that merger will render some portions of the software uncopyrightable.

Compilations are another context in which merger has been applied. Even if a compilation involves a sufficiently original selection or arrangement of facts to be eligible for copyright under *Feist* (see § 2.8 below), courts have sometimes applied the merger doctrine to deny copyright protection. (It may be sounder, however, to decide such cases on the ground that the principles underlying the particular selection and arrangement lack originality.)

More often, courts have declined to apply the merger doctrine to compilations. In some cases, courts have found that there are multiple ways to express the idea underlying the compilation. In other cases, courts have declined to apply merger on the ground that the idea underlying a particular selection of materials is a subjective or "soft" idea, meaning an idea that involves "matters of taste and personal opinion." *See, e.g., Kregos v. Associated Press,* 937 F.2d 700 (2d Cir. 1991) (selection of nine pitching statistics as predictors of baseball game); *Eckes v. Card Prices Update,* 736 F.2d 859, 863 (2d Cir. 1984) (classification of certain baseball cards as "premium" cards); *CCC Information Services, Inc. v. Maclean Hunter Market Reports, Inc.,* 44 F.3d 61 (2d Cir. 1994) (database of used-car valuations). Courts have often expressed the concern that too liberal an application of the merger doctrine to compilations would swallow up the idea/expression dichotomy, and/or eviscerate the rule of § 103, which extends copyright to compilations that involve original selection and arrangement. Copyright in compilations is discussed in § 2.8 below.

Compilation copyrights have occasionally been asserted with respect to valuations—for example, commodity futures contract settlement prices and used car valuations. Claims of copyright in such numbers are based on the argument that the numbers are expressions of the author's conclusions based on underlying data. The Second Circuit has reached inconsistent conclusions in these cases; one panel held the merger doctrine inapplicable to used car valuations, treating them as "predictions" that were copyrightable because they were "infused with opinion," *CCC Information Services, Inc. v. Maclean Hunter Market Reports, Inc.*, 44 F.3d 61 (2d Cir. 1994), while a later panel both distinguished this holding and treated it as dicta in concluding that the merger doctrine precluded copyright protection for futures contract settlement prices, *New York Mercantile Exchange, Inc. v. IntercontinentalExchange, Inc.*, 497 F.3d 109 (2d Cir. 2007). The Ninth Circuit, however, embraced the earlier panel's approach, declining to apply merger to valuations of collectible coins in *CDN Inc. v. Kapes*, 197 F.3d 1256 (9th Cir. 1999).

§ 2.6 Laws, Model Codes, and Standards

The Supreme Court has consistently held, as a matter of public policy, that "the law" is not copyrightable. *See, e.g., Banks v. Manchester*, 128 U.S. 244 (1888). This principle applies to court decisions as well as statutes, regulations, and agency rulings.

In contrast, model codes—which are typically drafted by private nonprofit organizations—are copyrightable. Copyright protection ends, however, once the code has been adopted as law. At this point, courts have held that the merger doctrine applies. Because the precise wording of a statute is essential to its interpretation, the expression is inextricably intertwined with the underlying idea. Courts often express this conclusion by saying that the statute enters the public domain. *See, e.g., Veeck v. Southern Bldg. Code Congress Int'l, Inc.*,

293 F.3d 791 (5th Cir. 2002) (en banc) (referring to laws both as "facts" and as "ideas"). There are sometimes slight differences between the wording of a model code and the wording of the code as adopted; in that event, the code as adopted enters the public domain, but copyright continues to protect the model code itself.

At times, rather than enact a privately written set of standards into law, a government will simply adopt those standards by reference. For example, a government entity may adopt a privately-created set of medical codes for its medical reimbursement programs, may require auto insurance companies to use a specific publisher's list of used car values, may require attorneys practicing before its courts to use Blue Book citation formats and/or West reporter citations, or may dictate which textbooks will be used in its public schools. Courts have held that such official adoptions do not place the extrinsic standards in the public domain. In some situations, however, such an adoption could be a significant factor in favor of fair use. (Fair use is discussed at § 10.2 below.)

§ 2.7　Subject Matter Uncopyrightable Due to Origin

Some works are excluded from copyright protection due to their origins, even if they satisfy the requirements of § 102. These are works created by employees of the federal government, and certain works of foreign origin.

A. United States Government Works

Under § 105, copyright does not extend to any work prepared by an officer or employee of the federal government as part of his or her official duties. Thus, for example, reports issued by Congress and federal agencies are ineligible for copyright protection. However, this provision does not prevent the federal government from owning copyrights either by assignment or pursuant to work-made-for-hire agreements with independent contractors.

Section 105 does not apply to works created by employees of state governments. States may therefore own copyright in such works, subject to the judge-made rule that laws are ineligible for copyright protection, and the otherwise-applicable limitations on copyright, such as fair use. For example, if state employees prepare original teaching materials as part of their assigned duties, or if the state tourist bureau produces T-shirts and bumper stickers with copyrightable graphics, a defendant that copies and distributes those materials may be liable for infringement.

B. Works of Foreign Origin

Under § 104, unpublished works are protected by United States copyright laws, regardless of their country of origin.

In the case of published works, however, federal copyright protection depends on a work's country of origin, which is determined by the nationality or domicile of the author(s) and by the place of first publication. Generally speaking, copyright protection for published works under § 104 depends on whether those works originate in countries which respect copyright in works originating in the United States. Specifically, § 104(b) extends copyright protection to a published work that is otherwise eligible under § 102 and § 103, provided that:

(1) on the date of its first publication, at least one of the authors is a national or domiciliary of the United States, or a national, domiciliary, or sovereign authority of a treaty party, or a stateless person (regardless of domicile); or

(2) the work is first published in the United States or in a foreign nation that, on the date of first publication, is a treaty party; or

(3) the work is a sound recording that was first fixed in a country that is a treaty party; or

(4) the work is a pictorial, graphic, or sculptural work that is incorporated in a building or other structure, or an architectural work that is embodied in a building, and the building or structure is located in the United States or a treaty party; or

(5) the work is first published by the United Nations or any of its specialized agencies, or by the Organization of American States; or

(6) the work comes within the scope of a Presidential proclamation.

The term "treaty party" is defined in § 101 to include any foreign country or international organization that is a party to any of the following agreements: the Universal Copyright Convention (UCC), the Geneva Phonograms Convention, the Berne Convention, the WTO Agreement, the WIPO Copyright Treaty, the WIPO Performances and Phonograms Treaty, and any other copyright treaty to which the United States is a party.

For purposes of § 104(b)(2), if a work is published in the United States (or a treaty party) within thirty days after publication in a foreign nation that is not a treaty party, then the work is considered to have been first published in the United States (or such treaty party).

Finally, § 104(b)(6) recognizes that copyright protection may also be appropriate for works originating in certain foreign countries that do not qualify as treaty parties. Accordingly, this provision authorizes (but does not require) the President, by proclamation, to extend federal copyright protection to works originating in any foreign country which provides copyright protection for works originating in the United States.

§ 2.8 Compilations

A *compilation* is a work formed by the assembling of preexisting materials or data which are selected, coordinated, or arranged in such a way that the resulting work as a whole constitutes an original work of authorship. Examples include customer lists and directories (assuming originality).

Collective works are a subset of compilations in which the preexisting materials are separate and independent works in themselves. The preexisting works must be works of authorship that independently meet the standard of § 102; however, they may be copyrighted or they may have entered the public domain due to expiration of their copyright. Examples of collective works include newspapers, magazines, journals, encyclopedias, and anthologies. The person responsible for making the original selection and/or arrangement of materials in a collective work is considered the author of the collective work. However, the underlying works included in the collection are separate works of authorship, and the copyright in the underlying works remains separate from the copyright in the collective work.

A. General Scope of Compilation Copyright

Although compilations (including collective works) are copyrightable under § 103, the compilation copyright extends only to the original material contributed by the creator of the compilation; it does not extend to the underlying materials. Section 103 does not specify a standard for determining which compilations are copyrightable. Instead, the general rule of § 102(a) applies, as it does to all copyrightable works: The compilation must be an *original work of authorship fixed in a tangible medium of expression.*

Under the 1909 Act, federal courts often found compilations to be copyrightable regardless of originality, applying the "sweat of the brow" doctrine, which focused on the question whether the compiler invested significant effort in obtaining the underlying information used in the compilation. For example, if the compiler of a telephone directory simply copied information from another directory, the compiler's work was not copyrightable. But if the compiler went door-to-door collecting this information, the information contained in the resulting directory was copyrightable. Under the sweat of the brow doctrine, therefore, facts were copyrightable, provided they were obtained through independent research rather than copying.

In *Feist Publications v. Rural Telephone Service*, 499 U.S. 340 (1991), the Supreme Court squarely rejected the sweat of the brow theory. In this case, plaintiff Rural brought an infringement claim against defendant Feist after the latter copied names and telephone numbers from Rural's white pages telephone directory. Rural argued that, under the sweat of the brow theory, its copyright extended to the information contained in its directory, and Feist was therefore not permitted to copy this information, but was obliged to send its employees door-to-door, or conduct a telephone survey, in order to obtain this information through independent research. The Court rejected this argument, along with the entire sweat of the brow theory. Copyright, the Court held, does not protect facts, regardless of the effort involved in collecting those facts. Instead, copyright applies only to works that are *original*. Facts, the Court held, are not original, because they "do not owe their origin to an act of authorship." 499 U.S. at 347. To be "original" means to originate from an author. A work is sufficiently original to be copyrightable only if it satisfies two requirements: (1) it must be independently created (that is, not copied from another work), and (2) it must possess at least a minimum degree of creativity.

The requirement of originality, the Court held, is imposed by the Patent and Copyright Clause itself—specifically, the framers' use of the terms "Writings" and "Authors."

In the context of compilations, the requisite element of originality is supplied not by the effort or resourcefulness of the person obtaining the underlying facts or other materials, but by the compiler's creativity in determining the *selection* and *arrangement* of those materials:

> The compilation author typically chooses which facts to include, in what order to place them, and how to arrange the collected data so that they may be used effectively by readers. These choices as to selection and arrangement, so long as they are made independently by the compiler and entail a minimal degree of creativity, are sufficiently original that Congress may protect such compilations through the copyright laws.

Id. at 348. If the selection or arrangement of material is sufficiently original, then the compilation is copyrightable expression.

In addition to original selection and arrangement, copyright applies to other elements of original expression that are supplied by the creator of a compilation. For example, a report may consist largely of uncopyrightable data, but may also include some textual discussion. Likewise, a book of recipes consists largely of uncopyrightable information, but may also contain significant literary expression and/or illustrations.

In *Feist*, the Court noted that the degree of creativity necessary for a work to qualify for copyright is small. Even if the work contains no literary or artistic expression, it is possible that the selection and arrangement of data alone may possess the minimal creativity required. Because Rural contributed no literary or artistic expression to its directory, the only aspect of the directory that could possibly constitute copyrightable expression was the selection and arrangement of names and telephone numbers. However, the selection and arrangement of information in Rural's white pages directory did not possess even the minimal level of creativity required to constitute copyrightable expression. Rural did not make any creative decisions in selecting which information to include; it included the names and phone numbers of all of its customers (and, in fact, it was required to do so by local law). Nor did it arrange this information in a creative way; it merely listed the names alphabetically, a choice which the Court described as "practically inevitable." Any other arrangement would have made it difficult for customers to use the directory. By choosing the most obvious and commonplace arrangement for its listings, Rural produced a directory that was useful, but not creative.

If Rural had exercised even minimal creativity in selecting or arranging the information in its directory, then it would have been able to claim copyright protection for its work. Even then, however, the copyright would have extended only to Rural's original expression—the selection and arrangement of data. In no event would copyright have extended to the underlying facts themselves—the names and telephone numbers of Rural's customers.

Even if a compilation is sufficiently original to satisfy *Feist*, the resulting copyright may be "thin." In other words, where selection and arrangement are only minimally creative, a defendant who copies the plaintiff's work may be able to avoid infringement liability by making only minor changes in either the selection or arrangement of material. In general, factual works have weaker copyrights than highly artistic or fanciful works.

In contrast to Rural's white pages directory, it is possible that a "yellow pages" directory could satisfy the minimal creativity requirement of *Feist*. The compiler of a yellow pages directory chooses which territory and types of businesses to include ("selection") and how to organize those businesses into categories and, perhaps, subcategories ("arrangement"). Nonetheless, plaintiffs have generally not fared well in cases alleging infringement of yellow pages listings; some courts have found insufficient originality, while others have found that the plaintiff's selection or arrangement of listings was original enough to warrant protection, but that slight differences in the selection or arrangement in the defendant's directory were sufficient to avoid infringement due to the "thinness" of the plaintiff's copyright.

Although the advertisements that appear in a yellow pages directory may themselves contain enough original literary or artistic expression to qualify for copyright protection, the compiler's copyright typically does not extend to the advertisements, because they are authored by others. However, the compiler's copyright may extend to the way that the advertisements are arranged on a page.

In some contexts, courts have had difficulty determining what constitutes an original "selection" or "arrangement." Plaintiffs have asserted copyright in medical procedure codes, parts numbers (for example, for replacement parts), and various other kinds of codes and numbering systems. In general, if the code or number is randomly assigned, courts have rejected claims of copyright. However, if the code or number is assigned in a way that conveys meaning (for example, where each digit corresponds to an item of information), some courts (but not all) have been more receptive to copyright protection, finding that the resulting number is an original expression of an idea.

B. Scope of Copyright in Collective Works

Copyright in a *collective work* is determined in the same way as copyright in any other compilation.

However, the underlying materials in a collective work are works of authorship rather than facts or other materials. Section 103 provides that one who assembles separate works of authorship into a collective work can claim copyright only in his or her original contributions to the collective work, not in the underlying works of authorship (unless, of course, those copyrights have been transferred to the compiler by assignment). Under *Feist*, however, copyright in a collective work does not arise as a result of the effort expended in assembling the underlying works; instead, a collective work is copyrightable only if and to the extent that it is (1) not copied, and (2) minimally creative.

Accordingly, the editor of the collective work can claim copyright in any original literary or artistic expression that he or she contributes to the collection, such as an introduction, annotations, or illustrations. Apart from these contributions, the editor can claim copyright only if and to the extent that his or her selection or arrangement of the underlying materials is original. A volume of the "Complete Works of Emily Dickinson," for example, will not meet the creativity requirement in terms of *selection* if it is indeed a comprehensive collection of Dickinson's works. If the *arrangement* of the works is also uncreative—for example, if it is alphabetical or chronological—then the collection will be completely ineligible for copyright protection (except to the extent of any literary or artistic expression added by the editor). In contrast, if the arrangement is more creative, or if the editor selects only certain works for inclusion, it is possible the collection will satisfy *Feist* (albeit probably with a "thin" copyright).

If the individual contributions are protected by copyright, then the creator of a collective work must obtain the consent of the copyright owner(s) to reproduce and publicly distribute their contributions as part of the collective work. In contrast, no permission would be required to create and publish a compilation of Shakespeare's plays, because those are in the public domain.

§ 2.9 Derivative Works

Section 101 defines a *derivative work* as follows:

A "derivative work" is a work based upon one or more preexisting works, such as a translation, musical arrangement, dramatization, fictionalization, motion picture version, sound recording, art reproduction, abridgment, condensation, or any other form in which a work may be recast, transformed, or adapted. A work consisting of editorial revisions, annotations, elaborations, or other modifications which, as a whole, represent an original work of authorship, is a "derivative work".

All derivative works are based on underlying works which themselves are copyrightable subject matter, even if the underlying work is no longer protected by copyright because it has entered the public domain. Thus, for example, if an art student paints a variation on the Mona Lisa which mimics the original except that a frown replaces the famous smile, the student has created a derivative work. Even though the Mona Lisa is too old to enjoy copyright protection, nonetheless it is Leonardo da Vinci's work of authorship, and the student's work is derivative, because it is a creative adaptation of Leonardo's work. In contrast, if the student had painted an original depiction of a frowning woman that he noticed while riding on the subway, his work would not be derivative, but painted from life, because it would not incorporate a preexisting work of authorship.

A. Scope of Derivative Work Copyright

Under § 103, copyright in derivative works extends only to the original material contributed by the person who created the derivative work. If the underlying work is in the public domain, it remains so. If the underlying work is protected by copyright, that copyright is independent of, and unaffected by, the derivative work copyright.

For example, when a stage play is made into a motion picture, the filmmaker's copyright extends only to the differences between the play and the movie (that is, the script changes plus the audiovisual components that bring the story to life, such as the appearance and voices of the actors, the specific set and costume designs, and any accompanying music created for the film). If the play is in the public domain, then a person seeking to stage a public performance of the play does not need the filmmaker's permission; if the play is still under copyright, then any public performance of the play would require only the consent of the play's copyright owner.

The duration of the copyright in a derivative work has no effect on the duration of the copyright in the underlying work. Thus, incorporating a public domain work into a derivative work does not revive the copyright in the underlying work.

Conversely, when we say that a derivative or collective work has entered "the public domain," this does not necessarily mean that *every component* of the work is in the public domain. It means only that the original contributions made by the creator of the derivative work or the compiler of the collective work have entered the public domain. This mirrors the practice of referring to a work as copyrighted when in fact only *some portion* of the work is copyrighted; all copyrighted works include some uncopyrightable elements.

Copyright in a derivative work is thus independent of copyright in any underlying work. In most cases, the underlying work will enter the public domain before the derivative work, because it is the older of the two. In that case, others are free to copy the underlying work, but not the original material added by the creator of the derivative work until that work, too, enters the public domain. For example, if a copyrighted poem is turned into a song by the addition of original music, and the poem enters the public domain ten years later, others are free to copy the poem, but not the music, and not the song, since the latter incorporates the still-copyrighted music.

Until recently, it was also possible that, due to noncompliance with formalities (see Chapter 4), a derivative work could enter the public domain while the underlying work was still protected by copyright. For example, the film "Pygmalion" entered the public domain when its copyright owner failed to renew its copyright, but the copyright in the underlying stage play had been timely renewed and was still in effect. Although the film itself was in the public domain, any party that wanted to publicly perform or copy the film could not do so without obtaining the consent of copyright owner of the stage play. *Russell v. Price,* 612 F.2d 1123 (9th Cir. 1979). In this situation, if the elements of the stage play could have been removed from the film, the remaining portions of the film could have been exploited due to their public domain status. On these facts, of course, it was unlikely that the public domain portions of the film, by themselves, had any exploitation value, because the characters, plot, and dialogue of the stage play were the dominant components of the film. In contrast, if a film were largely original, but included a copyrightable piece of music, then if the film (a derivative work) entered the public domain prematurely, removing the copyrighted music (the underlying work) would enable someone to exploit the public domain elements of the film.

B. Originality in Derivative Works

Although the creator of a derivative work must combine an underlying work with original elements in order to have a copyrightable work, the statutes and the legislative history do not indicate the *degree* of originality that is required. In principal, if a derivative work is too similar to the underlying work, then it will not be entitled to copyright protection, because it lacks originality, and is therefore merely a copy of the underlying work. As discussed below, however, it is difficult to draw a clear line between copies and derivative works.

The leading case is *Alfred Bell & Co. v. Catalda Fine Arts, Inc.*, 191 F.2d 99 (2d Cir. 1951), in which the plaintiff claimed a derivative work copyright in mezzotint engravings of public domain paintings. The engravings were fairly accurate reproductions of the underlying paintings, but they were not identical to the paintings, nor were any two engravings of the same painting identical to one another. Because the court found that there were "substantial variations" between the engravings and the paintings they reproduced, it held that the engravings were copyrightable derivative works rather than mere copies of the public domain works.

Alfred Bell also held that it was irrelevant whether these substantial variations resulted from deliberate choices by the artist, or mere accidents:

> [E]ven if their substantial departures from the paintings were inadvertent, the copyrights would be valid. A copyist's bad eyesight or defective musculature, or a shock caused by a clap of thunder, may yield sufficiently distinguishable variations. Having hit upon such a variation un-

intentionally, the "author" may adopt it as his
and copyright it.

Id. at 105.

Portions of the *Alfred Bell* opinion emphasize the
difference between the underlying works and the
engravings, pointing out the artistic choices made
by the engraver. These passages imply that copyright depends on the level of creativity reflected in
the engraving. Elsewhere, however, the opinion
notes that the engraving process was difficult, expensive, and time-consuming, and required substantial skill. These passages could be interpreted to
suggest that copyright in a derivative work depends
of the amount of effort expended to produce it.
Because *Alfred Bell* was decided before the Supreme
Court repudiated the "sweat of the brow" doctrine
in *Feist*, these passages reflect an outdated standard.

Indeed, prior to *Feist,* a number of courts invoked
Alfred Bell to support holdings that merged the
"sweat of the brow" approach with the "substantial
variations" analysis. One court held that a scale
model reproduction of Rodin's "Hand of God"
sculpture was copyrightable because of the skill,
effort, and precision required to produce it. Another
held that a plastic reproduction of a cast iron "Un-
cle Sam" bank was not copyrightable, partly because the differences were insubstantial, but also
partly because the variations between the plastic
and iron versions reflected not artistic skill, but the
practicalities of mass-producing a plastic object.

The case law after *Feist* is more faithful to the pure "substantial variations" standard, focusing on whether the differences are substantial or trivial, and whether those differences reflect the author's creativity, without considering the amount of skill, time, or effort involved. It is clear, for example, that mechanically transposing music from one key to another involves so little creativity that it results in a trivial variation that is ineligible for a derivative work copyright, while turning a simple melody into an elaborate orchestral arrangement would clearly involve substantial variations that would be protected by copyright.

The changes that are made to convert an underlying work into a derivative work must, of course, be the result of human authorship. Decisions that are dictated entirely by a computer or other device do not qualify. For example, copyright in a colorized film depends on the range of color choices from which selections were made, and the extent to which these choices were made by individuals rather than by a computer.

Some courts suggest that the differences between the underlying work and the derivative work must not only be substantial, but must reflect deliberate artistic choices, a standard that is difficult to reconcile with *Alfred Bell*'s recognition of accidental variations. All courts agree, however, that the derivative work must contain "substantial variations" or "distinguishable variations." In addition, most courts agree that merely transferring a work to a different medium will not, without more, produce a derivative work, because the differences are likely to be trivial and mechanical rather than substantial and creative.

Except in the most extreme cases, courts have had difficulty drawing the line between substantial variations and those that are merely trivial. Some courts are more rigorous than others, treating changes as trivial which another court might treat as substantial. For example, courts have had particular difficulty determining whether and to what extent a realistic photograph of an underlying copyrightable work is separately copyrightable as a derivative work. Because each case is fact-specific, it is difficult for courts to articulate a standard that can be applied in different situations.

Some courts take the position that the standard of originality should be higher for derivative works than for other works of authorship. Under *Feist* (see § 2.1 above), the level of creativity required to obtain copyright protection for a work is ordinarily quite low. However, if an artist copies a public domain work and makes only minor changes to produce a derivative work, there is a risk that this artist might file an infringement claim against another party that copies the same public domain work. Because all three of the works would be so similar, it could be difficult for a court to determine whether the defendant copied the plaintiff's work or the public domain work. Thus, if courts are too liberal in recognizing minor variations as copyrightable, this could enable the first creator of a derivative work to use the threat of litigation to prevent others from copying the same underlying public domain work. *See, e.g., Gracen v. Bradford Exchange,* 698 F.2d 300 (7th Cir. 1983); *L. Batlin & Son, Inc. v. Snyder,* 536 F.2d 486, 490 (2d Cir. 1976).

§ 2.10   Works that Infringe Underlying Works

Under § 103(b), copyright in derivative works and compilations (including collective works) extends only to the original material contributed by their creators. The compilation, collective work, or derivative work copyright is independent of any copyright in the underlying materials, and therefore does not affect the scope, duration, ownership, or subsistence of any copyright in those materials. Thus, if the underlying work is in the public domain, its incorporation into a compilation or derivative work does not change that status. Likewise, incorporating a copyrighted work into a derivative or collective work will not prolong the copyright in the underlying work. And if the copyright in the derivative or collective work has entered the public domain prematurely, this does not, by itself, cause the underlying work to enter the public domain.

Section 103(a) addresses the copyright status of derivative or collective works that infringe their underlying works, stating that "protection for a work employing preexisting material in which copyright subsists does not extend to any part of the work in which such material has been used unlawfully." As discussed above, § 103(b) already provides that the copyright in a collective or derivative work does not extend to the underlying material, but only to the original contributions made by the compiler or derivative work creator. What does § 103(a) add to this analysis? It prevents the infringer from asserting *any copyright at all* in those portions of the new work which are inseparably intertwined with the underlying work. For example, consider an English-language translation of a copyrighted French novel. The translation is a derivative work, but is completely intertwined with the underlying work; one cannot exploit the translation without also exploiting the underlying work. The author of an authorized translation of a copyrighted French novel may sue an infringer who copies the translation (although not an infringer who copies the novel in the original French). But the author of an *unauthorized* translation of the French novel may not sue the person who copies that translation, because the author of the unauthorized translation has no copyright protection.

A similar result would apply to an infringing film adaptation of a copyrighted novel, short story, or play, because while the film itself is a derivative work, it is typically so intertwined with the underlying work that any exploitation of the film would amount to an exploitation of the underlying work. Accordingly, the author of an infringing film adaptation would not be able to assert a copyright claim against someone who copied or publicly performed the film. In contrast, if the filmmaker had permission to adapt the underlying novel, short story, or play, but used infringing music in several portions of the film, the filmmaker might be able to enforce his or her derivative work copyright against someone who copied or publicly performed the film, because there would, at least arguably, be copyright protection for those portions of the film which did not incorporate the infringing music. The actual disposition of such a case might depend on how intertwined the infringing music was with the rest of the film.

CHAPTER 3

COPYRIGHT OWNERSHIP

§ 3.1 Introduction

Copyright ownership arises initially through authorship, and may be transferred by assignment, inheritance, or any other means by which property may be conveyed. Copyright interests may also be licensed, on either an exclusive or non-exclusive basis. Thus, copyright ownership issues involve matters of authorship, assignments, and licensing. Ownership issues may also involve determining the respective rights of persons who own copyrights in collective or derivative works, on the one hand, and the persons who own copyrights in the underlying works that are included in those collective or derivative works.

§ 3.2 Copyright Ownership is Separate from Ownership of Physical Object

Section 202 provides that ownership of the copyright in a work is separate from ownership of a physical embodiment of a work. Thus, when an art collector purchases a painting, the collector owns the physical object but, absent a separate conveyance of the copyright, acquires no interest in the copyright. Conversely, a party may own the copyright in a work, or an interest in the copyright, without owning the original embodiment or any other copy of the work.

§ 3.3 Authorship

The author of a work initially owns the entire copyright in the work. The simplest scenario is where an individual acts alone in creating a work, and the work is not a work made for hire. As the sole author and copyright owner, the creator is free to license or assign any or all of the copyright, or retain full ownership.

The rights of any assignee or licensee of a copyright depend on the work's chain of title, which ultimately must be traceable to the author. Thus, any uncertainty about the authorship of a work can lead to subsequent problems in determining the rights of assignees and licensees.

. Uncertainty can arise whenever there are several individual participants in the creative process that produces a copyrightable work, because it is possible that the work is a *joint work*. Uncertainty can also arise when one or more participants may be acting as employees or independent contractors of another party, because it is possible that the work is a *work made for hire*. In each situation, the authorship question must be resolved in order to determine the respective rights of the participants, the duration of the copyright, and the rights of any subsequent assignees and licensees.

§ 3.4 Works Made For Hire

Many valuable copyrighted works result from creative collaborations. Absent an enforceable agreement among the collaborators, the authorship and ownership of a collaborative work would have to be determined under the uncertain standards of joint authorship. (See § 3.5 below.) In order to minimize uncertainty as to authorship, many collaborative works are created as works made for hire.

In the case of a work made for hire, § 201(b) provides that the author of the work is not the person whose individual creative efforts produced the work, but the party that employed or commissioned that person. As the author of the work made for hire, the employer or commissioning party owns the entire copyright, except as otherwise provided in an express, written agreement signed by the parties.

For the employer or commissioning party, the legal consequences of creating something as a work made for hire differ from the consequences of acquiring the copyright in that work by assignment. As the author, the employer or commissioning party owns the copyright free and clear of any inalienable author's rights—specifically, moral rights under § 106A (see § 7.8 below) and termination rights under §§ 203 and 304(c) (see § 6.6 below). In contrast, if that party had acquired the copyright by assignment or license from the creators, the creators would retain their authorship status, and thus the right to protect their moral rights and to terminate the assignment or license.

The concept of a work made for hire is unique in copyright law, in three respects. First, it represents the only situation in which a work may have an author that is not a natural person; many works made for hire are authored by corporations. Second, it is the only situation in which the authorship of a work (as opposed to the ownership of the copyright) may be determined by contract. Third, it is the only situation in which a party that has made no creative contribution to a work may be recognized as the author of that work. As discussed below, the concept of a work made for hire is extremely useful in fixing the authorship of works which result from collaborative activities such as filmmaking, and eliminates many of the complexities that arise under joint authorship arrangements.

Although § 26 of the 1909 Act defined the term "author" to "include an employer in the case of works made for hire," it provided no other guidance as to what constituted a work made for hire. Over time, courts began interpreting § 26 broadly, and by the 1970s they were treating most specially commissioned works as works made for hire.

Against this background, the 1976 Act narrowed and clarified the meaning of a work made for hire, in large part to provide greater protection to artists working as independent contractors. Under the two-part statutory definition in § 101, a work made for hire is either (1) a work prepared by an employee within the scope of his or her employment; or (2) a specially ordered or commissioned work that fits into one of several specified subject matter categories, and which is the subject of a signed, written work-made-for-hire agreement.

A. Employee–Created Works

Any copyrightable work created by an employee acting within the scope of his or her employment is a work made for hire, regardless of the nature of the work. This result applies even if the parties did not address works made for hire in their employment agreement or negotiations.

Unlike works created by independent contractors, work-made-for-hire status arising from an employment relationship can apply to any type of copyrightable work. Furthermore, no written agreement is required. Even an oral or implied employment agreement can lead to a work made for hire.

In enacting this employer-friendly work-made-for-hire rule, Congress thought it reasonable to give the employer full rights to any copyrightable work that was produced by the specific efforts for which an employee was hired and was being compensated— that is, a work produced within the scope of that person's employment. In contrast, it would not be reasonable to give the employer exclusive rights in a work produced by an employee acting outside the scope of his or her employment—for example, where an employee writes greeting cards for an employer but writes free-lance screenplays on the side. Such an outcome would give the employer a benefit that the parties never bargained for, and for which the employee is not being compensated, and it would deny the true creator of the work the opportunity to reap the rewards of his or her creative efforts. Similarly, in the case of specially ordered or commissioned non-employee works, it would be unreasonable to assume that both parties implicitly understand that the commissioning party will own all the rights to the work; in many cases, the parties may intend that the commissioning party will own only the physical embodiment, and no interest at all in the copyright. This is why, in the case of specially ordered or commissioned works, § 101 requires that the parties enter into an express, written agreement specifying that the work is a work made for hire (see Part B below).

In determining whether the rule for employee-created works applies, therefore, it is essential to determine whether the creator of the work is an employee or an independent contractor.

Section 101 does not define the term "employee." However, the controlling case distinguishing employees from independent contractors for copyright purposes is *Community for Creative Non–Violence v. Reid*, 490 U.S. 730 (1989). Here, a nonprofit organization (CCNV) engaged an artist (Reid) to create a sculpture depicting homeless persons. Although the parties did not sign a written agreement, Reid offered to donate his services, and CCNV agreed to pay costs up to $15,000. Throughout the creative process, CCNV exercised a significant degree of creative control over the final design of the sculpture. However, the parties did not discuss authorship or copyright ownership.

When a dispute over copyright ownership arose, the Supreme Court was asked to determine whether the sculpture was a work made for hire. Because the sculpture did not qualify as a work made for hire under the "specially commissioned" prong of the definition (discussed in Part B below), it could be a work made for hire only if Reid was acting as CCNV's employee when he created it. Thus, the Court was squarely faced with the problem of defining an "employee."

CCNV v. Reid holds that the question whether a person is an "employee" under the work-made-for-hire rules must be determined under the general common law of agency, which considers the hiring party's right to control *the manner and means* by which the product is accomplished. In other words, it is not sufficient that the hiring party exercises control over the end result; the hiring party must also control the process by which that result is achieved. Thus, even if the hiring party issues specific guidelines to which the end result must conform, this does not establish the existence of an employment relationship under the work-made-for-hire rules.

CCNV lists a number of factors that are relevant to determining whether the hiring party controls the manner and means of production. These factors, which are derived from the *Restatement (Second) of Agency* § 220(2), include the following: the skill required; the source of the instrumentalities and tools; the location of the work; the duration of the relationship between the parties; whether the hiring party has the right to assign additional projects to the hired party; the extent of the hired party's discretion over when and how long to work; the method of payment; the hired party's role in hiring and paying assistants; whether the work is part of the regular business of the hiring party; whether the hiring party is in business; the provision of employee benefits; and the tax treatment of the hired party. The list is nonexhaustive, and no single factor is determinative. Depending on the specific facts and circumstances, some factors will have more importance in some situations than in others. Based on these factors, the Court concluded that Reid was an independent contractor.

CCNV rejected several alternative tests for employee status. It rejected a test based on the right to control the end result (as opposed to the process of creating it), because even in an independent contractor scenario the hiring party will often dictate the end result, and Congress clearly intended to impose a different work-made-for-hire standard on independent contractors, as illustrated by part (2) of the § 101 definition (see Part B below). The Court also rejected a test based on the hiring party's exercise of *actual* control over the creative process, finding no support for such a test in the statute or its legislative history, and noting also that such a test would impede Congress's goal of enhancing predictability, because it would make work-made-for-hire status dependent on events that take place after the parties enter into their agreement, thus making it difficult for them to predict, at the time of contracting, whether the end product would be a work made for hire. Finally, the Court rejected the suggestion that "employee" refers only to formal, salaried employees, finding this test unsupported by the language of § 101.

Even where it is clear that the creator of a work is someone's employee, uncertainty can arise if the creator of the work has multiple employers, or if he or she performs some creative activities as a freelancer, and thus outside the scope of any employment arrangement. Because an employment relationship gives rise to a work made for hire only when the creation of that work falls within the scope of a person's employment, in these situations it is essential to determine whether the creative activity in question falls within the scope of the duties assigned by a specific employer.

B. Specially Ordered or Commissioned Works

Part (2) of the § 101 definition applies to works created outside of employment relationships—that is, works created by independent contractors. The definition refers to these as works that have been "specially ordered or commissioned."

Unlike works arising from employment relationships, specially ordered or commissioned works constitute works made for hire only if they satisfy each of two statutory requirements. Specifically, the work must fall into one of several eligible categories of works, and the parties must expressly agree, in a written instrument signed by both parties, that it is a work made for hire. Unless both of these requirements are met, the independent contractor, and not the hiring party, will be considered the author of the work. In that event, the hiring party may still be able to obtain an assignment of the copyright, but the independent contractor will retain the inalienable authors' rights (termination rights and, where applicable, moral rights) even after assigning the copyright.

1. *Eligible Categories*

Under part (2) of the § 101 definition, works created by independent contractors cannot be works made for hire unless they are:

specially ordered or commissioned for use as a contribution to a collective work, as a part of a motion picture or other audiovisual work, as a translation, as a supplementary work, as a compilation, as an instructional text, as a test, as answer material for a test, or as an atlas.

This list of eligible works was the result of extended congressional deliberation in the years leading up to the 1976 Act, and was intended to encompass works that are normally prepared at the instance and expense of a hiring party. In contrast, works that ordinarily proceed from individual inspiration—such as novels, poetry, paintings, musical compositions, and sculptures—are typically ineligible for work-made-for-hire status under part (2). However, in appropriate circumstances, even works of an individualistic nature may still be eligible.

For example, even a musical composition or a sculpture can be a work made for hire if it is created specifically for use in a motion picture. And, of course, works ineligible under part (2) may still be works made for hire under part (1) if they are created in an employment relationship.

Notably, the list of works eligible for "specially commissioned" status does not include sound recordings. Because of this omission, it is not clear whether sound recordings can be the subject of valid work-made-for-hire agreements. Record companies have consistently entered into work-made-for-hire agreements with non-employee recording artists, and naturally take the position that these contracts are enforceable. Although this may have been supportable under the liberal concept of works made for hire that evolved under the 1909 Act, the definition in the 1976 Act is much narrower, and while few courts have addressed the question, several opinions issued in the late 1990s held that the specially-commissioned sound recordings at issue in those cases were not works made for hire.

In response to those rulings, the recording industry managed to insert language into the Satellite Home Viewer Improvement Act of 1999 amending the definition of works made for hire to include sound recordings. When recording artists protested this change, Congress retroactively repealed the amendment, and added new language to the definition which expressly leaves the question undecided. With no guidance from Congress, the question is once again left to the courts.

In some cases, "specially commissioned" sound recordings may qualify as works made for hire under one of the remaining enumerated categories, such as collective works. However, with sound recordings increasingly being marketed and digitally delivered as individual works, the argument that they are created as contributions to collective works may become less persuasive. Alternatively, the recording industry could opt to include a video component in every recording, effectively converting what would have been a sound recording into an audiovisual work. Because audiovisual works are one of the enumerated categories, the resulting work could be the subject of an enforceable work-made-for-hire agreement (and, incidentally, would enjoy an exclusive general public performance right under § 106(5) that would be unavailable to a sound recording, and would also be ineligible for the § 115 compulsory license and the copying privilege under § 1008 of the Audio Home Recording Act).

Although the recording industry may, prospectively, avoid the work-made-for-hire uncertainty by creating audiovisual works instead of sound recordings, this self-help strategy does not resolve the status of existing sound recordings. Congress's failure to resolve this simple problem may lead to inconsistent judicial determinations.

2. *Written Agreements*

Even if an independent contractor's work falls into one of the categories of eligible works, it cannot be a work made for hire unless the contractor and the commissioning party expressly agree to this status in a written agreement that is signed by both parties.

Although § 101 does not dictate any specific wording, the written agreement must unambiguously reflect the parties' shared intent that the work in question will be a work made for hire. Stating that the work is a "work made for hire" (or a common variation, "work for hire") will ordinarily suffice for this purpose. In contrast, statements that the creator "surrenders all right, title and interest" or "waives copyright" in the work, or that the commissioning party will own "all rights" in the work, are ambiguous, and are likely to be construed as a mere assignment of copyright, leaving the creator with the inalienable rights of authorship, including moral rights (where applicable) and the right to terminate the assignment. Similarly, a statement that the commissioning party is the "owner" of the work could be construed as conferring ownership only of the individual tangible object (such as a painting or sculpture), in which case the independent contractor would retain the copyright as well as all author's rights in the work. Either of these scenarios can easily be avoided by including more precise work-made-for-hire language.

Even a well-written work-made-for-hire agreement can prove unenforceable if the work in question is ineligible for status as a "specially commissioned" work made for hire. For example, the sculpture at issue in *Community for Creative Non–*

Violence v. Reid, 490 U.S. 730 (1989) did not fit into any of the categories listed in the "specially commissioned" prong of the work-made-for-hire definition. The same problem could arise in the case of a sound recording, since Congress has failed to resolve the question whether a sound recording may qualify as a "specially commissioned" work. If a work-made-for-hire agreement proves invalid for lack of eligible subject matter, a court may construe it as an assignment of the copyright.

When multiple parties contribute to a creative work, a party that seeks to be recognized as the sole author of that work must ensure that all creative participants either (1) are bona fide employees or (2) are bound by valid work-made-for-hire agreements. If even a single creative participant is overlooked, that participant may subsequently raise a claim of joint authorship. Thus, establishing an iron-clad work-made-for-hire arrangement requires the party seeking sole authorship status to be vigilant in anticipating the extent of the creative contributions likely to be made by various participants in a project, and to be diligent in establishing employment relationships or entering work-made-for-hire contracts with each of those parties before the creative activity begins. Film producers, for example, should secure work-made-for-hire arrangements with anyone who might later be deemed to have made a creative contribution to the film in a non-employee capacity. Because it can be hard to predict where creative inputs might come from, it is better to be over-inclusive than under-inclusive in these arrangements. For example, in *Aalmuhammed v. Lee,* 202 F.3d 1227 (9th Cir. 2000), the producers of the film *Malcolm X* hired the plaintiff to act as an advisor, but failed to bind him to either an employment or a work-made-for-hire agreement. Later, he filed suit, alleging that his creative contributions made him a joint author of the film, and forcing the producers of the film to engage in costly litigation over the exact nature of his contribution to the film.

3.   *Pre– versus Post–Creation Agreements*

To be valid, the work-made-for-hire agreement must be entered into *before* the specially commissioned work is created. After creation, it is too late. At the moment of creation, authorship vests in the actual creator, and from that point onward it is no longer possible to change the authorship of the work; only the ownership of the copyright and the ownership of the tangible object itself can be transferred after the work's creation.

It is well settled that a work-made-for-hire agreement must be a written instrument, signed by both parties, and that an oral agreement is insufficient. However, on some occasions parties have entered into an oral work-made-for-hire agreement before creating a work, then reduced their agreement to writing only *after* the work has been created. This can happen, for example, where the parties have an oral or implied work-made-for-hire relationship, but do not realize until after the work's completion that the law requires a signed writing. Will a subsequent writing retroactively validate their otherwise-unenforceable oral or implied agreement? The statutes do not address this timing question, and courts have reached conflicting conclusions. Some courts have held unequivocally that the signed writing must precede creation of the work, in order to achieve Congress's goal of providing certainty of authorship so that the work will be readily marketable. *E.g., Schiller & Schmidt, Inc. v. Nordisco Corp.,* 969 F.2d 410 (7th Cir. 1992). Other courts have held that, depending on the circumstances, the writing can be validly executed after the work's creation, provided that it ratifies an agreement that was entered into *before* the work's creation. *E.g., Playboy Enterprises, Inc. v. Dumas*, 53 F.3d 549 (2d Cir. 1995). This split of authority is unlikely to be resolved soon.

Courts that are reluctant to uphold written agreements executed after a work's creation are concerned about the possibility that a hiring party may act in bad faith, withholding payment for the completed work until the artist signs a work-made-for-hire agreement, and falsely asserting that the written agreement simply ratifies a pre-existing oral agreement. Thus, if the artist later challenges the validity of the written contract, disputing the existence of a preexisting oral agreement, courts are likely to treat the written contract as invalid unless there is strong proof of the oral agreement. Because the purpose of the signed writing requirement is to give artists adequate notice that they are giving up their authorship rights, so that they can bargain accordingly, a hiring party that fails to obtain the artist's signature on a written agreement before a work's creation will ordinarily have to bear the consequences of that oversight if there is a subsequent dispute

C. Legal Consequences of Work-Made-for-Hire Status

The determination that a copyrighted work is a work made for hire has several important legal consequences.

First, the authorship of the work vests *ab initio* in the employer or commissioning party. As a result, that party enjoys rights which are broader than those of a copyright assignee. As the legal author of the work, the employer or commissioning party owns the copyright free and clear of the inalienable authorship rights which the work's creator would have retained in the case of a mere assignment of copyright. Those rights include the right to terminate assignments or licenses of the copyright under § 203 or § 304(c), and, where applicable, moral rights under § 106A. Also, with respect to works made for hire that were published prior to January 1, 1978, the vesting rules for the copyright renewal term were very different from the rules applicable to works by individual authors. (See § 5.1 below.)

Under the 1976 Act, works made for hire also have a different term of copyright protection compared to works by individual authors. (See Chapter 5.)

D. Divided Ownership of Works Made for Hire

If a work meets the definition of a work made for hire, then regardless of whether it is created by an employee or an independent contractor, § 201(b) provides that the person for whom the work was prepared (1) is considered to be the author, and (2) absent a signed, written agreement to the contrary, owns all of the rights comprised in the copyright. Accordingly, even in a work-made-for-hire scenario, it is possible in for the parties to enter an enforceable agreement to divide ownership of the copyright.

§ 3.5 Joint Works

Although the concept of joint authorship was already well established in case law, it was not codified until the 1976 Act. Section 101 defines a "joint work" as "a work prepared by two or more authors with the intention that their contributions be merged into inseparable or interdependent parts of a unitary whole." The legislative history explains that contributions are interdependent when each has some meaning standing alone, like the music and lyrics of a song, while contributions are inseparable when they have little or no independent meaning standing alone, as might be the case where two writers collaborate on a screenplay. The legislative history also indicates that the authors of a joint work need not work together at the same time, but each must intend, at the time of making his or her contribution, that this contribution will eventually be merged with that of another author to create a unitary whole.

The statutory definition of a joint work actually defines a work of joint *authorship*. Joint ownership of a copyright may also arise through assignment of the copyright to multiple parties, or through inheritance. Absent a written agreement to the contrary, however, the ownership rights of joint owners are the same as those of joint authors. While it is typically not difficult to determine whether a copyright is jointly owned as a result of assignment or inheritance, courts have often had difficulty determining whether a work is jointly authored, for reasons discussed below.

A. Derivative and Collective Works Distinguished

Authorship of a joint work differs from authorship of a derivative work or a collective work. The differences are based on the intentions of the parties as well as the nature and timing of their contributions. A derivative work involves an underlying work of authorship and a subsequent adaptation thereof. At the time the underlying work is created, its author does not intend to merge his or her contribution with the work of another author. Rather, the first author intends the first work to stand on its own, even if he or she also contemplates that the work may someday be adapted into a new form. For example, the author of a novel may hope to sell the motion picture rights someday, but still views the novel itself as a completed work. In contrast, when a joint work is created, each contributor intends, *at the time of making his or her contribution*, that this contribution will be merged with that of another author to produce a single unitary work. Neither contribution is underlying, and neither is derivative. They are simply two parts of a single work. The parts may be interdependent (like the music and lyrics of a song) or inseparable (like the contributions of two writers who collaborate on a script). It is not necessary that the first contributor know the identity of the person who will eventually become the collaborator on the joint work; it is enough that the first contributor intends to find such a collaborator.

A song resulting from the efforts of a composer and a lyricist is an example of a work that may be either joint or derivative, depending on the process through which it is created. If a composer writes a melody in hopes of finding a lyricist to contribute the words to produce a completed song, the resulting song is a joint work, authored by both of them. In contrast, if the composer writes an instrumental piece, not initially intending for words to be added, the subsequent addition of lyrics by another party gives rise to a derivative work, authored by the lyricist. The composer, of course, remains the author of the instrumental piece, which means that the derivative work (the song) cannot be exploited without the composer's consent. The lyrics alone, however, can be exploited with only the permission of the lyricist, because the composer is not a joint author of the song.

A joint work also differs from a collective work, in which each author's creative contribution stands on its own as an independent copyrightable work. Unlike the authors of a joint work, the authors of the individual works that are combined into a collective work do not intend to merge their contributions as inseparable or interdependent parts of a single unitary work. Rather, they intend for their individual contributions to retain their identities as separate copyrightable works. Each author owns the copyright in his or her individual contribution, and the compiler is the author and copyright owner of the collective work.

B. Complexities of the Collaborative Process

Merely because several persons contribute to the creation of a work, each with the intent of merging their individual contributions to produce a single unitary work, does not mean that the resulting work is joint, or that each contributor is an author. Collaborative works may involve a wide variety of contributions from numerous persons, and while all of them may be share a common goal, copyright law may not recognize all of them as joint authors.

The difficulty in identifying the authors of a joint work arises from several sources. Some participants in a collaborative work may make greater contributions than others, either qualitatively or quantitatively, and any assessment of the relative magnitude of their contributions is likely to be highly subjective. The nature of their contributions may vary as well—some providing general ideas, others providing more detailed suggestions, and still others providing labor or skill but little creative input. One collaborator may exercise more decision-making authority than the others with respect to the final product, deciding which of the other parties' suggestions will be adopted, without necessarily providing many creative suggestions of his or her own. The creative process is likely to be unstructured and largely undocumented, and the participants' later recollections may be vague or unreliable. Some contributions may have been fixed in a tangible medium of expression from the start, while others may have been introduced verbally, and then significantly altered by other collaborators before being recorded. Parties may enter the collaboration with unstated and conflicting expectations about their ultimate authorship status. Frequently, the creative process is well underway, or complete, before any of the participants consider the legal question of authorship status.

C. Legal Consequences of Joint Authorship

According to the legislative history, joint works are subject to the common law presumption that, in the absence of a contract, each owner (that is, each author) is a tenant in common with an equal and undivided ownership share; this rule applies even if the authors' creative contributions were not equal. Thus, when a joint work is created, each author owns an equal share of the copyright in that work, unless they have agreed to a different arrangement. (Because such an agreement would amount to an assignment of a copyright interest, it would have to be in writing to be enforceable.) Such an assignment would affect only the relative ownership interests of the authors; it would not change the fact that the work is a joint work, nor would it eradicate any of the inalienable rights of authorship, such as moral rights under § 106A or the right to terminate the assignment under § 203.

Absent an agreement to the contrary, each owner of a joint work is free to exploit the work without the consent of the other owners, but must account for the profits of that exploitation by splitting them equally among all of the joint owners. This exploitation right applies to *non*exclusive licenses; thus, for example, if a song is jointly authored and the copyright has not been assigned, one joint author of the song can grant a non-exclusive license for the song to be used in a motion picture, but would have to split the licensing proceeds equally with the other joint owner. In contrast, assignments, exclusive licenses, and mortgages require the consent of *all* joint owners. In some foreign jurisdictions, the consent of all joint owners is required even for a nonexclusive license.

The common law rule that equal ownership arises even where the authors' respective contributions are unequal contributes to the cautiousness with which courts approach joint authorship claims. Where one author's contribution is significantly greater than that of another, courts may be reluctant to recognize the minor contributor as a joint author at all. Because the common law rule would give the "minor" author an ownership share equal to that of the "major" author, courts sometimes reject the minor contributor's authorship status altogether, rather than give that contributor ownership rights that seem disproportionate.

Because an assignment or exclusive license of a joint work requires the consent of all owners, a joint work may be less marketable than a work that has a single author. A copyright is likely to be considerably less valuable when it cannot be sold, licensed, or mortgaged without the consent of multiple parties. If there are any doubts about whether a particular work is a joint work, it is likely to be unmarketable until those doubts are resolved. Thus, recognizing a work as jointly authored can make the work significantly more difficult to exploit commercially.

D.   Standards for Joint Authorship

Joint authorship disputes frequently turn on one or both of two questions: First, what was the nature of each person's contribution, and was it sufficient to support an authorship claim? Second, did each collaborator have the requisite intent to create a joint work? Because any uncertainty in the authorship of a work can impair its marketability, courts have tried to develop bright-line tests for making these determinations. As discussed below, they have had limited success.

1. *Nature of the Contribution*

In attempting to define what contributions are sufficient to support joint authorship claims, courts and commentators generally agree that the contribution must be original, meaning (1) not copied and (2) at least minimally creative. There also appears to be a consensus that the contribution must be more than *de minimis,* although there is no clear standard for determining when a contribution is too trivial to satisfy this test.

The circuits are split, however, on whether a joint author's creative contribution may consist entirely of abstract ideas, or whether the contribution must qualify independently as copyrightable expression. The joint work definition does not say that each contribution must be independently copyrightable, and some courts and commentators have argued that, in the context of joint works, copyright's goal of fostering creativity is best served by rewarding those who contribute ideas as well as those who turn those ideas into detailed expression. Several courts, however, have disagreed, requiring each contribution to consist of independently copyrightable expression. This requirement enables courts to reject joint authorship claims that might be considered legitimate if contributions of abstract ideas gave rise to joint authorship status, and thus is likely to lead to fewer works being recognized as joint works.

Whatever the merits of its gatekeeping function, the independent copyrightability requirement can be problematic in its application. For example, in *Gaiman v. McFarlane*, 360 F.3d 644 (7th Cir. 2004), the Seventh Circuit declined to apply this requirement to comic book characters that were the product of creative inputs from several collaborators, suggesting that, in some contexts, it is possible that none of the individual contributions to a finished work would satisfy the independent copyrightability requirement, and yet the resulting work would still qualify for copyright. More generally, the difficulty of drawing a clear line between abstract ideas and copyrightable expression can make it difficult to determine whether, in a particular case, the independent copyrightability standard has been met, because the distinction often turns simply on the level of detail. (See § 2.3 above on the idea/expression dichotomy.) For example, if one writer suggests adding a subplot or character to a script, the question whether that contribution is an abstract idea or copyrightable expression depends on the level of detail the writer provides.

The requirement of independent copyrightability is also difficult to reconcile with the joint works definition, which explicitly recognizes that contributions to a joint work may be interdependent *or inseparable*. Arguably, the independent copyrightability requirement impermissibly reads the "inseparable" language out of the definition.

Uncertainty over what types of contributions support authorship claims also arises when authorship is asserted by individuals featured in copyrighted photographs and recorded performances. In the case of a recorded performance, each individual performer may be an author of the recorded work, if his or her performance contains creative expression. For example, a group of musicians who permit their musical performance to be recorded will typically, absent an enforceable work-made-for-hire agreement, be joint authors of the recording. They may also share authorship with those who make creative decisions about the recording and editing process. In the case of a posed photograph, the person who poses may be a joint author along with the photographer who took the picture; although there is little authority on this question, the answer should depend on the level of creativity contributed by the person who poses.

In the case of photographs or recordings of persons who are engaged in real-life events as opposed to intentional creative performances, courts have not addressed the question whether the person who is the subject of the candid photograph or recording qualifies as an author. A court would most likely decline to recognize such an authorship claim, for any of several reasons (assuming factual support): First, the subject did not authorize the recording to take place. Second, merely being the subject of the recording, without more, may not be a sufficiently creative contribution. Third, because the subject lacks the intent to create a work of authorship in the first place, the subject by definition cannot intend to merge his or her "contribution" with that of another in order to create a single unitary work.

2. Interpreting the Intent Requirement

A second issue in the joint works analysis is whether each putative joint author must harbor a specific intent to share authorship with the others. Although there is no foundation for such a requirement in either the statutes or their legislative history, there is significant support in the case law.

The only explicit intent requirement in the joint works definition is the requirement that joint authors have "the intention that their contributions be merged into inseparable or interdependent parts of a unitary whole." The statute does not state that the parties must intend to share credit for the work or to share in any of the legal rights of authorship, such as the right to exploit the joint work, to share in the exploitation proceeds, and to participate in decisions regarding assignments and exclusive licenses. Nonetheless, several circuits have denied joint authorship claims solely on the ground that another author of the work did not intend to share authorship.

The seminal case requiring intent to share authorship, *Childress v. Taylor*, 945 F.2d 500 (2d Cir. 1991), involved two women who collaborated on a biographical play. One viewed herself as the sole author, and viewed her collaborator as a mere assistant, whereas the latter viewed herself as a full co-author. The Second Circuit held that a joint work could not arise unless *both* parties viewed one another as joint authors; thus, the subjective intent of one collaborator could unilaterally defeat the authorship claim of the other. Even though the statutory intent requirement was satisfied—because both women intended to merge their contributions into a single unitary work—the court held that this was insufficient to give rise to a joint work. If the intent to merge contributions were enough, the court observed, this "would extend joint author status to many persons who are not likely to have been within the contemplation of Congress"—persons such as editors and research assistants.

However, even the Second Circuit had difficulty defining the requisite intent. Although it rejected a standard which would require the authors to intend the legal consequences of joint authorship (consequences which many collaborators would not even be aware of), it suggested that "some distinguishing characteristic of the relationship must be understood in order for it to be the subject of their intent." While noting that the parties' understanding as to "credit" or "billing" might be relevant in some cases, the court conceded that there were some situations—such as ghost-written works—in which this factor would not be determinative.

The Second Circuit also suggested that the parties' intent to share authorship with one another might be more important where, as in the stage play at issue, the party who lacked the requisite intent is "indisputably the dominant author of the work," and that this factor would be less important in "traditional forms of collaboration, such as between the creators of the words and music of a song."

Subsequent case law in the Second Circuit has adhered to *Childress,* denying joint authorship status even where an ousted collaborator's contribution was substantial and copyrightable, *see Thomson v. Larson,* 147 F.3d 195 (2d Cir. 1998) (also emphasizing the dominant author's decisionmaking authority). *Childress* has also been adopted by the Seventh Circuit. *See Erickson v. Trinity Theatre, Inc.,* 13 F.3d 1061 (7th Cir. 1994). The Ninth Circuit has adopted a slightly different approach, which considers three factors: (1) the extent of each collaborator's control over the creative process; (2) the existence of any objective manifestations of intent to share authorship (in contrast to the Second Circuit's focus on subjective intent); and (3) whether the audience appeal of the work turns on both contributions and "the share of each in its success cannot be appraised." *Aalmuhammed v. Lee,* 202 F.3d 1227 (9th Cir. 2000) (adding, however, that "[c]ontrol in many cases will be the most important factor"). The Fourth Circuit adopted the *Aalmuhammed* approach in an unpublished opinion. *Brown v. Flowers,* 196 Fed. Appx. 178 (4th Cir. 2006).

E.   Effect of Subsequent Modifications

Assuming that a work is determined to be joint, if one author modifies the joint work to create a derivative work, should all of the authors of the joint work also be considered authors of the derivative work?

The rules governing authorship of a derivative work are the same regardless of whether the underlying work is a joint work or a work of sole authorship. When sufficient original content is added to an underlying work, the result is a new derivative work, authored by the person who added the original content. The person who does the adapting is the author of the derivative work, and the authors of the underlying work do not share in that authorship. This is true regardless of whether the adapter was also one of the original joint authors, or is a complete stranger to that authoring group. The original joint authors intended to merge their contributions to create the original joint work, but their intent is not deemed to carry over to a derivative work in which they did not participate.

These rules can be difficult to apply, however, when it is not clear whether the underlying work and the derivative work are truly separate works. If it is clear that the joint work is finished, and the collaboration ended, before the creation of the derivative work begins, then the works would be considered separate. For example, where a comedy troupe collaborated on a screenplay which was then licensed to a producer for filming as a motion picture, the Ninth Circuit held that the screenplay and the film were not a single unitary work jointly authored by the troupe and the producer, and that the members of the troupe were the only authors of the screenplay. *Gilliam v. American Broadcasting Cos.*, 538 F.2d 14 (2d Cir. 1976). Absent a work-made-for-hire agreement, on these facts the question whether the troupe members were also joint authors (with the producer) of the finished film would depend on what contributions they made to the film apart from licensing their underlying screenplay.

In some cases, however, it is less clear that the joint work was indeed finished before one of the collaborators—perhaps bringing in a new partner— begins to alter the work. Case law prior to the 1976 Act addressed several variations on this problem. Where a composer and a lyricist collaborated on a song, but the composer later consented to the substitution of lyrics by a different lyricist, the Second Circuit held that the composer and the second lyricist were the joint authors of the revised song, because the composer's intent to merge his contribution carried over to the version with the new lyrics. *Shapiro, Bernstein & Co. v. Jerry Vogel Music Co., Inc.*, 161 F.2d 406 (2d Cir. 1946) (the "Melancholy Baby" case). The court reached the same conclusion a few years later, when a composer assigned the copyright in his instrumental solo, and the assignee then hired a writer to add lyrics. *Shapiro, Bernstein & Co. v. Jerry Vogel Music Co., Inc.*, 221 F.2d 569 (2d Cir. 1955), *modified on rehearing*, 223 F.2d 252 (2d Cir. 1955) (the *"Twelfth Street Rag"* case). The latter decision, however, was roundly criticized for blurring the distinction between joint and derivative works, and is generally understood to have been overruled by the 1976 Act.

Both of these pre–1976 cases involved modifications by persons who did not participate in the underlying joint work. In contrast, *Weissmann v. Freeman*, 868 F.2d 1313 (2d Cir. 1989), which was decided under the 1976 Act, involved revisions to a joint work that were made by one of its original joint authors. There, a professor and his assistant jointly authored a series of academic articles. When the assistant then incorporated some material from those articles into a new article, the professor asserted joint authorship rights in that article. The district court ruled in the professor's favor, characterizing the series of articles as "a single evolutionary joint work," but the Second Circuit reversed. Using an analysis similar to *Gilliam*, the court treated the last article as a separate derivative work individually authored by the assistant, and refused to find that the professor's joint authorship intent with respect to the underlying works carried over to the new work in which he did not directly participate.

F. Joint Authorship Involving Work-Made-for-Hire Arrangements

Sometimes several employers (and/or commissioning parties) may collaborate with one another to create a joint work. In this case, the authorship rights of the employers and/or commissioning parties are determined under the work-made-for-hire rules. If they indeed qualify as authors, then their rights with respect to one another are determined under the rules for joint works.

Joint works may also be created under circumstances in which some, but not all, of the creative contributors are acting under work-made-for-hire arrangements. For example, an independent contractor who is not bound by a work-made-for-hire agreement might create a computer program in collaboration with a corporate employee who is acting within the scope of his or her duties. In this case, the independent contractor and the corporation will be joint authors of the computer program. The normal rules of joint authorship will determine the respective rights and duties of each author— *e.g.,* their rights to license or assign the joint work, and their duties to account to one another for the profits.

In the latter situation, however, an unsettled question is how to measure the duration of the copyright in a joint work that has one or more individual authors *as well as* one or more authors whose rights derive from work-made-for-hire arrangements: Should the copyright endure for the works-made-for-hire term (95 years from publication, or 120 years from creation, whichever ends first), or for the joint works term (the life of the last surviving author, plus 70 years)? Because a corporation does not have a "life" in the sense that a human author does, a strict application of the joint works term would be impossible. Among the possible alternatives approaches, then, are (1) to apply the works-made-for-hire term, even though the work is not purely a work made for hire; (2) to apply the joint works term, based only on the life of the last surviving author who did not act under a work-made-for-hire arrangement; (3) to allow copyright to endure until the *later* of the work-made-for-hire term or the last-surviving-author-plus-70 term; or (4) to allow copyright to endure until the *earlier* of the work-made-for-hire term or the last-surviving-author-plus-70 term. Although choosing among these options would be a simple matter for Congress, it has not done so.

§ 3.6   Authorship in Collective Works

If a collective work is original enough to be copyrightable, then the party that selects and arranges the underlying contributions is considered the author of the collective work. However, the copyright in the collective work is separate from the copyright in the underlying contributions. In the absence of an express transfer, the creator of the collective work is not the owner of the contributions authored by others. Instead, under § 201(c) the owner of the collective work copyright is presumed to have acquired only the right to reproduce and distribute each contribution as part of the collective work, any revision of the collective work, and any later collective work in the same series.

In *New York Times v. Tasini*, 533 U.S. 483 (2001), the Supreme Court held that § 201(c) did not permit the republication of free-lance articles, originally published in newspapers and other print periodicals, in searchable electronic databases (such as Lexis/Nexis, Westlaw, or CD–ROMs), because these databases allowed users to select and view individual articles in isolation from the other materials originally included in the collective work. In contrast, reproduction in typical microfiche format would normally be permitted by § 201(c), because this format reproduces the entire collective work, and is thus comparable to the original print version. In light of *Tasini*, publishers of print periodicals will need to obtain assignments or licenses from their free-lance authors in order to reproduce those authors' works in searchable electronic databases that permit each work to be viewed in isolation. Absent such permission, these articles may have to be removed from the databases to avoid infringement liability.

The Supreme Court in *Tasini* did not decide whether the § 201(c) rights can be transferred or licensed by the owner of the collective work copyright; however, several courts have held that they can.

CHAPTER 4

FORMALITIES

The role of formalities in federal copyright law has significantly decreased under the 1976 Act. In most cases, compliance with formalities is no longer essential to owning the copyright in a work. However, certain formalities are still essential to pursuing infringement claims, and others can enhance the remedies available to a successful infringement plaintiff. In addition, certain formalities that are no longer required for newly created works continue to play a significant role in determining the copyright status of works that were first published as late as February, 1989.

Three types of formalities are associated with federal copyright law: notice, deposit, and registration. For newly created works, none of these formalities is currently a prerequisite to owning a copyright. However, deposit and registration affect the copyright owner's ability to enforce a copyright and to enjoy certain remedies against infringers. Even though copyright notice is no longer required for works first published on or after March 1, 1989, copyright notice still offers some practical benefits. Because many people still equate the absence of a copyright notice with a lack of copyright protection, a prominent copyright notice can deter potential infringers. Also, by identifying the copyright owner, the notice facilitates a potential user's efforts to locate the copyright owner in order to secure the appropriate permissions. When infringement occurs, a defendant that had access to a copy or phonorecord of the work that displayed a copyright notice cannot raise a defense of innocent infringement, based on lack of awareness of the copyright, to mitigate actual or statutory damages. 17 U.S.C. §§ 401(d), 402(d). Finally, in any countries which adhere to the Universal Copyright Convention but not to the Berne Convention, copyright notice in the form prescribed by §§ 401 and 402 will satisfy any formalities imposed as a condition to copyright protection.

§ 4.1 Notice

While notice is no longer essential to obtain copyright protection for newly published works, the notice requirement which was in effect prior to March 1, 1989 (the effective date of the Berne Implementation Act of 1988 (BCIA)) may have a significant impact on the current copyright status of works that were first published prior to that date. Two different notice requirements were in effect during the relevant period: the notice requirement of the 1909 Act, which was in effect through 1977, and the notice requirement of the original 1976 Act, which remained in effect through February, 1989.

A. Notice Under the 1909 Act

Under the 1909 Act, federal copyright ordinarily did not attach to any work until that work was publicly distributed with copyright notice affixed. However, unpublished works enjoyed perpetual protection under common law copyright. Once a work was published with a proper copyright notice, common law protection ended, and federal copyright law attached, with its limited statutory term of protection. If a work was published without proper copyright notice, however, common law copyright ended, and the work entered the public domain, because the publication without notice disqualified the work from federal copyright protection.

In the case of works that were not reproduced for sale, the 1909 Act provided that federal copyright protection could be secured through registration even without publication. This was accomplished by filing a copyright claim with the Register of Copyrights, and satisfying a deposit requirement. In the case of literary, dramatic, musical and photographic works, this requirement was satisfied by depositing one complete copy of the work. Different deposit requirements applied to certain other categories of works as to which depositing a complete copy was not feasible (*e.g.,* works of art).

Sections 19 and 20 of the 1909 Act prescribed the form for the mandatory copyright notice. In general, it consisted of either the word "Copyright," the abbreviation "Copr.," or the symbol ©, accompanied by the name of the copyright proprietor and, in the case of a printed literary, musical, or dramatic work, the year in which copyright was secured by publication. In the case of sound recordings, beginning in 1972 notice took the form of the ℗ symbol accompanied by the name of the copyright owner and the year of first publication. For printed publications, musical works, and sound recordings, § 20 prescribed the proper placement of the copyright notice. Courts varied in their tolerance for deviations from the required form, some treating minor errors as the equivalent of omissions, while other courts were more forgiving, especially where the copyright owner had demonstrated a good faith effort to comply with the statutory requirements.

Under § 10 of the 1909 Act, copyright notice was required to appear on all copies of a work that were publicly distributed or offered for sale in the United States under the authority of the copyright owner. Omission from even a single copy could cause the work to enter the public domain. Section 21 recognized an exception where the copyright proprietor sought to comply with the notice requirement, but by accident or mistake omitted the notice from a particular copy or copies; in such a case, the copyright was still enforceable against anyone who had actual notice of the copyright, but the copyright owner could not recover damages against an innocent infringer who was misled by the omission of the notice, and could, as a condition to obtaining a permanent injunction, be required to reimburse the infringer's reasonable outlay that was innocently incurred. In applying § 21, courts tended to interpret "accident or mistake" narrowly, applying it to mechanical failures during printing but not to omissions resulting from negligence or oversight.

B. Notice Under the 1976 Act

The notice requirement was significantly modified in the 1976 Act. Effective January 1, 1978, common law copyright was abolished for all fixed works. Instead, federal copyright attached from the moment an original work of authorship was fixed in tangible form. Thus, publication with notice no longer served as the dividing line between common law and federal copyright protection. However, copyright notice was still mandatory for all published works, and public distribution without notice could still cause a work to enter the public domain. Technically, this occurred through a *forfeiture* of federal copyright protection, since federal copyright subsisted in a work from the moment it was fixed, and was lost only when the work was published without notice.

Under § 405(a) of the 1976 Act, if notice was omitted from copies or phonorecords that were publicly distributed by authority of the copyright owner prior to March 1, 1989, the copyright was forfeited unless one of the following exceptions applied:

(1) notice was omitted from only a relatively small number of publicly distributed copies or phonorecords; or

(2) the copyright was registered before, or within five years after, the publication without notice, and a reasonable effort was made to add notice to all copies or phonorecords of the work that were distributed to the public in the United States after the omission was discovered; or

(3) notice was omitted in violation of an express requirement in writing that, as a condition of the copyright owner's authorization of the public distribution of the copies or phonorecords, they bear the prescribed notice.

Even where the publication without notice took place outside the United States, it has been held that copyright was forfeited unless one of the § 405(a) exceptions applied. *Hasbro Bradley, Inc. v. Sparkle Toys, Inc.,* 780 F.2d 189 (2d Cir. 1985). This is consistent with the wording of § 405(a), which refers to the omission of notice from copies and phonorecords that are "publicly distributed" without specifying where that distribution takes place. In contrast, § 405(a)(2) allows the copyright owner to cure this omission by adding notice only to copies or phonorecords that are publicly distributed "in the United States" after the omission is discovered.

Completing the cure under § 405(a)(2) requires a copyright owner to add notice to copies of the work that are distributed "after the omission has been discovered." When the omission was truly inadvertent, it is generally accepted that the date of "discovery" is the date on which the copyright owner first learns that notice was omitted. In contrast, where a copyright owner omitted notice intentionally, with full knowledge that notice was legally required, it is generally accepted that the omission was "discovered" at the time the distribution without notice took place. More difficult, however, is the situation where a copyright owner knowingly omitted the copyright notice without realizing that notice was legally required. Courts and commentators have endorsed different approaches to this scenario. One view is that discovery occurs when the existence of copyright protection becomes an issue (*e.g.,* when infringement occurs), *O'Neill Devs., Inc. v. Galen Kilburn, Inc.,* 524 F.Supp. 710 (N.D. Ga. 1981). However, the better view, and the one adopted by the First Circuit in *Charles Garnier, Paris v. Andin International, Inc.,* 36 F.3d 1214 (1st Cir. 1994), is that discovery occurs when the copyright owner discovers the legal significance of the omission.

There is no fixed standard for determining whether a copyright owner has made a "reasonable effort" to add notice to all copies and phonorecords that are distributed to the public in the United States after the omission has been discovered. However, in the *Garnier* case the owner's efforts were found to be unreasonable as a matter of law, because after discovering the omission the owner began adding notice only to newly produced goods, and failed to add notice to goods that were already in retailers' inventories.

C. Notice After the BCIA

In order to bring federal copyright law into compliance with the Berne Convention, Congress abolished the notice requirement in the Berne Convention Implementation Act of 1988 ("BCIA"), effective March 1, 1989. Thus, any copyrightable work first published on or after March 1, 1989 is exempt from the notice requirement.

If a copyright owner distributed copies without notice before March 1, 1989, but satisfied the requirements of § 405(a)(2) by registering the work within five years and adding copyright notice to all copies publicly distributed in the United States thereafter, does the obligation to affix notice continue even after March 1, 1989? Because the statute is silent on this question, technically the obligation to affix notice under § 405(a)(2) continues indefinitely, and the First Circuit adopted this interpretation in *Garnier, supra*. However, because Congress completely eliminated the notice requirement for works *first* published after March 1, 1989, in order to comply with the Berne Convention, it seems unlikely that Congress intended this result.

Under § 406 of the 1976 Act, if a work was published before March 1, 1989, under the authority of the copyright owner, but bears an incomplete or erroneous copyright notice, the consequences depend on the nature of the error or omission:

If the notice identifies the wrong person as the copyright owner, the validity and ownership of the copyright are unaffected. However, an accused infringer has a complete defense if he or she was misled by the notice and began the infringing actions in good faith under a purported transfer or license from the person identified in the notice as the copyright owner, unless, before the infringing actions commenced, either (1) the work had been registered in the name of the copyright owner, or (2) a document executed by the person named in the notice and identifying the correct copyright owner had been recorded.

If the notice incorrectly identifies the year of first publication, then if the year shown in the notice is earlier than the year of first publication, the year shown in the notice is treated as the publication year for purposes of calculating the duration of copyright under § 302. If the year shown in the notice is more than one year later than the actual year of first publication, the work is considered to have been published without notice, and is therefore subject to the provisions of § 405.

If the notice omitted either the copyright owner's name or the year of first publication, the work is considered to have been published without notice, and is therefore subject to the provisions of § 405.

Because the question whether a work was publicly distributed with or without copyright notice was of crucial importance prior to March 1, 1989, courts were often asked to determine whether a particular distribution was private or public. Where the distributed copies bore a proper copyright notice, the copyright owner typically sought a ruling that the distribution was public, thus causing statutory copyright to attach the work (and thereby enabling the copyright owner to invoke federal court jurisdiction and obtain federal remedies against an infringer). Such distributions were known as "investive" (or "investitive") publications. Where copyright notice was omitted or inadequate, the copyright owner typically sought a ruling that the distribution was private, so that the work could retain its perpetual common law copyright and avoid being thrown into the public domain. In these cases, public distributions were referred to as "divestive" (or "divestitive") publications.

D. Meaning and Effect of Publication

Section 26 of the 1909 Act generally indicated that the term "publication" included selling, offering to sell, and publicly distributing a work under the authority of the copyright owner, but otherwise the meaning of publication was determined by the courts, which held that the term also included *offers* to distribute to the public, if made under the copyright owner's authority. Interpretive problems arose, however, in determining which distributions were public, and in determining whether public performances and displays were publications.

Where copies of a work were actually distributed, courts interpreting the 1909 Act drew a distinction between general distributions, which were treated as publications, and "private" or "limited" distributions, which were not. For example, the Ninth Circuit held that a distribution of no more than 20 copies of a manuscript lacking copyright notice to persons not known to the author, with no restriction on further distribution, was a general publication. In the Ninth Circuit's view, a limited distribution must be made to "a definitely selected group for a limited purpose, and without the right of diffusion, reproduction, distribution or sale.... [T]he circulation must be restricted both as to persons and purpose, or it cannot be called a private or limited publication." *White v. Kimmell*, 193 F.2d 744 (9th Cir. 1952). In close cases, many courts interpreting the 1909 Act appeared to be reluctant to rule that a particular distribution was public, if the result would be a divestitive publication; some courts expressly stated that a broader dissemination was necessary for a divestitive publication than for an investitive one. *See, e.g., Hirshon v. United Artists Corp.*, 243 F.2d 640 (D.C. Cir. 1957); *American Visuals v. Holland*, 239 F.2d 740 (2d Cir. 1956). Some of the decisions under the 1909 Act, however, are questionable. *See, e.g., Academy of Motion Picture Arts & Sciences v. Creative House Promotions, Inc.*, 944 F.2d 1446 (9th Cir. 1991) (holding that distribution of 158 Oscar statuettes to Academy Award winners without copyright notice and with no express restriction on further distribution was not divestitive); *compare King v. Mister Maestro, Inc.*, 224 F.Supp. 101 (S.D.N.Y. 1963) (finding "limited" distribution where Martin Luther King distributed advance copies of "I Have a Dream" speech to reporters with no restriction on further distribution or copying) *with Estate of Martin Luther King, Jr., Inc. v. CBS, Inc.*, 13 F. Supp. 2d 1347 (N.D. Ga. 1998) (reaching the opposite conclusion), *rev'd,* 194 F.3d 1211 (11th Cir. 1999).

The distinction between limited and general distributions persisted under the 1976 Act. Accordingly, the pre–1978 case law interpreting that distinction continues to be relevant.

The question whether a public performance constituted a publication under the 1909 Act was answered in the negative in *Ferris v. Frohman*, 223 U.S. 424 (1912). In the case of public displays, courts generally held that a public display without notice was not a publication if circumstances indicated that the author did not intend to forfeit copyright—for example, where the viewers were subject to restrictions on copying.

The definition of publication in § 101 of the 1976 Act is more detailed than in the 1909 Act. While it includes "the distribution of copies and phonorecords of a work to the public" either by transfer of ownership or by rental, lease, or lending, it expressly excludes public performances and displays. Furthermore, while a mere offer to distribute a work generally constituted publication under the 1909 Act, the 1976 Act adopts a narrower interpretation, stating that publication includes an offer to distribute a work "for purposes of further distribution, public performance, or public display."

However, the 1976 Act failed to resolve one problem which arose in determining the meaning of publication under the 1909 Act. Several courts had reached conflicting conclusions on whether a pre–1978 public distribution of a sound recording or other derivative work constituted a publication of the underlying work(s) incorporated in that derivative work. In the context of sound recordings, for example, phonorecords were frequently distributed to the public without a copyright notice for the underlying musical compositions (and typically without any copyright notice at all, since sound recordings were not eligible for federal copyright protection if they were first recorded prior to February 15, 1972), thus raising the question whether this public distribution caused the underlying musical compositions to enter the public domain. Section 401 of the 1976 Act did not require copyright notice to appear on publicly distributed phonorecords (because it referred only to "copies," and not "phonorecords"), but it failed to address the status of pre–1978 phonorecord distributions. Congress finally resolved this issue in 1997 when it enacted § 303(b), which provides that a pre–1978 distribution of a phonorecord was not a publication of the musical compositions embodied therein. The Ninth Circuit has held that § 303(b) should be applied retroactively, because it clarified rather than changed the law. *ABKCO Music, Inc. v. LaVere*, 217 F.3d 684 (9th Cir. 2000).

However, Congress has not resolved the analogous question whether, prior to March 1, 1989, the public distribution without notice of a derivative work caused the underlying work to enter the public domain (or, during the period of January 1, 1978 to March 1, 1989, caused a forfeiture of the underlying work's copyright, subject to the cure provisions of § 405(a)). There is little authority on this question, but the Second Circuit has held that the public distribution of a motion picture in 1960 without a copyright notice caused the underlying (and previously unpublished) screenplay to enter the public domain. *Shoptalk, Ltd. v. Concorde–New Horizons Corp.*, 168 F.3d 586 (2d Cir. 1999).

§ 4.2 Registration

Under the 1909 Act, statutory copyright in works that were not reproduced for sale could be secured through registration. Otherwise, registration was not essential to securing copyright protection; however, under § 13 of the Act, it was a prerequisite to filing an action for infringement.

Under the 1976 Act, registration is not essential to securing copyright protection, with one exception. The exception applies to works that were published without copyright notice on or after January 1, 1978 and before March 1, 1989. As discussed in § 4.1 above, copyright in such works was forfeited unless the copyright owner could satisfy one of the exceptions set forth in § 405(a)(1)-(3); one of these exceptions required, *inter alia*, registration of the work within five years of the publication without notice.

Under § 411 of the 1976 Act, registration continues to be a prerequisite to filing an action for copyright infringement of a United States work, although it is not a prerequisite for bringing an action for moral rights violations under § 106A. Registration is also not a prerequisite for bringing an action for infringement of certain works of foreign origin; hence the use of the term "United States work" in § 411. Such foreign works are exempt from the registration requirement because the Berne Convention, as incorporated in the

TRIPS provisions of the World Trade Organization (WTO) Agreement and the WIPO Copyright Treaty (WCT), forbids member countries from imposing formalities as a condition of copyright protection; Congress chose to comply with this requirement by eliminating the registration requirement for foreign works protected by Berne, but it did not eliminate this requirement for United States works. Section 101 provides a detailed definition of a "United States work," which considers the place of publication in the case of published works, and, in the case of unpublished works, the nationality, domicile, and residency of the authors; for pictorial, graphic, or sculptural works incorporated in a building or structure, the building or structure must be in the United States.

Registration procedures are governed by §§ 409–10 and by the Copyright Office Regulations at 37 C.F.R. § 202.3–12. In general, registration is accomplished by submitting the appropriate registration form (which depends on the type of work being registered) together with the registration fee (currently $45 for most works), and depositing a copy or phonorecord of the work with the Register of Copyrights (see details on deposit requirement at § 4.3 below). In some cases, a single registration may cover an entire group of works, such as newspapers and other periodicals. The registration form requires the applicant to disclose, *inter alia*, information pertaining to the author(s) as well as the copyright claimant, and information pertaining to any preexisting works that have been incorporated into the material sought to be registered.

If the Register of Copyrights determines that the work is eligible for copyright registration, a certificate of registration will issue. The effective date of such registration is the date on which the completed application for registration (including fee and deposit) was received by the Copyright Office. A certificate of registration issued before or within five years of the first publication of a work constitutes prima facie evidence of the validity of the copyright and of the facts stated on the certificate. For registrations made later than five years from first publication, the evidentiary value of the certificate is left to the court's discretion.

Section 408(f) and accompanying Copyright Office regulations permit preregistration of works that fall into certain categories that have a history of infringement prior to publication, including motion pictures, sound recordings, musical compositions, books, computer software, and photographs used in advertising and marketing. Preregistration does not constitute prima facie evidence of copyright validity, but it does satisfy the registration prerequisite for an infringement action under § 411. When a work has been preregistered, registration must be completed no later than three months after the work is published. If infringement of a preregistered work commences within two months after the work is published, an action for infringement will be dismissed unless a completed registration application (including fee and deposit) is submitted to the Copy-

right Office by the earlier of three months after
publication or one month after the copyright owner
learns of the infringement.

In addition to serving as a prerequisite to an
action for infringement of a United States work,
and as prima facie evidence of copyright validity,
registration has several other benefits. As discussed
in § 9.5 below, a work must be registered *before* it
is infringed in order for the copyright owner to be
eligible to recover statutory damages or attorneys
fees in an infringement action. This requirement
applies even to works originating in Berne Convention countries. Under § 205(c), the constructive notice provisions of the Copyright Office recording
system (see § 6.5 below) apply only to registered
works. Also, registration is required in order to
obtain relief against infringing imports through the
U.S. Customs Service under § 603 or in an action
before the International Trade Commission. Finally,
compulsory licensing fees under § 115 can only be
collected by the owner of the copyright as reflected
in the records of the Copyright Office.

In order to register a work, the copyright claim-
ant must satisfy the deposit requirement of
§ 408(b), discussed below. In some cases, copyright
owners seeking to register works in order to file
infringement actions have been unable to satisfy
this requirement because they no longer possess the
original or copies of the infringed work, and thus
they have been unable to pursue infringement actions.

§ 4.3 Deposit

The copyright statutes contain two different deposit requirements—one which is essential to copyright registration, and one which is designed to enhance the collections of the Library of Congress.

Under § 408(b) of the 1976 Act (as under § 12 of the 1909 Act), an application for copyright registration must be accompanied by a deposit of the material for which registration is sought. The specific deposit requirements depend on the nature of the work, and are set forth in the Copyright Office Regulations, 37 C.F.R. §§ 202.20–.23. Based on practical considerations, § 408(c) authorizes the Register of Copyrights to permit registration of some works without deposit of a complete copy. For example, the secure test regulations of 37 C.F.R. § 202.20(c)(2)(vi)—which apply to tests such as the SAT and the GRE—provide that the Copyright Office will return deposited copies of such tests, and their answer materials, to the registrant, but will retain a sufficient portion or description of the materials to constitute an archival record of the deposit.

Section 407 sets forth a separate deposit requirement, unrelated to copyright registration, which requires the deposit of copies or phonorecords of published works within three months of their publication. (A similar requirement applied under § 13 of the 1909 Act.) The deposited materials are added to the collections of the Library of Congress. Failure to comply with this deposit requirement has no impact on the copyright status of the work, but can subject the copyright owner to a fine. Some categories of works are exempt from the § 407 deposit requirement—*e.g.,* sculptural works, individual contributions to collective works, and most advertisements. *See* 37 C.F.R. § 202.19.

§ 4.4 Renewal Registration

Under the 1909 Act, timely renewal of a copyright registration was necessary to obtain the benefits of the renewal and extended renewal terms. Even after the 1976 Act, this requirement continued to apply to works that had been copyrighted under the 1909 Act. Failure to make a timely renewal registration caused the work to enter the public domain. Starting in 1992, renewal registration became automatic. A renewal registration still offered some benefits, however. If the renewal term vested in the author's § 304(a) statutory heirs (because the author died before vesting), then the failure of those heirs to file a timely renewal registration caused them to lose their right (recognized under *Stewart v. Abend,* see § 5.1 below) to prevent continued exploitation of a derivative work created under a grant during the first term of copyright. Also, a certificate showing timely renewal registration constitutes prima facie evidence of the validity of the copyright during its renewal and extended renewal term. The evidentiary weight accorded a non-timely renewal registration certificate is left to the discretion of the court.

The last works copyrighted under the 1909 Act entered their renewal terms at the end of 2005. Although it is no longer possible to make a *timely* renewal registration, renewal registrations are permitted throughout the renewal and extended renewal terms of these works, for whatever evidentiary value a court may decided to accord to them. Works copyrighted under the 1976 Act, however, have no renewal terms.

For a detailed discussion of copyright duration and renewals, see Chapter 5.

CHAPTER 5

COPYRIGHT DURATION

The duration of a work's copyright protection depends on the year in which the work was created or first published. The term of protection for works first fixed in a tangible medium of expression on or after January 1, 1978 is determined by § 302 of the 1976 Act. For works first published between 1909 and December 31, 1977, the term of protection is determined by the 1909 Act. Another set of rules determines the term of protection for works created before January 1, 1978, but still unpublished as of that date. However, all copyrightable works published before 1923 are now in the public domain. Finally, because sound recordings that were fixed before February 15, 1972, receive no federal copyright protection, the duration of their copyright, if any, is determined by state law.

§ 5.1 Works Published Before January 1, 1978

The term of copyright protection for works published prior to January 1, 1978 is determined under the 1909 Copyright Act (except for works published prior to 1909, all of which are now in the public domain). The statutory copyright term under the 1909 Act commenced upon publication with notice, and consisted of an initial 28–year term followed by a renewal term. As originally enacted, the renewal term lasted 28 years. However, as a result of a series of congressional enactments culminating in the 1976 Act, the renewal term was extended for an additional 19 years, giving these works a total renewal term of 47 years. By 1998, many of the works published under the 1909 Act had entered the public domain. However, any works which were still protected by copyright as of October 27, 1998 received an additional 20–year extension under the Sonny Bono Copyright Term Extension Act of 1998 (CTEA), which increased their total renewal term to 67 years, giving them a total copyright term of 95 years. Because the copyright term of the 1909 Act applies to works published as late as December 31, 1977, the last works copyrighted under the 1909 Act will enter the public domain on December 31, 2072 (unless Congress enacts another extension of the renewal term).

All copyright terms under the 1909 Act run until the end of the calendar year in which they expire.

A. Copyright Renewal

In the case of works that were published under the 1909 Act, until § 304 was amended in 1992 it was necessary for a copyright owner to file a renewal registration during the final year of the initial 28–year copyright term in order to obtain the benefit of the renewal term (including any extensions thereof). Failure to file a timely renewal registration caused the work to enter the public domain. In

1992, however, Congress amended § 302 to make renewal automatic. These automatic renewals took place between 1992 and 2005, which was the last year in which any copyrighted work was eligible for renewal. Thus, as of 2006, all works published between 1909 and December 31, 1977 had either entered the public domain or begun their second term of copyright.

B. Vesting of Renewal Term

When a copyright was renewed under the 1909 Act (automatically or otherwise), the owner(s) of the renewal term were determined under § 304(a). In the case of works made for hire, posthumous works, works copyrighted by corporate bodies, and certain composite works, the renewal term vested in the party that owned the copyright at the commencement of the renewal term, even if that party was an assignee. For all other works, the rules were more complex. If the author was still living at the end of the first term, the renewal term vested in the author, so that if the author had executed an assignment or license of the renewal term, the assignment or license took effect at this time. However, if the author died before the end of the first term, then the owner(s) of the renewal term were determined according to a hierarchy established by § 304(a): (1) the author's spouse and children, if any were still living, (2) in the absence of a living spouse or child, the author's executors, (3) in the absence of a will, the author's next of kin. If the author died before the end of the first term of copyright, then any assignment or license of the renewal term executed by the author during his or her lifetime was void. Thus, the author could not "contract around" the § 304(a) rules of succession.

This rule had harsh consequences for grantees that had, prior to the author's death, acquired an interest in the renewal term. If the author was no longer living at the commencement of the renewal term, then any assignment or license of the renewal term which the author purported to make while living was invalid, and the assignee or licensee did not receive any interest in the renewal term as a result of the inter vivos transfer. Instead, the renewal term vested in the author's statutory heirs, as determined under § 304(c). The heirs were then free to enforce their exclusive rights, provided they filed a timely renewal registration. If the grantee had prepared a derivative work in reliance on the inter vivos grant, the grantee could not exercise any of the § 106 rights in that derivative work during the renewal term. For example, the makers of the film *Rear Window* were forced to cease exploiting their film when the author of the underlying short story died before his renewal term vested; the author's executor assigned the renewal right to a third party, who then brought a successful infringement claim, overcoming the defendants' arguments for reading an implied "derivative works exception" (analogous to the one that Congress explicitly included in the termination provisions, discussed in § 6.6 below) into the renewal provisions. *Stewart v. Abend,* 495 U.S. 207 (1990).

§ 5.2 Works Created on or After January 1, 1978

Under the 1976 Act, works created on or after January 1, 1978 receive a single term of copyright protection, which commences as soon as the work is fixed in a tangible medium of expression. For works with individual authors, the 1976 Act originally provided that the copyright would endure for the life of the author plus 50 years. For joint works, the term consisted of the life of the last surviving author plus 50 years. In the case of works made for hire, copyright expired at the earlier of 75 years from publication or 100 years from creation. Anonymous and pseudonymous works received the same copyright term as works made for hire.

In 1998, however, the CTEA added an additional 20 years to each of these copyright terms. Accordingly, all copyrighted works created on or after January 1, 1978 currently enjoy the following terms of protection:

Individually authored works: Life of author + 70 years.

Joint works: Life of last surviving author + 70 years.

Works made for hire: Shorter of 95 years from publication, or 120 years from creation.

Anonymous and pseudonymous works: Same as works made for hire.

Under § 302(c), if the identity of the author(s) of an anonymous or pseudonymous work is properly disclosed to the Copyright Office before the end of the copyright term, then the appropriate life + 70 term will apply. No works created under the 1976 Act will enter the public domain until 2048 at the earliest.

§ 5.3 Works Created but Unpublished as of January 1, 1978

Yet another set of rules governs works that were created prior to January 1, 1978 but still unpublished as of that date. Under the 1909 Act, these unpublished works were protected by common law copyright, which was perpetual until publication, at which point the work either entered the public domain or began its limited term of statutory copyright, depending on whether it was published with notice. (See § 4.1 above.) Under § 102 and § 301 of the 1976 Act, however, common law copyright in fixed works was abolished, and all fixed works became subject to the limited term of statutory copyright under § 302. Accordingly, works created but unpublished as of January 1, 1978 lost their perpetual copyright on that date, and instead received the same term of protection as works created on or after that date—that is, the life of the author plus 50 years (now 70 years due to the CTEA), or, in the case of works made for hire, the shorter of 75 years (now 95) from initial publication or 100 years (now 120) from creation.

Congress realized, however, that imposing this limited statutory term on older unpublished works that had heretofore enjoyed perpetual copyright protection would cause many such works to enter the public domain immediately (for example, if the author had already been dead for 50 years), and others soon thereafter. To mitigate this harsh result, Congress created a special minimum term of protection for these works. Section 303(a) provided that copyright in these works would not expire before the end of 2002. Furthermore, to encourage publication of these works, § 303(a) also provides that if such a work was published on or before the end of 2002, its copyright will expire no sooner than the end of 2047 (originally 2027 under the 1976 Act, then extended by 20 years under the CTEA).

§ 5.4   Sonny Bono Copyright Term Extension Act

As discussed above, the current term of protection includes the 20–year extension which applied to all federal copyrights that were still in effect on October 27, 1998, pursuant to the Sonny Bono Copyright Term Extension Act (CTEA) of 1998. In *Eldred v. Ashcroft*, 537 U.S. 186 (2003), the Supreme Court considered a challenge to the constitutionality of the CTEA from a plaintiff who argued that extending the term of protection for subsisting copyrights (that is, not limiting the extended term to newly created works) (1) violated the "limited Times" restriction in the Patent and Copyright Clause, (2) failed to "promote the Progress of Science," (3) overlooked the constitutional requirement of originality, (4) ignored a *quid pro quo* implicit in copyright protection, and (5) violated the

First Amendment. The Court rejected each of these arguments, and upheld the CTEA.

§ 5.5 Works No Longer Protected by Copyright

If a work was published before 1923, then even if its copyright was timely renewed, it entered the public domain no later than 1997. Works published in 1923 or later are still protected by copyright (assuming compliance with applicable notice and renewal requirements), and will not begin entering the public domain until 2018.

§ 5.6 Author's Date of Death

In the case of copyright terms that expire 70 years after an author's death, ascertaining the author's date of death will be essential to determining the date on which the copyright term expires. Unfortunately, because there is no single repository of death records, this date will not always be easy to determine.

Sections 302(d) and (e) provide some assistance. Under § 302(d), any person with an interest in a copyright may at any time record in the Copyright Office a statement indicating the date of the author's death or declaring that the author is still alive as of a specific date. The Register of Copyrights is required to maintain these records, and may include pertinent information obtained from other sources as well. Under § 302(e), 95 years after a work's publication or 120 years after its creation (whichever comes first), a presumption arises that the author has been dead for at least 70 years unless the records of the Copyright Office indicate that this is not the case. If a person obtains a certified report from the Copyright Office showing that the presumption is warranted, reliance in good faith on this presumption is a complete defense to infringement.

§ 5.7　Orphan Works

The increased duration of copyright, combined with the elimination of mandatory notice and registration, as well as automatic renewal, has given rise to a phenomenon referred to as "orphan works." These are works in which copyright subsists, but the copyright owners of which either cannot be identified or cannot be located. Without the ability to contact the copyright owner to obtain consent, a party wishing to avoid infringement liability, and the attendant possibility of a significant damages award as well as an injunction against continued use of the work, will be reluctant to use the work. This is of particular concern to persons who are considering investing in the creation of a derivative work that incorporates the orphan work.

In response to this concern, the Copyright Office has recommended legislation that would permit the use of a work whose copyright owner cannot be identified or located, subject to an obligation to pay a reasonable license fee to the copyright owner if and when that person comes forward. In addition, the copyright owner would be foreclosed from obtaining injunctive relief against the continued use of a derivative work which the user created after being unable to identify or locate the copyright owner of the underlying work. These limitations on remedies would be available only if the user performed a reasonably diligent search for the copyright owner, and gave attribution to the author and copyright owner if their identities could be ascertained with reasonable certainty.

§ 5.8 Sound Recordings Fixed Before February 15, 1972

Because federal copyright does not extend to sound recordings fixed in the United States before February 15, 1972 (see § 2.2 above), the existence and duration of copyright protection for such recordings is a matter of state law. Under § 301(c), federal copyright law will not preempt this state law protection until February 15, 2067.

State law protection for these early sound recordings is highly variable, and in many states the existence and nature of such protection has yet to be determined. Where protection is available, it typically falls into one or more of three categories: criminal laws prohibiting record piracy, state statutes specifically addressing sound recording copyrights, and common law tort claims (whether denominated as common law copyright, unfair competition, or misappropriation).

Roughly half the states have adopted criminal statutes prohibiting the copying and distribution of these early sound recordings, including California, Illinois, Michigan, New York, and Virginia. In *Gold-*

stein v. California, 412 U.S. 546 (1973), the Supreme Court upheld an earlier version of California's criminal statute, Cal. Penal Code § 653h, against a preemption claim, holding that, with respect to the sound recordings at issue in that case, Congress had not precluded states from providing protection.

California's civil statute, Cal. Civ. Code § 980(a)(2), provides that the "author" of a pre–February 15, 1972 sound recording "has an exclusive ownership therein until February 15, 2047."

In most states, there have not yet been definitive rulings on the nature or extent of common law protection against copying or sale of these early sound recordings. Where no statutory protection exists, however, most states are likely to rule favorably rather than leave these recordings unprotected. It is difficult to predict how courts will determine the precise duration and scope of protection for these works. If they attempt to provide protection that is roughly comparable to that of federal copyright law, they will still have to decide whether to model their protection on the 1909 Act or the 1976 Act. Difficult questions may also arise with respect to copyright ownership, infringement defenses (such as fair use), and remedies.

The existence and scope of common law copyright protection under New York law was recently addressed by the New York Court of Appeals in *Capitol Records, Inc. v. Naxos of America, Inc.*, 4 N.Y.3d 540, 797 N.Y.S.2d 352, 830 N.E.2d 250 (2005), in response to questions certified to the court by the Second Circuit. The Court of Appeals held that, with respect to New York common law: (1) publication of a sound recording did not divest it of common law copyright; (2) the expiration of copyright in the recording's country of origin did not cause the recording to lose its common law copyright; (3) common law copyright protection of sound recordings will continue until 2067, the year in which federal preemption takes effect; (4) copyright infringement consists of two elements, a valid copyright and unauthorized copying; (5) no showing of bad faith, market competition, or commercial benefit is required to establish infringement; (6) the absence of a significant market for the copyrighted work is not a defense to infringement; and (7) it is no defense to infringement that the defendant's recording constitutes a "new work" because it has been remastered to enhance sound quality. Note that all of these holdings are specific to the common law of New York; the common law of other states may differ.

§ 5.9 Restoration of Copyrights in Foreign Works

When the United States joined the Berne Convention in 1988, the Convention required signatories to extend copyright to works originating in member countries if those works had not yet entered the public domain in their countries of origin. However, many such works had already lost their federal copyright protection due to failure to comply with formalities such as notice and renewal registration. Although the Berne Convention Implementation Act of 1988 ("BCIA") instituted a number of statutory changes in order to implement the requirements of Berne, including elimination of the notice requirement, it did not restore the copyright in foreign works that had entered the public domain due to failure to comply with formalities.

However, in order to implement the United States' obligations under the North American Free Trade Agreement and the TRIPS provisions of the WTO Agreement, Congress amended the copyright statutes in 1994 and 1995 by adding § 104A to the Copyright Act. Section 104A restored the remaining term of copyright protection for certain foreign works (known as "restored works") which had entered the public domain in the United States prematurely due to, *inter alia*, failure to comply with formalities.

To qualify as a "restored work" under § 104A, a work must meet several requirements. It must be an original work of authorship that has not yet entered the public domain in its source country through expiration of its copyright term. It must have entered the public domain in the United States for any of three reasons: (i) noncompliance with formalities, including nonrenewal, publication without proper notice, or failure to comply with the now-obsolete manufacturing requirements of the 1909 Act (which required all English language books and periodicals to be printed in the United States), (ii) in the case of sound recordings fixed before February 15, 1972, lack of subject matter protection, or (iii) lack of national eligibility. At least one of the work's authors or rightholders must, at the time the work was created, have been a national or domiciliary of an eligible country. In addition, in the case of published works, the work must have been first published in an eligible country and must *not* have been published in the United States within 30 days after such publication. If the source country is an eligible country only by virtue of adherence to the WIPO Performances and Phonograms Treaty (1996) (WPPT), then the restored work must be a sound recording.

The "source country" of a restored work must be a country other than the United States. In the case of *unpublished* works, the source country is the eligible country in which the author or rightholder is a national or domiciliary, except that: (1) if the work has more than one author or rightholder, then the source country is the eligible country of which the majority of the work's foreign authors or rightholders are nationals or domiciliaries, and (2) if the majority of authors or rightholders are not foreign, then the source country is the nation other than the United States which has the most significant contacts with the work. (The term *rightholder* in § 104A refers specifically to the person who makes the first authorized fixation of a sound recording, or to any person who acquires rights from that person.) In the case of *published* works, the source country is the eligible country of first publication, unless the restored work was published on the same day in two or more eligible countries, in which case the source country is the eligible country which has the most significant contacts with the work.

As defined in § 104A(h)(3), the term "eligible country" excludes the United States, but applies to any country which: (1) became a WTO member after December 8, 1994 (the date of enactment of the Uruguay Round Agreements Act (URAA), implementing the United States' obligations under the WTO Agreement); (2) adheres to the Berne Convention, the WIPO Copyright Treaty (WCT), or the WIPO Performances and Phonograms Treaty (WPPT); or (3) becomes eligible by proclamation after December 8, 1994. A nation can become eligible by proclamation if the President of the United States finds that the nation extends to authors who are United States nationals or domiciliaries restored copyright protection substantially similar to that provided by § 104A. When a nation so qualifies, the Presidential proclamation may restore protection to any work of which at least one author is, on the date of first publication, a national, domiciliary, or sovereign authority of that nation, or which was first published in that nation. Such proclamations may be revised, suspended, or revoked, and may be subject to conditions or limitations.

If a work qualified as a restored work under § 104A, then its federal copyright has now been restored. In other words, even though that work was previously in the public domain in the United States, it is once again under copyright. The date on which the copyright was restored depends on the date on which the source country became an eligible country. Copyright was restored as of January 1, 1996, with respect to any work whose source country already adhered to the Berne Convention or was already a WTO member as of that date. For all other works, copyright was restored on the date that the source country became an eligible country (*i.e.,* by adherence to Berne, the WCT, or the WPPT; by joining the WTO; or by Presidential proclamation). As additional countries become eligible in the future, even more copyrights will be restored.

Pursuant to § 104A(a), federal copyright in restored works vests automatically on the date of restoration, and continues for the remainder of the term of federal copyright protection that the work would have received if it had not entered the public domain in the United States. The statutory term of protection is *not* lengthened to compensate for the years that the work was in the public domain. Thus, the total number of years of copyright protection afforded to a restored work will typically be less than the total number of years of protection it would have received had it never entered the public domain at all. For example, if a restored work was published without notice in 1946, and its copyright was restored in 1996, then its copyright will expire in 2041, just as if it had never entered the public domain at all. The work will *not* receive an extra 50 years of protection to make up for its half-century in the public domain.

Works whose source country is the United States are not eligible for copyright restoration under § 104A. Thus, if work sourced in the United States entered the public domain due to publication without notice (and if this omission was not corrected under § 405(a)(2)) or failure to file a timely renewal registration, that work remains in the public domain.

Once copyright is restored to a work, § 104A(b) provides that the copyright vests initially in the author or initial rightholder of the work as determined by the law of the source country. Subject to a statutory exception for certain "reliance parties," the copyright owner is thereafter entitled to the full array of infringement remedies with respect to acts of infringement that commence on or after the date of restoration, until the remaining copyright term has expired.

In the case of a "reliance party," the rights of the owner of a restored copyright are subject to certain limitations. Generally speaking, a reliance party is any party that relied on a work's public domain status during the time it was unprotected by copyright—that is, from the date it entered the public domain until the date on which copyright was restored. As discussed below, in order to avoid undue hardship to these parties, § 104A(d)(2) places certain limits on the remedies available against reliance parties.

In the case of a restored work, § 104A(d)(2) makes the full array of infringement remedies available against a reliance party that undertakes infringing acts on or after the date of restoration, but *only if* the acts take place after the reliance party has received actual or constructive notice of the restored copyright. Actual notice is served on the reliance party, whereas constructive notice is accomplished by filing a notice of intent with the Copyright Office. More specifically, the conditions for invoking infringement remedies against reliance parties are as follows:

When constructive notice is utilized, § 104A(d)(2)(A) provides that infringement remedies are available where the owner of the restored copyright (or the owner of an exclusive right in the restored work), or the owner's agent, has filed with the Copyright Office, within 24 months after the date of restoration, a notice of intent to enforce the copyright; *and either* (I) the infringing conduct began more than 12 months after the notice of intent was published in the Federal Register, *or* (II) the infringing conduct began before the end of that 12–month period, but continued after the end of that period (in which case remedies are available only for the conduct that took place after the end of the period); *or* (III) copies or phonorecords of the work were made after the notice of intent was published in the Federal Register.

In the case of actual notice, § 104A(d)(2)(B) provides that infringement remedies are available where the owner of the restored copyright (or the owner of an exclusive right in the restored work), or the owner's agent, serves upon the reliance party a notice of intent to enforce the copyright; *and either* (I) the infringing conduct began more than 12 months after the notice of intent was received, *or* (II) the infringing conduct began before the end of that 12–month period, but continued after the end of that period (in which case remedies are available only for the conduct that took place after the end of the period), *or* (III) copies or phonorecords of the work were made after receipt of the notice of intent. Actual notice of intent to enforce is effective as to the reliance party on whom the notice is served, as well as any other reliance parties having actual knowledge of the service and the contents of the notice. 17 U.S.C. § 104A(c).

If the notice of intent to enforce is filed with the Copyright Office and also served directly on the reliance party, then the 12–month period described in the two preceding paragraphs runs from the *earlier* of the date of actual service or the date on which the notice is published in the Federal Register.

In order to be valid, a notice of intent to enforce a restored copyright—whether served on the reliance party directly or filed with the Copyright Office— must comply with strict statutory requirements set forth in § 104A(e).

Regardless of which type of notice is utilized, the effect of the 12–month window is to allow the reliance party a reasonable period to sell off copies or phonorecords already in hand at the time notice is received.

Under § 104A(d)(3), special rules apply in certain situations where a reliance party has incorporated a restored work into a derivative work that was created before the date of copyright restoration. If the source country of the derivative work was an eligible country on December 8, 1994 (the date of the URAA's enactment), then subsection (d)(3) applies to derivative works created before that date. Otherwise, subsection (d)(3) applies only to derivative works created before the date on which the source country became an eligible country by Presidential proclamation or by adherence to the WTO Agreement, Berne, the WCT, or the WPPT. If a derivative work meets these criteria, a reliance party may continue to exploit the derivative work notwithstanding the restoration of copyright in the underlying work, but only if the reliance party pays the copyright owner "reasonable compensation" for any activities that would constitute infringement but for these provisions. If the parties cannot agree on the amount of compensation, the amount will be determined by a federal district court. In determining the amount of compensation, the statute instructs the district court to consider any harm to the actual or potential market for, or value of, the restored work which will result from the reliance party's continued exploitation of the derivative work, as well as the relative amounts of expressive material which the reliance party and the restored work's author contributed to the derivative work.

Section 104A(h)(4)(A)-(C) identifies each of the following parties as a "reliance party" with respect to a restored work: (A) a person who engages in acts, *before* the source country of the work becomes an eligible country, which would have violated § 106 if the restored work had been protected by copyright at that time, *and* who continues to engage in such acts after the source country becomes an eligible country; (B) a person who makes or acquires one or more copies or phonorecords of a work *before* the source country becomes an eligible country; and (C) a person who, as a result of the sale or other disposition of a derivative work covered by § 104A(d)(3) or of significant assets of a reliance party described in (A) or (B) above, is a successor, assignee or licensee of that person.

The removal of works from the public domain under § 104A is unprecedented and controversial. In *Golan v. Gonzales*, 501 F.3d 1179 (10th Cir. 2007), the Tenth Circuit questioned the constitutionality of § 104A, ordering a district court to subject the statute to First Amendment scrutiny. If § 104A is held to be unconstitutional, restored works will lose their copyright protection, and the United States will be in violation of its international obligations under the Berne Convention and the WTO Agreement.

CHAPTER 6

ASSIGNMENTS AND LICENSES

§ 6.1 Divisibility

Although copyright ownership vests initially in the author of a work, any interest in the copyright may be the subject of an assignment or an exclusive or non-exclusive license.

Under § 201(d) of the 1976 Act, copyright is infinitely divisible. In other words, copyright is considered a "bundle of rights," and any portion of that bundle may be assigned through a conveyance or by operation of law, and may be inherited under a will or through intestate succession. Furthermore, any interest in a copyright may be the subject of an exclusive or non-exclusive license. In the case of a literary work, for example, one party may own (or hold a license for) the print publication rights, another may own or license the film adaptation rights, and yet another may own or license the electronic publication rights. Both owners and exclusive licensees (but not non-exclusive licensees) may register their interests in a copyright, and both have standing to sue infringers.

In contrast, copyright was indivisible under the 1909 Act. For an assignment to be valid, it had to include the entire copyright. An attempt to assign anything less was treated as a license. Only the owner of the entire copyright could register the copyright and sue infringers.

Under the 1909 Act, a licensee (exclusive or otherwise) could not re-sell or sublicense its interest without the copyright owner's consent. Under § 201(d) (2) of the 1976 Act, courts have reached conflicting conclusions on this question. Thus, in the absence of an express contractual provision limiting the licensee's rights, it is unclear whether current law permits exclusive licensees to transfer or sublicense their rights. In the case of non-exclusive licensees, the answer is probably no, because, as discussed below, even the 1976 Act treats non-exclusive licensees differently from holders of exclusive rights. Only the latter are recognized as copyright owners.

§ 6.2 Transfers

Under § 204, a transfer of copyright ownership, other than by operation of law, is enforceable only if it is evidenced by a writing signed by the grantor or the grantor's authorized agent.

Which transactions qualify as "transfers" for purposes of the § 204 requirement of a signed writing? Section 101 defines a "transfer of copyright ownership" as "an assignment, mortgage, exclusive license, or any other conveyance, alienation, or hypothecation" of any of the copyright owner's exclusive rights, even when limited in time or place of effect. The definition thus includes both assignments and exclusive licenses, but expressly excludes non-exclusive licenses (often referred to as "permissions" or "clearances"). Thus, any time a grantee receives rights that are exclusive (even if they are limited in duration and/or restricted to a particular geographic area), the grant is a "transfer." In contrast, if the grantee merely receives permission to exploit the copyrighted work, and does not acquire any right to exclude the grantor or third parties from exploiting the work, this is not a "transfer," and thus no writing is required.

Several courts have held that an oral transfer of copyright can be valid under § 204 if it is subsequently ratified in a signed writing. Where the parties to the agreement do not dispute the validity of the transfer, this approach is consistent with the purpose of § 204, which, like the Statute of Frauds, is intended to protect copyright owners from false assertions by parties claiming oral licenses or assignments, and to provide certainty as to the ownership of rights. These holdings have enabled transferees to obtain standing to sue third-party infringers even though the original transfer was not in writing. In contrast, if the putative transferor disputes the validity of the written ratification, it is less likely that a court will treat the ratification as valid under § 204, since the transferee could have protected itself by obtaining a signed writing at the time of the transfer.

A written instrument was also required for assignments of statutory copyrights under § 28 of the 1909 Act, although here, too, some courts allowed subsequent written ratifications of oral assignments. Unlike current law, however, § 28 did not require exclusive licenses of statutory copyrights to be in writing, nor did it require an assignment or exclusive license of a *common law* copyright to be in writing. Because some of these works are still under copyright today, these unwritten agreements can create problems in identifying the current copyright owners.

A copyright transfer may also occur by operation of law. Thus, for example, an interest in a copyright may be transferred in a bankruptcy proceeding. Outside of the bankruptcy context, however, § 201(e) precludes the government from seizing or transferring any interest in an individual author's copyright until it has been voluntarily transferred by the author.

§ 6.3 Nonexclusive Licenses

Because the § 101 definition of a "transfer of copyright ownership" expressly excludes non-exclusive licenses, such a license is not governed by § 204, and thus does not require a written instrument to be enforceable. Thus, oral and implied licenses can be enforced if they are non-exclusive. However, if a dispute should arise between the parties, the absence of a writing can make it difficult, as an evidentiary matter, to prove the existence, scope, and other specific terms of the license.

The burden of establishing an implied license is on the party claiming the protection of that license (typically, an accused infringer). Courts have been willing to find implied nonexclusive licenses where the conduct of the parties indicates a shared understanding that one party will have the right to exploit the other's copyrightable work—for example, where the copyright owner delivers a copy of the work in exchange for a sum far in excess of the value of the tangible copy.

In determining whether the facts support the existence of an implied license, however, courts do not always make clear whether they are relying on state law or judicially-developed federal law. Although the copyright statutes offer no criteria for this determination, some courts have adopted a three-part test derived from *Effects Associates, Inc. v. Cohen*, 908 F.2d 555 (9th Cir. 1991). Under this test, an implied nonexclusive license for use of a copyrighted work is created when: (1) a person (the licensee) requests the creation of a work, (2) the creator (the licensor) makes that particular work and delivers it to the licensee who requested it, and (3) the licensor intends that the licensee copy and distribute the work. In applying this test, some courts give the greatest weight to the licensor's intent.

Implied license questions frequently arise in the context of architectural plans. In this context, several circuits have adapted the *Effects Associates* test to develop a more specific set of non-exhaustive criteria: (1) whether the parties were engaged in a short-term discrete transaction as opposed to an ongoing relationship; (2) whether the creator utilized written contracts, such as the standard American Institute of Architects (AIA) contract, which provide that copyrighted materials can be used only with the creator's future involvement or express permission; and (3) whether the creator's conduct during the creation or delivery of the copyrighted material indicated that use of the material without the creator's involvement or consent was permissible.

Because non-exclusive licensees have no right to exclude others from exploiting the licensed copyright, they do not have standing to sue infringers, and may not register their interest in the copyright, although they may record that interest. (See § 6.5 below.)

§ 6.4   Interpreting Assignments and Licenses

Although copyright law provides the default rules governing copyright assignments and licenses (such as the § 204 writing requirement for transfers of exclusive rights), the interpretation of assignment and licensing agreements is generally a matter of state law. However, if the application of state law would lead to a result that conflicts with federal copyright policy, the state law will be preempted. (See Chapter 13.)

As noted earlier (see § 6.3 above), in cases involving implied copyright licenses, courts do not always make clear whether they are relying on state law or judicially-developed federal standards when determining whether the parties' conduct gives rise to an implied license.

Problems often arise in interpreting older copyright assignments and licenses in light of new technological modes of exploitation that were not considered by the parties that negotiated and drafted these agreements. For example, older book publishing agreements may refer to "books" without specifying whether this term includes e-books, and older film adaptation or synchronization agreements may not mention videocassettes, DVDs, or newer media.

§ 6.5   Recordation

Under § 205 of the 1976 Act, copyright transfers and any other documents pertaining to a copyright can be recorded with the Copyright Office.

Recordation serves several purposes:

First, under § 205(c), if copyright in the work has been registered, then recordation of any document pertaining to the work provides all persons with constructive notice of the facts stated therein, provided that the document identifies the work to which it pertains with sufficient specificity that, once indexed by the Register of Copyrights, the document can be found by a reasonable search under the title or registration number of the work.

Second, under § 205(d), when there are conflicting transfers, the one executed first prevails if it is timely recorded in the manner required to give constructive notice. A transfer is timely recorded if it is recorded within one month after its execution in the United States, or within two months after its execution abroad, or at any time before recordation of the later transfer. If the earlier transfer is not recorded within these time limits, then the later transfer will prevail if (1) it is recorded in the manner required to give constructive notice, and (2) it is taken in good faith, for valuable consideration or on the basis of a binding promise to pay royalties, and without notice of the earlier transfer. These priority rules apply only to registered copyrights.

Third, recordation is also relevant to establishing priority between a transfer and a conflicting non-exclusive license. Under § 205(e), a non-exclusive license, even if unrecorded, prevails over a conflicting transfer if the non-exclusive license is evidenced by a written instrument signed by the licensor or an agent thereof, provided that either (1) the license was taken before execution of the transfer, or (2) the license was taken in good faith before recordation of the transfer and without notice of it.

In addition to transfers, § 205(a) provides that any other documents pertaining to a copyright may be recorded in the Copyright Office. This privilege applies to both registered and unregistered copyrights.

In *In re Peregrine Entertainment, Ltd.,* 116 B.R. 194 (C.D. Cal. 1990), a federal district court held that any state recordation system pertaining to interests in copyrights is preempted by the recording rules of § 205, so that a security interest in a copyright can be perfected only by recording that security interest with the Copyright Office, and not by filing a UCC–1 financing statement under state law. Thus, under *Peregrine*, the UCC Article 9 method of perfecting a security interest does not apply to copyrights. However, a well-reasoned Ninth Circuit opinion has suggested that the *Peregrine* analysis should be limited to security interests that pertain to *registered* copyrights, because the priority system established in § 205 does not apply to unregistered copyrights, and thus provides no mechanism for perfecting a security interest in such copyrights. *See In re World Auxiliary Power Co.*, 303 F.3d 1120 (9th Cir. 2002) (holding that a security interest in an unregistered copyright may be perfected by filing a UCC–1 financing statement with the appropriate state agency). The Ninth Circuit disagreed with those courts that had extended *Peregrine* to unregistered copyrights. *See Zenith Productions, Ltd. v. AEG Acquisition Corp.*, 161 B.R. 50 (9th Cir. BAP 1993); *In re Avalon Software, Inc.*, 209 B.R. 517 (D. Ariz. 1997).

However, to avoid the risk that the state filing could be preempted by a later registration of the copyright, the holder of a security interest in an unregistered copyright should record that interest with the Copyright Office as well. *In re World Auxiliary Power Co.*, 244 B.R. 149, 154 n.11 (C.D. Cal. 1999), *aff'd*, 303 F.3d 1120 (9th Cir. 2002).

§ 6.6 Termination

Under certain conditions, the grant of any interest in a copyright may be terminated by the grantor. Termination rights apply not only to transfers (*i.e.*, assignments and exclusive licenses), but also to non-exclusive licenses. However, termination rights do not apply to works made for hire. In addition, as discussed below, all termination rights are subject to a derivative works exception.

The 1976 Act contains two termination provisions. The termination right in § 304(c) applies to grants executed before January 1, 1978, while the termination right in § 203 applies only to grants executed on or after January 1, 1978. Each of these termination provisions will be examined in turn.

A. Provisions Common to Both Termination Rights

Certain provisions are common to both the § 203 and § 304 termination rights. These include the types of grants that are subject to termination, the notice requirement, the derivative works exception, the exclusion of works made for hire, and the ineffectiveness of waivers.

1. *Grants Subject to Termination*

Termination rights apply to assignments, exclusive licenses, and non-exclusive licenses of a copyright or of any right in a copyright, other than by will.

2. *Notice*

Termination can be effected only by serving written notice on the grantee between 2 and 10 years before the effective date of termination. The notice must state the effective date of termination and must otherwise comply with Copyright Office regulations, and a copy of the notice must be recorded in the Copyright Office before the effective date of termination. 17 U.S.C. §§ 203(a)(4), 304(c)(4).

3. Derivative Works Exception

Both termination rights are subject to a derivative works exception, which provides that a derivative work which was created under the authority of the grant before the effective date of termination may continue to be exploited, under the terms of the grant, after termination. However, after termination the grantee may not create any new derivative works based on the copyrighted work covered by the terminated grant. 17 U.S.C. §§ 203(b)(1), 304(c)(6)(A).

Application of the derivative works exception depends on whether the grantee in fact created a derivative work. If the alterations to the copyrighted work are not substantial, then the grantee has merely copied that work rather than created a new derivative work; in that case, the derivative works exception will not apply, and the grantee must cease exploiting the copy. For a detailed discussion of derivative works, see § 2.9 above.

4. Works Made for Hire

Termination rights do not apply to works made for hire. The actual person who creates a work made for hire lacks a termination right because he or she is not considered its "author" for copyright purposes; rather, the author is the employer or other person who commissioned the work. (See

§ 3.4 above.) Even the employer or commissioning party, however, lacks a termination right. Congress's purpose in enacting termination rights was to protect individual authors from being locked into unfavorable contracts resulting from the individual's weak bargaining position; Congress did not have this same concern about the bargaining position of employers or commissioning parties. Thus, assignments and licenses of works made for hire are not subject to termination under either § 203 or § 304.

5. *Agreements to the Contrary Notwithstanding*

Both termination provisions provide that termination may be effected "notwithstanding any agreement to the contrary, including an agreement to make a will or to make any future grant." 17 U.S.C. §§ 203(a)(5), 304(c)(5). Thus, the termination right cannot be waived or assigned. In *Marvel Characters, Inc. v. Simon*, 310 F.3d 280 (2d Cir. 2002), the Second Circuit held that a settlement agreement in which parties agreed that a previously-created work was a work made for hire (which would make it ineligible for termination rights) was an "agreement to the contrary" under § 304(c)(5); accordingly, it had no effect on the individual author's § 304 termination right. This decision is probably correct, since the question whether something is a work made for hire is based on the agreement between the parties at the time of creation, and not on a subsequent agreement entered into to settle a dispute.

B. Termination Under § 304

The termination right in § 304 is closely related to, and was enacted at the same time as, the 19–year extended renewal term established by the 1976 Act for works copyrighted under the 1909 Act. This 19–year extension increased the renewal term from 28 years to 47 years (which was later extended to 67 years under the CTEA). Without a termination right, this copyright extension would have produced a windfall for the assignees and licensees of authors that had already executed grants of their renewal terms. In order to shift the benefits of this windfall to authors and their families, Congress gave these parties the right to terminate grants that had already been executed before January 1, 1978, the effective date of the 1976 Act.

Consistent with its purpose, the § 304 termination right applies only to a pre–1978 grant of an interest in copyright (other than by will) which includes the renewal term, and only when the grant was executed by one of the parties in whom a renewal term could vest under § 304(a)(1)(C)—that is, the author, or the author's widow(er), children, executors, or next of kin. Thus, § 304 termination right cannot be exercised by a mere assignee. The termination right also does not apply if the work was created as a work-made-for-hire.

1. *Who May Terminate*

If the grant was executed by one or more of the author(s) of the work, then the granting author, if still living, may terminate the grant to the extent of his or her share in the ownership of the renewal copyright. If the granting author is dead, then that author's power to terminate belongs to the person(s) entitled to exercise a total of more than 50% of that author's termination interest, according to the following priority list established by § 304(c)(2):

- The widow(er) receives 100% of the author's termination interest unless the author has surviving children or grandchildren, in which case the widow(er) owns 50% of the author's interest;

- The author's surviving children, and the surviving children of any dead child of the author, receive 100% of the author's termination interest unless there is a widow or widower, in which case they receive only 50%;

- The rights owned by the author's children and grandchildren (as determined above) are divided among them and exercised on a *per stirpes* basis according to the number of the author's children; the children of a dead child of the author may exercise their share of the termination interest only by action of a majority of them;

- If the author has no living widow(er), children, or grandchildren, then the author's executor, administrator, personal representative, or trustee receives that author's entire termination interest.

If the grant was executed not by the author, but by one of the other parties in whom the renewal term can vest under § 304(a)(1)(C)—the author's widow(er), children, executors, or next of kin—then the grant may be terminated by the surviving person(s) who executed it.

2. *When Termination May Occur*

Because the § 304 termination right applies only to the *extended* portion of the renewal term for works published under the 1909 Act, termination of a grant can be effected no sooner than the expiration of the original 28–year renewal term. Therefore, § 304(c)(3) provides that termination may take place no earlier than 56 years from the commencement of the federal copyright term. Beginning at the 56–year point, there is a 5–year window during which termination can be effected. However, in the case of works that had already been protected by federal copyright for more than 56 years as of the effective date of the 1976 Act, § 304(c)(3) provides that the 5–year termination window commenced on January 1, 1978.

3. *Notice of Termination*

Termination under § 304 is effected by serving the grantee (or the grantee's successor in interest) with a written notice, signed by the person(s) entitled to terminate the grant, that conforms to the requirements of § 304(c)(4).

4. *Reversion of Terminated Rights*

Section 304 also specifies who owns the terminated rights after the effective date of termination. If the original grant was executed by one of the author's statutory successors under § 304(a)(1)(C) (for example, the author's widower), then the rights that were covered by the grant revert to the surviving person or persons who executed the grant. If the original grant was executed by one or more of the work's authors, then all of a particular author's rights that were covered by the grant revert to that author, if he or she is still living, or, if that author is deceased, to the persons who own that author's termination right under § 304(c)(2), including any who did not join in signing the notice of termination.

The reverted rights vest as soon as the notice of termination is served.

If a deceased author's rights vest in two or more persons under § 304(c)(2) (*e.g.*, the author's widower and children), then they vest according to the proportionate shares specified in that provision (in this example, 50% to the widower and 50% split among the author's surviving children and the children of any dead child of the author, *per stirpes*).

5. *Post–Termination Grants of Reverted Rights*

The parties in whom reverted rights vest are entitled to execute further grants of those rights— either to the original grantee, under a newly negotiated contract, or to a new grantee. Where the rights have vested proportionately under § 304(c)(2), the new grant must be signed by the same number and proportion of the newly-vested owners as were required to terminate the grant in the first place. However, the new grant is binding on all of the newly-vested owners, even those who did not join in signing it.

In general, a grant of reverted rights is valid only if it is made after the effective date of termination. However, where the new grant is made to the original grantee or that party's successor in title, the new grant may validly be executed anytime after the date on which notice of termination is served.

6. *Effect of Copyright Term Extension Act*

As discussed in § 5.4 above, the CTEA added 20 years to the terms of all subsisting copyrights in 1998. Thus, any work that was in its 19–year extended renewal term as of 1998 saw its extended renewal term increase to 39 years.

As discussed earlier, § 304(c) allows termination only during a 5–year window commencing at the start of the extended renewal term (that is, after 56 years of copyright protection). However, some works that received an additional 20 years of protection under the CTEA were already beyond this window in 1998, so that it was too late for the grantors to exercise their termination right under § 304(c) if they had not already done so. Without a second window of opportunity, these grantors would lose the benefit of the 20–year extension, which would instead be a windfall to their grantees.

Section 304(d) was added by the CTEA to ensure that the benefit of the 20–year extension for works in this category would go to the author or owner of the termination right rather than to the grantee. It does this by providing a second window of opportunity for grantors whose § 304(c) termination rights had expired, unexercised, as of the effective date of the CTEA (October 27, 1998). Thus, for these works, § 304(d) provides that termination may be effected during a 5–year window beginning at the end of 75 years from the date on which copyright was originally secured. All of the other provisions of § 304(c) apply to § 304(d) terminations.

C. Termination Under § 203

Because Congress established a single unitary term of copyright in the 1976 Act, the families of deceased authors of works copyrighted on or after January 1, 1978 do not receive the benefit of a renewal term that is free and clear of grants executed by the author during his or her lifetime. (See § 5.2 above.) Nonetheless, Congress remained concerned that an author might execute a long-term grant under unfavorable terms due to an imbalance in bargaining power, only to find in later years that the value of the rights surrendered has significantly increased. In order to give these authors (and their families) a "second bite at the apple," § 203 of the 1976 Act creates a right to terminate these copyright grants after a fixed number of years.

The § 203 termination right applies only if a grant was executed (1) by the author of the work, and (2) on or after January 1, 1978. Both of these requirements distinguish it from the § 304(c) termination right.

1. *Who May Terminate*

If the grant was executed by one author, it can be terminated by that author, if living, or if the author is dead, then by the person or persons who own and are entitled to exercise a total of more than 50% of that author's termination interest according to the order of priority established in § 203(a)(2) (which is identical to the order of priority under § 304(c)(2)):

- The widow(er) receives 100% of the author's termination interest unless the author has surviving children or grandchildren, in which case the widow(er) owns 50% of the author's interest;

- The author's surviving children, and the surviving children of any dead child of the author, receive 100% of the author's termination interest unless there is a widow or widower, in which case they receive only 50%;

- The rights owned by the author's children and grandchildren (as determined above) are divided among them and exercised on a *per stirpes* basis according to the number of the author's children; the children of a dead child of the author may exercise their share of the termination interest only by action of a majority of them;

- If the author has no living widow(er), children, or grandchildren, then the author's executor, administrator, personal representative, or trustee receives that author's entire termination interest.

In the case of a joint work, termination of a grant executed by two or more authors of the work may be effected by a majority of the authors who executed the grant. If any of the granting authors is dead, then that author's termination interest may be exercised by the persons who own and are entitled to exercise a total of more than one-half of that author's termination interest, according to the same order of priority that is set forth in § 203(a)(2) above.

2. *When Termination May Occur*

Termination may occur anytime during a 5–year window that begins 35 years after execution of the grant, unless the grant covers publication rights, in which case the 5–year window begins 35 years after publication under the grant or 40 years after execution of the grant, whichever term ends earlier.

3. *Notice of Termination*

Termination under § 203 is effected by serving the grantee (or the grantee's successor in interest) with a written notice, signed by the person(s) entitled to terminate the grant, that conforms to the requirements of § 203(a)(4).

4. *Reversion of Terminated Rights*

On the effective date of termination, the rights covered by the terminated grant revert to the author(s) and other persons owning termination rights, including any who did not sign the notice of termination.

The reverted rights vest as soon as the notice of termination is served. Those rights vest in the author(s) and other persons entitled to terminate, according to their proportionate shares under § 203(a)(2) above.

5. *Post–Termination Grants of Reverted Rights*

The parties in whom reverted rights vest under § 203 are entitled to execute further grants of those rights—either to the original grantee, under a newly negotiated contract, or to a new grantee. The new grant must be signed by the same number and proportion of the newly-vested owners as were required to terminate the grant in the first place. However, the new grant is binding on all of the newly-vested owners, even those who did not join in signing it.

In general, a grant of reverted rights is valid only if it is made after the effective date of termination. However, where the new grant is made to the original grantee or that party's successor in title, the new grant may validly be executed anytime after the date on which notice of termination is served.

CHAPTER 7
EXCLUSIVE RIGHTS

§ 7.1 Overview

The six exclusive rights of a copyright owner are set forth in § 106. Three of the six exclusive rights apply to all categories of copyrightable works; these are the exclusive rights to (1) reproduce the copyrighted work in copies or phonorecords; (2) prepare derivative works based on the copyrighted work (also known as the "adaptation" right); and (3) distribute copies or phonorecords of the copyrighted work to the public. The remaining three rights apply only to certain categories of copyrighted works, as discussed in greater detail below; these are the exclusive rights to (4) perform the copyrighted work publicly; (5) display the copyrighted work publicly; and (6) perform the copyrighted work publicly by means of a digital audio transmission. With respect to the activities encompassed by the six exclusive rights, the copyright owner has the exclusive right both to engage in the activity and to authorize others to engage in that activity. Each of these exclusive rights is discussed in detail below.

The § 106 exclusive rights are subject to a number of statutory limitations, spelled out in §§ 107–122. For a detailed discussion of these limitations, see Chapter 8.

In addition to the exclusive rights of a copyright owner under § 106, authors (as opposed to copyright assignees) enjoy certain moral rights under § 106A. Moral rights are discussed in § 7.8 below.

Unauthorized exercise of any of these rights may give rise to an infringement claim, as discussed in Chapter 9. However, not every action that implicates one of the § 106 rights necessarily constitutes infringement; some actions may be permitted by statutory privileges (such as the first sale rule of § 109), some may be considered noninfringing by virtue of being *de minimis,* and some will not give rise to infringement liability because an affirmative defense applies (such as fair use or copyright misuse). Thus, in analyzing an infringement claim, it is necessary first to determine which, if any, of the copyright owner's exclusive rights has been *exercised* by the defendant, and then to determine whether the exercise of that right constitutes infringement.

The exclusive rights are not affirmative rights to engage in the activities described in § 106. Rather, each of the exclusive rights is a right to *exclude* others from engaging in those activities. Thus, for example, ownership of copyright in an obscene film does not give the copyright owner an affirmative right to perform the film publicly, because such performances may violate local obscenity laws, but it does allow the copyright owner to prevent someone else from publicly performing the film.

§ 7.2 Reproduction Right

The reproduction right of § 106(1) gives the copyright owner the exclusive right to reproduce the work in copies or phonorecords, and to authorize such reproductions. Reproduction, in this context, means copying, whether the copying is conscious or unconscious. Reproduction does not apply to independent creation, in which a new work resembles a pre-existing work but was not copied from it either consciously or unconsciously. Instead, it applies to producing a second copy of a work through imitation. Thus, if two artists paint the same landscape independently, neither of them imitating the other's work, then even if the two works are identical, neither artist has reproduced the other's work within the meaning of § 106(1). In contrast, if one artist chooses to paint the same landscape already painted by another, and consciously or unconsciously imitates the other's artistic choices, then the later artist may be found to have reproduced the other's copyrighted work. Thus, reproduction in this context does not literally mean "to produce again," but to produce a work *that imitates another*.

To fall within § 106(1), the reproduction must take the form of a "copy or phonorecord," meaning that it must be expressed in a tangible form. Thus, a live performance is not a reproduction. The tangibility requirement is imposed by § 101, which defines both copies and phonorecords as "material objects" in which a work is "fixed by any method now known or later developed," and from which that work "can be perceived, reproduced, or otherwise communicated, either directly or with the aid of a machine or device."

The tangibility requirement applies to both copies and phonorecords. Under § 101, the only difference between these two categories of tangible fixations is that a phonorecord is a tangible fixation of sounds (other than those accompanying a motion picture or other audiovisual work), while a copy is any tangible fixation other than a phonorecord. Thus, an mp3 file of a sound recording is a phonorecord, while a DVD, or any other tangible embodiment of an audiovisual work, is a copy.

Straightforward examples of reproduction by copying include duplicating a work on a photocopying machine, or duplicating a CD, DVD, video game or mp3 file on a computer or other electronic recording device. Reproductions like these typically produce exact (or near-exact) duplicates of the copyrighted work. As discussed in § 9.3 below, however, for a reproduction to infringe, it need not be an exact copy of the copyrighted work; it need only be "substantially similar."

On a more challenging set of facts, the Second Circuit held that a series of still photos could "reproduce" copyrighted choreography within the meaning of § 106. *Horgan v. Macmillan, Inc.,* 789 F.2d 157 (2d Cir. 1986). Although the essence of choreography is movement, a series of still photos can make those movements perceptible to a viewer who looks at a sufficient number of sequential photos that were taken close together in time. Thus, the question whether a series of still photos infringes a choreographic work depends on the number, frequency, and sequencing of the photos. It is less clear, however, whether the mere *existence* of the photos would reproduce the choreography, or whether the photos would have to be arranged in sequence before reproduction would be found. This question did not arise in *Horgan*, because the defendant had already arranged the photos in sequence in a book that he was preparing to publish.

Copying a work into a different medium of expression will not avoid a finding of reproduction under § 106. Thus, a photograph may reproduce a sculpture, and vice versa. Reproducing a painting in fabric used for clothing is also a reproduction. Similarly, using copyrighted artwork in the background of a movie or television scene is also a reproduction. Isolating a still image from a movie and turning it into a poster is a reproduction as well.

Copying also occurs when material is scanned or downloaded onto the permanent memory of a computer, when material is uploaded from a computer to a server, and when computer users "swap" or "share" files by transmitting material from one computer to another, adding the material to the permanent memory of the recipient's computer while retaining a copy in the permanent memory of the sender's computer.

It remains unsettled, however, whether copying occurs when a work is reproduced only temporarily in a computer's random access memory ("RAM").

The uncertainty arises from the § 101 definition of "fixation," which is limited to embodiments that make the work perceptible "for a period of more than transitory duration." The legislative history on this point is conflicting. The 1976 House Report states that the concept of fixation excludes "purely evanescent or transient reproductions such as those projected briefly on a screen, shown electronically on a television or other cathode ray tube, or captured momentarily in the 'memory' of a computer." H.R. Rep. No. 94–1476, 94th Cong., 2d Sess. 51 (1976). However, in 1978 a Congressionally-authorized commission of experts recommended the opposite result. The *Final Report of the National Commission on New Technological Uses of Copyrighted Work*s (1978) ("CONTU Report") stated that the assertion in the legislative history "should be regarded as incorrect and should not be followed." CONTU Report, at 55. The CONTU Report states that § 106 "seemingly would prohibit the unauthorized storage of a work within a computer memory," and that the process of "inputting" material into a computer is one in which "a reproduction is created within the computer memory." *Id.* at 98 & n.169. While only a few courts have squarely addressed this question, a majority of these have held that temporary storage on RAM is a fixation, and therefore can support an infringement claim. As discussed in § 8.10 below, the 1998 amendments to § 117 arguably imply congressional ratification of this interpretation. One court, however, has suggested that storage on RAM is not a fixation when it is automatic and transitory (as in the case of a transmission through the facilities of an Internet service provider), but that it is a fixation when the copyrighted content is actually used. *CoStar Group, Inc. v. LoopNet, Inc.*, 373 F.3d 544 (4th Cir. 2004).

The reproduction right is independent of the public distribution right. Thus, the reproduction right is implicated as soon as a copy is made, regardless of whether that copy is sold or otherwise publicly disseminated, and regardless of whether it is publicly performed or displayed. As a result, liability for infringing reproduction may be found even where no distribution has occurred.

The scope of the reproduction right for sound recordings is narrower than for other classes of copyrighted works. Under § 114(b), the exclusive right to reproduce a sound recording is limited to the right to duplicate the actual sounds that are fixed in the recording. It does not encompass the making of a "soundalike" recording—that is, a recording that closely imitates the copyrighted recording, but which consists of an independent fixation of sounds. Thus, while copying an mp3 file of a popular song from one computer to another could infringe the reproduction right, hiring singers and musicians to produce a virtually identical recording of that song through imitation would not (although it could infringe the reproduction right in the underlying musical composition). In contrast, with respect to all categories of copyrightable works other than sound recordings, an independent fixation can infringe as long as it is substantially similar. For example, if a photographer chooses a model, pose, setting, angle, and lighting and camera equipment in order to produce a close imitation of a famous photograph, the resulting photo is a reproduction under § 106(2).

§ 7.3   Right to Create Derivative Works

The adaptation right of § 106(2) gives the copyright owner the exclusive right to make, and to authorize the making of, derivative works that are based on the copyrighted work. Section 101 defines a "derivative work" as follows:

> A "derivative work" is a work based upon one or more preexisting works, such as a translation, musical arrangement, dramatization, fictionalization, motion picture version, sound recording, art reproduction, abridgment, condensation, or any other form in which a work may be recast, transformed, or adapted. A work consisting of editorial revisions, annotations, elaborations, or other modifications which, as a whole, represent an original work of authorship, is a "derivative work."

The right to create derivative works often overlaps with the reproduction right. When a copyrighted work is altered, and the changes are fixed in a tangible medium of expression, portions of the resulting work may be "substantially similar" to the copyrighted work, while other portions contain substantial alterations. In such a case, both the reproduction right and the derivative work right are implicated. This is true, for example, of a motion picture adaptation of a short story or a foreign language translation of a novel.

According to the 1976 House Report, however, a derivative work need not be fixed in a tangible medium of expression in order to infringe the derivative work right. Thus, for example, an authorized public performance of a copyrighted play or choreographic work may be an unauthorized derivative work if the script or choreography is altered, even if the altered performance is not recorded. Even if the copyright owner authorized a public performance, the unauthorized alterations included in that performance may infringe the derivative work right. Accordingly, the House Report makes clear that the derivative work right may be infringed even where no reproduction takes place. In contrast, in order for a derivative work to be *protected by copyright*, it must, like any other copyrightable work, be fixed in tangible form. (See § 2.1 above.)

Although the legislative history makes clear that even an unfixed derivative work can be actionable as an infringement of the § 106(2) right, courts have had difficulty applying this concept to certain types of altered performances. For example, in cases presenting similar facts, the Second and Seventh Circuits reached opposite conclusions on the question whether derivative works are created when devices are used to alter the performance of a video game—for example, by speeding up the overall rate of play, or by allowing the player to change certain characteristics of the game or its characters—without permanently storing these alterations. The Seventh Circuit held that a speeded-up performance of a video game was a derivative work, because it was "a substantially different product from the original game," which required "some creative effort to produce," and because there was market demand for such a work. *Midway Manufacturing Co. v. Artic International, Inc.*, 704 F.2d 1009 (7th Cir. 1983). In contrast, the Second Circuit held that the derivative right was not implicated by a device that enabled players to alter the performance of a video game by changing certain characteristics. Although it acknowledged that fixation was not required under § 106(2), the court nonetheless held that a derivative work "must incorporate a protected work in some concrete or permanent 'form.'" *Lewis Galoob Toys, Inc. v. Nintendo of America, Inc.*, 964 F.2d 965 (9th Cir. 1992). However, nothing in the Copyright Act or its legislative history supports the court's assertion that incorporation must be "concrete or permanent," and the Ninth Circuit's imposition of this requirement is difficult to reconcile with the statement in the House Report that a derivative work need not be fixed in order to infringe.

Despite the House Report language evincing Congress's intent to encompass unfixed derivative works in § 106(2), several federal district court decisions involving Internet "pop-up" ads that temporarily obscure portions of the copyrighted material on a website have held that pop-up ads do not create derivative works because, *inter alia*, any alterations they cause are not "fixed." *See, e.g., Wells*

Fargo & Co. v. WhenU.com, Inc., 293 F.Supp.2d 734 (E.D.Mich. 2003); *1–800 Contacts, Inc. v. WhenU. com*, 309 F.Supp.2d 467 (S.D.N.Y. 2003). Although the ultimate conclusion in these cases may be correct (as discussed later in this section), this part of their rationale is probably incorrect as a matter of law.

Courts narrowly avoided addressing the question of unfixed derivative works in yet another context in 2005, when Congress enacted the Family Movie Act (FMA). The FMA was prompted by the development of software which enables consumers to view edited performances of motion picture DVDs. This technology does not alter the content fixed on the DVD. Instead, it alters the *performance* of the DVD by temporarily deleting, obscuring, or replacing content that viewers may find offensive, such as graphic violence, profanity, or nudity. The FMA added § 110(11) to the Copyright Act, providing that no infringement occurs when a consumer uses such technology to make portions of a performance "imperceptible." Neither the FMA nor its legislative history makes clear whether this immunity from liability applies only to deletions, or whether it also immunizes the insertion of substitute content (*e.g.,* substituting a non-profane word for a profanity, or digitally adding clothing to a nude figure). It is clear, however, that the FMA applies only to altered performances; it does not authorize the creation or distribution of a DVD or videocassette in which the altered content has been *fixed*.

Unfixed derivative works such as live performances represent one situation in which the derivative right may be infringed without copying the underlying work. Another situation in which a derivative work is created without copying is the direct alteration of a copy of the copyrighted work. For example, if the purchaser of a painting or sculpture alters the painting or sculpture in a significant way—perhaps by adding additional colors or details to the painting, or changing the shape or colors of the sculpture—the altered work is a derivative work, even though no copy was made of the underlying work (and, indeed, the underlying work no longer exists in its original form).

Courts have encountered difficulty in determining which alterations to a work are substantial enough to give rise to derivative works. Part of the difficulty stems from the two-sentence structure of the "derivative work" definition in § 101 (reproduced above). The first sentence can be read broadly to indicate that a derivative work arises anytime an underlying work is recast, transformed, or adapted. However, the second sentence can be read to suggest that a derivative work must also be "original." In order for a derivative work to be *copyrightable*, of course, it must be original. However, it is not clear that Congress intended the originality requirement to apply also to determining when an unauthorized alteration work *infringes* under § 106(2). Courts and commentators are currently divided on this question. If a derivative work must be original in order to infringe, then minor alterations will not give rise to infringement claims under § 106(2).

Even among those courts that do not treat originality as a prerequisite to establishing infringement under § 106(2), there is no consensus on what degree of alteration is required to find that a work has been "recast, transformed, or adapted." The Seventh and Ninth Circuits, for example, reached opposite conclusions on nearly identical facts in *Lee v. A.R.T. Co.,* 125 F.3d 580 (7th Cir. 1997) and *Mirage Editions, Inc. v. Albuquerque A.R.T. Co.,* 856 F.2d 1341 (9th Cir. 1988). In both cases, the defendants purchased authorized copies of the plaintiff's artwork (pages cut from books in *Mirage Editions*, and note cards and small lithographs in *Lee*), and mounted the artwork on tiles. The Ninth Circuit held that the defendants had created unauthorized derivative works. The Seventh Circuit disagreed, treating the mounting process as a trivial alteration, much like traditional framing, and therefore concluded that the plaintiff's artwork had not been "recast, transformed, or adapted." On these facts, the Seventh Circuit's view is widely regarded as more persuasive. However, other factual scenarios present an infinite spectrum of possible alterations, and the line between those changes that are substantial enough to give rise to derivative works and those which are not remains elusive.

Both the video game and the altered artwork examples highlight the difficulty of determining which changes are substantial enough to give rise to the creation of a derivative work. This question is less often posed in scenarios that involve unauthorized copying as well as alteration—for example, an unauthorized translation of a book, or an unauthorized film adaptation of a short story—only because in such cases the plaintiff can win on a claim of infringing reproduction, without even addressing the question whether the alterations are significant enough to infringe the derivative work right. Nonetheless, the derivative work question could arise in circumstances that also involve copying—specifically, where the copyright owner has consented to copying but has not consented to any alteration of the work. For example, if a print publication license permits the publisher to print copies of a text, but does not permit any editing, if the publisher makes changes to the text without the copyright owner's consent then the publisher can be held liable for unauthorized creation of a derivative work only if a court concludes that the changes are substantial enough to satisfy the definition of a derivative work.

A comparable scenario arose in *Gilliam v. American Broadcasting Companies, Inc.,* 538 F.2d 14 (2d Cir. 1976), where the copyright owners of a television script retained the copyright in their script, and did not agree to allow the filmed version (itself an authorized derivative work) to be edited for the insertion of commercials. When the defendants edited out substantial portions of the program and inserted commercials, the plaintiffs prevailed in a suit for infringement of their exclusive right to create derivative works. Although the copying, public distribution, and public performance of the script were authorized, the editing for insertion of commercials was not. On these facts, the editing was unquestionably substantial enough to satisfy the "derivative work" definition.

Derivative works claims have also arisen in the context of Internet "pop-up" ads, in which a defendant's advertisement briefly appears on a user's computer screen so as to temporarily obscure the user's ability to see a portion of the content being displayed on the plaintiff's website. Thus far, courts have consistently rejected these claims, holding that the temporary obscuring of the plaintiff's copyrighted screen display does not create a derivative work, and noting that a contrary holding would give rise to an infringement claim whenever a Windows user views one "window" inside another.

Like the reproduction right, the adaptation right is defined more narrowly for sound recordings than for other categories of works. Under § 114(b), the adaptation right is limited to the right to prepare a derivative work "in which the actual sounds fixed in the sound recording are rearranged, remixed, or otherwise altered in sequence or quality." The exclusive right does not extend to the creation of work in which there is an independent fixation of sounds that closely imitate those of the sound recording. Thus, the adaptation right does not apply if musicians are hired to make a new recording that imitates the sounds of the copyrighted recording, but it does apply if the new recording "samples" the actual sounds of the copyrighted recording through the use of analog or digital copying equipment.

§ 7.4 Public Distribution Right

Under § 106(3), the copyright owner enjoys the exclusive right to distribute copies or phonorecords of the work to the public, and the exclusive right to authorize such distributions, whether by "sale or other transfer of ownership, or by rental, lease, or lending." The terms "copy" and "phonorecord" have the same definition here as in § 106(1) (defining the reproduction right).

Just as liability for infringing reproduction may be found even if the copies are not publicly distributed, liability for infringing public distribution may arise even where the defendant engaged only in public distribution, and did not actually make the infringing copies. The defendant need not even be aware that the copies are infringing.

The exclusive distribution right applies only to *public* distributions. Private, or "limited," distributions do not require the copyright owner's consent. The rules used to distinguish between public and private distributions in the § 106(3) context are generally the same as the standards used to draw this distinction in determining whether a work has been "published" for such purposes as the registration provisions of § 412 (see § 9.5 below) and the pre–1989 copyright notice provisions of § 405(a) (see § 4.1 above). However, while the § 101 definition of publication also includes a mere *offer* to distribute copyrighted material "for the purpose of further distribution, public performance, or public display," it is unsettled whether this part of the publication definition also applies to § 106(3). Thus, courts have reached conflicting conclusions on whether a public distribution takes place when material is "made available" on the Internet, without proof that anyone has actually received and copied or distributed the material.

A major limitation on the public distribution right is the first sale rule of § 109(a). (See § 8.2 below.) In brief, the first sale rule permits the owner of a copy or phonorecord that was lawfully made in the United States to sell or otherwise dispose of that particular copy or phonorecord. In the case of sound recordings and software, however, the first sale rule does not permit rentals. Because the first sale rule applies only to lawfully made copies, it does not apply to any public distributions of infringing copies.

Importation. Under § 602(a), an infringing public distribution under § 106(3) occurs whenever copies or phonorecords of a work that were acquired overseas are imported into the United States without the consent of the U.S. copyright owner, subject to three exceptions: (1) importation under authority of a state or local government or the federal government, except for works imported for use in schools and audiovisual works imported for non-archival purposes; (2) importation, solely for the importer's private use, of (i) no more than one copy or phonorecord of a work at any one time or (ii) copies or phonorecords that are in the person's personal baggage; and (3) importation by or for a scholarly, educational, or religious organization, neither for private gain nor in connection with systematic reproduction or distribution in violation of § 108(g)(2) (see § 8.1 below), of (i) a single copy of an audiovisual work for archival purposes, and (ii) no more than five copies or phonorecords of any other work for library lending or archival purposes. In contrast, under § 601(b), importation is completely prohibited with respect to copies or phonorecords the making of which would have been an infringement of copyright if the federal copyright statutes applied.

It remains unsettled whether, and under what circumstances, an electronic transmission is a public distribution. The copyright statutes do not define a "distribution." Both the § 101 definition of "publication" and the language of § 106(3) refer to "the distribution of copies or phonorecords of a work to the public by sale or other transfer of ownership," without indicating whether the copies or phonorecords must be in a tangible form throughout the distribution process, or whether it is sufficient that recipients can create their own tangible copies by downloading the transmitted material. When Congress was drafting the current copyright statutes in the late 1960s and early 1970s, Congress simply did not contemplate that copies of copyrighted material might be disseminated in other than tangible form. However, in *New York Times Co., Inc. v. Tasini*, 533 U.S. 483, 498 (2001), the Supreme Court stated that it is "clear" that distribution occurs when a publisher sells copies of an article through an electronic database.

Even if a particular electronic transmission is a distribution, § 106(3) is infringed only if the distribution is public. Some electronic transmissions are private, or limited, distributions. For example, sending copyrighted material as an attachment to an email sent to one individual might be a distribution, but it would be private rather than public, and thus would not infringe under § 106(3) (although it may involve a reproduction under § 106(1)). In contrast, posting copyrighted material on the Internet so that it is widely available for downloading would be a *public* distribution (assuming, of course, that it is a "distribution" in the first place).

Although it has been argued that electronic dissemination is not distribution, most courts that have addressed this question in the context of downloadable Internet transmissions have treated this as a form of public distribution, because persons who receive a downloadable transmission can save a permanent copy, a position supported by *Tasini*, as noted above. If this analysis is correct, it raises the additional question whether a public distribution occurs only when a recipient actually downloads the material, or whether the distribution occurs as soon as the material is made available for downloading. This question, too, is unresolved. In the context of peer-to-peer networks, some courts have held that distribution occurs whenever material is made available in a computer file that is accessible to others in a peer-to-peer file sharing network, even though the material resides on the user's hard drive (rather than on a separate, centralized server) until it is accessed by another user. A related question is whether inline linking and framing, without more, constitute distribution where the infringing materials are located on a third-party website; the Ninth Circuit has held that a defendant cannot be liable for public distribution of a work if no copy actually resides on the defendant's system. *Perfect 10, Inc. v. Amazon.com, Inc.*, 508 F.3d 1146 (9th Cir. 2007).

Some Internet transmissions provide a public performance or display of copyrighted material without enabling the recipient to download a permanent copy of the material. Streaming audio and video fall into this category. If the streaming transmission cannot be saved on a recipient's computer, the argument for treating this as a distribution is weakened. On the other hand, because the streaming performance or display is temporarily captured in the RAM of the recipient's computer, which many courts would treat as a fixation, it might be argued that this tangible fixation is sufficient to characterize the streaming transmission as a distribution.

§ 7.5 Public Performance Right

Under § 106(4), certain copyright owners have the exclusive right to publicly perform their works, and to authorize public performances thereof.

Unlike the reproduction, adaptation, and public distribution rights, the public performance right applies only to certain categories of works, which are listed in § 106(4): literary, musical, dramatic, and choreographic works, pantomimes, and motion pictures and other audiovisual works. Thus, the

§ 106(4) right does not apply to pictorial, graphic, and sculptural works, architectural works, or sound recordings.

The concept of performance is defined in § 101:

To "perform" a work means to recite, render, play, dance, or act it, either directly or by means of any device or process or, in the case of a motion picture or other audiovisual work, to show its images in any sequence or to make the sounds accompanying it audible.

Under § 106(4), it is crucial to distinguish between the rights in a sound recording and those in a musical composition. When a CD or mp3 file is played by a deejay in a dance club, for example, this implicates the public performance rights of the copyright owner of any musical composition embodied in the sound recording, but not the public performance rights of the record company that owns the copyright in the sound recording itself. As discussed in § 7.7 below, sound recordings enjoy a different kind of public performance right, under § 106(6), which is not implicated when a CD or mp3 file is played by a deejay in a dance club.

The copyright owner's exclusive right extends only to *public* performances, not to private ones. According to § 101, to perform a work publicly means:

(1) to perform or display it at a place open to the public or at any place where a substantial number of persons outside of a normal circle of a family and its social acquaintances is gathered; or

(2) to transmit or otherwise communicate a performance or display of the work to a place specified by clause (1) or to the public, by means of any device or process, whether the members of the public capable of receiving the performance or display receive it in the same place or in separate places and at the same time or at different times.

For purposes of this definition, "transmit" means to communicate a performance "by any device or process whereby images or sounds are received beyond the place from which they are sent." 17 U.S.C. § 101.

Applying these definitions, courts have identified three distinct situations in which a performance is public:

(a) when it occurs in a place "open to the public";

(b) when it occurs in a nonpublic place where members of the public are gathered;

(c) when it is transmitted or communicated to a place open to the public or to a place where members of the public are gathered, or when it is transmitted to individual members of the public by means of a device or process, regardless of how many people are receiving the transmission at any given time, and regardless of whether the recipients are located in separate places, including non-public places, when receiving the transmission.

In addition, secondary retransmissions, or further communication to the public, of a public performance may infringe the § 106(4) right even if the initial public performance was authorized. Each of these four situations is discussed below.

A. Places Open to the Public

In addition to areas that are open to the public without restriction (streets, sidewalks, public parks, etc.), this category includes privately owned spaces which members of the public are ordinarily entitled to enter, even if admission is charged. Thus, this category includes retail stores, shopping malls, restaurants, bars, nightclubs, arenas, movie theatres, live theatres, public transportation vehicles, commercial airplanes, cruise ships, campgrounds, golf courses, skating rinks, parking lots, and most areas of a hotel other than private guestrooms.

B. Places Where Public Is Gathered

Even if a performance takes place in a location to which the general public is not ordinarily invited, the performance is public if the persons present for the performance include a "substantial number" of persons other than the "normal circle" of a family and their social acquaintances. Examples include private clubs, lodges, summer camps, factories, conference rooms, military bases and vessels, schools (including classrooms, libraries, auditoriums, and dormitories), hospitals, and prisons. Even a performance in a hotel room or in an individual's private home may be a public performance under this standard, depending on who is present for the performance.

There is no clear rule for determining what constitutes a gathering of a "substantial number" of persons. However, the 1976 House Report states that "routine meetings of businesses and governmental personnel" would not qualify; thus, performances at such meetings would ordinarily be treated as private. In contrast, a performance that was open to all employees gathered at the annual retreat or holiday party of a large company would almost certainly be public.

A performance in a church will ordinarily be a public performance, if it takes place in the part of the church to which the public is ordinarily invited or in an area where members of the public are in fact gathered (such as an auditorium).

C. Transmission Clause

A public performance also occurs when the sounds or images of a work are transmitted or communicated to a public place, or to members of the public, by means of any device or process, even if members of the public receive it at different times and in different places.

This category includes, *inter alia*, performances via television or radio (including both ordinary broadcasts and pay-per-view performances), as well as performances over the telephone (for example, recorded music played while a caller is on "hold") or transmitted through the Internet. With respect to entertainment systems available to hotel guests, when a movie is transmitted to an individual guest room from another location, this is a public performance. In contrast, if the hotel provides the guest with the tangible DVD, and the guest then plays the DVD on a device located in the room, this is a private performance because no transmission is deemed to occur. This is consistent with the treatment of DVD performances in a person's home as private performances, whereas television performances transmitted to the same home would be public performances.

A performance by means of a transmission is a public performance even if is received by individual members of the public in different places and at different times. This can be the case, for example, with television and radio broadcasts, and with audio performances transmitted to telephone callers on "hold." It is also typical of public performances by means of Internet transmissions. A transmission will be a public performance even if the recording is stored at a central location (such as a server) and is performed at a time chosen by the individual member of the public.

However, a copyright owner alleging an infringing public performance by means of a transmission need not prove that the transmission was actually received; it is enough that it was *capable* of being received by members of the public. Thus, the copyright owner alleging an infringing television broadcast need not prove that any person within range of the broadcast was watching the broadcast or was operating a television at all.

Under the "transmission" prong of the public performance definition, streaming audio and/or video transmissions on the Internet are public performances if they can be received by members of the public. As is true of television and radio broadcasts, a digital transmission via the Internet is a public performance if it can be received by various members of the public, even if it is received by different people, in different places, and at different times. Thus, even if a streaming transmission to members of the public does not constitute a public distribution because it cannot be downloaded (as discussed in § 7.4 above), it nonetheless constitutes a public performance.

In contrast, a transmission directed to one individual or to a select group not assembled in a public place would not be a public performance. For example, performing a copyrighted work over the telephone to a single listener would be private performance, whereas making a recorded performance available to every caller would be a public performance.

In the case of cross-border transmissions, the Ninth Circuit has held that a public performance occurs where the transmission is received, rather than where it originates. Thus, a broadcast or other transmission that originates in Canada and is received in the United States implicates § 106(4), but if it originates in the United States and is received in Canada, § 106(4) does not apply. Outside the Ninth Circuit, this question remains unsettled.

D. Further Communication or Retransmission to the Public

Even where a public performance has been authorized by the copyright owner, infringement may occur if that performance is further communicated or retransmitted to the public. For example, if the initial transmission is directed to a limited audience (such as a pay-per-view broadcast), but is then retransmitted to a larger audience without the copyright owner's consent, the retransmission is an unauthorized public performance. If the copyright owner has authorized only a live public performance to an audience gathered in a theatre, any further communication or transmission of that live performance to the public (*e.g.*, by a television broadcast, Internet transmission, or simply a public address system the makes the performance audible to passers-by on the street) is an unauthorized public performance.

In the case of an authorized radio or television broadcast, the public performance right will be infringed if, in the absence of a statutory privilege or the copyright owner's consent, the transmission is communicated to an audience gathered in a bar, restaurant, stadium, church, or skating rink, or in a public area such as a street or park, or if it is routed to telephone callers who have been placed "on hold," or if it is retransmitted over the Internet. (The general rule allowing a copyright owner to prevent further communication or retransmission of a licensed public performance explains why the NFL is able to limit the rights of certain establishments to host "Super Bowl Parties" for the general public.) Even a radio played loudly in a car or on the beach can be an unauthorized public performance. However, the 1976 Act recognizes several exceptions to this general rule, as discussed in Chapter 8. Thus, not all of these public performances are necessarily infringing, even in the absence of consent.

E. Performing Rights Organizations

While public performance rights are an important source of revenue for the copyright owners of musical compositions (typically, music composers and music publishers), the tasks of enforcing those rights, negotiating public performance licenses, and collecting performance royalties would be overwhelming if each copyright owner acted individually. For that reason, owners of music copyrights rely on performing rights organizations which act collectively on their behalf. The three such organizations active in the United States are: the American Society of Composers, Authors, and Publishers (AS-CAP), BMI (formerly "Broadcast Music, Inc."), and SESAC (formerly "the Society of European Stage Authors and Composers," but now representing United States copyright owners as well). Each of these organizations is empowered to execute blanket licensing agreements on behalf of their members, authorizing radio and television stations, clubs, and other performance venues to perform the organization's entire catalog of musical compositions in exchange for a licensing fee, which is then distributed among the organization's members. Outside of the blanket licensing context, public performance rights (like other § 106 rights) are typically negotiated individually for each copyrighted composition (often through an agent).

§ 7.6 Public Display Right

With respect to certain categories of works, § 106(5) grants copyright owners the exclusive right to publicly display the work, and to authorize others to do so. The categories of works to which the public display right applies are: literary, musical, dramatic, and choreographic works, pantomimes, and pictorial, graphic, or sculptural works, including the individual images of a motion picture or other audiovisual work. Although architectural works per se are not included in this list, when the design of an architectural work is depicted in a pictorial, graphic, or sculptural work (for example, in blueprints or drawings), the public display right will apply. The other category excluded from this list is sound recordings.

Section 101 defines "display" as follows:

To "display" a work means to show a copy of it, either directly or by means of a film, slide, television image, or any other device or process or, in the case of a motion picture or other audiovisual work, to show individual images nonsequentially.

The public display right closely parallels the public performance right, discussed in the previous section. The right extends only to public displays; private displays do not require the copyright owner's consent. Public displays are distinguished from private displays using the same § 101 definition of "publicly" that governs public performances; thus, the display is public if it occurs in place open to the public, or in a place where members of the public are in fact gathered, or if the display is transmitted or otherwise communicated to a public place or to members of the public, even if individuals receive the transmission at different times and in different places.

However, the public display right is subject to a different set of statutory limitations than the public performance right. For example, under the first sale rule of § 109(c), an authorized copy of a work may be publicly displayed by or under authority of its owner to persons gathered in the same place where that copy of the work is located. This and other limitations on the public display right are discussed in Chapter 8.

Infringing public displays most commonly occur in the context of television broadcasts, motion picture performances, and Internet transmissions, since none of these public displays is authorized by the first sale rule. For example, if a copyrighted work is visible in the background of a television program or a motion picture without the copyright owner's consent, this is an unauthorized public display (and also involves unauthorized reproduction and public distribution, and usually unauthorized creation of a derivative work). Similarly, posting a copyrighted photograph or book excerpt on the Internet without the copyright owner's consent is also an unauthorized public display. Although displaying a copy of a work to a classroom of students is authorized by the first sale rule, making that image visible via closed circuit television to students in another classroom probably exceeds the scope of the first sale privilege, and therefore constitutes an unauthorized public display.

In the Internet context, there is a question whether unauthorized inline linking and framing of copyrighted content on another's website is an unauthorized public display. If the content was placed on the Internet with the copyright owner's consent, the better answer appears to be that mere inline linking and framing does not constitute a second, unauthorized, public display. A 2002 Ninth Circuit decision to the contrary was withdrawn in *Kelly v. Arriba Soft Corp.*, 336 F.3d 811 (9th Cir. 2003), and a subsequent Ninth Circuit decision held that inline linking and framing alone do not infringe the public display right, because the image being displayed does not reside on the defendant's server. *Perfect 10, Inc. v. Amazon.com, Inc.*, 508 F.3d 1146 (9th Cir. 2007). In contrast, courts routinely find unauthorized public display when a work is posted on the Internet without the copyright owner's consent.

§ 7.7 Digital Audio Transmission Right

Section 106(6) gives the copyright owner of a sound recording the exclusive right to publicly perform the work by means of digital audio transmission, and the exclusive right to authorize others to do so. Enacted in 1995, this right applies only to sound recordings, and establishes a public performance right much narrower than the general public performance right which § 106(4) provides for other categories of works. Prior to 1995, there was no public performance right in sound recordings at all. Congress enacted § 106(6) in response to the recording industry's concerns that digital subscription services could supplant record sales, because it was possible for people to make high quality recordings from digitally transmitted performances.

Although § 106(6) is broadly worded, referring to the exclusive right "to perform the copyrighted work publicly by means of a digital audio transmission," the exclusive right is narrower than this language suggests. For example, the exclusive right does not apply to *all* digital audio transmissions; it exempts nonsubscription transmissions by FCC-licensed terrestrial broadcast stations, as well as certain transmissions to and within business establishments.

In many cases, the copyright owner's exclusive right under § 106(6) is subject to statutory licensing, and the statutory license fees must be distributed among a number of stakeholders, including not only the record company but also the performing artists.

The detailed limitations on the digital audio transmission right are spelled out in § 114(d)-(i). (See § 8.7 below.)

§ 7.8　Moral Rights

Until 1990, federal copyright law contained no explicit moral rights provisions. The exclusive rights under § 106 are considered to be economic rights that are freely assignable. Subject only to the termination rights of § 203 and § 304(c), an author that assigns his or her exclusive § 106 rights—or any portion of those rights—retains no control over the assigned rights, except as provided by contract.

In countries that recognize authors' moral rights, however, even where an author assigns all economic rights in a work, he or she retains certain inalienable moral rights. In their fullest realization (in France, for example), those rights include a right of divulgation (that is, the right to control the first public distribution), a right of attribution (the right to receive credit for the work), a right of integrity (the right to object to alterations in the work which will damage the author's honor and reputation), and a right to withdraw the work from circulation. Moral rights are especially well established in continental Europe.

With one major difference, the right of divulgation is roughly comparable to the § 106(3) public distribution right, and the right of integrity is roughly comparable to the § 106(2) adaptation right. The difference, however, is that, unlike the § 106 rights, in a true moral rights regime the author's divulgation and integrity rights (like the other moral rights) are unassignable.

In some circumstances, federal trademark law provides a right somewhat comparable to the rights of attribution and integrity. For example, in *Gilliam v. American Broadcasting Cos.*, 538 F.2d 14 (2d Cir. 1976), the Monty Python troupe argued successfully that broadcasting an edited version of their television program without their consent involved a false attribution under § 43(a) of the Lanham Act, 15 U.S.C. § 1125(a), because the broadcast falsely implied that they approved of the edited version. While in the past some authors have also won § 43(a) actions against defendants who failed to give them authorship credit, such claims are less likely to succeed today, after the Supreme Court held in *Dastar Corp. v. Twentieth Century Fox Film Corp.*, 539 U.S. 23 (2003), that § 43(a) does not require attribution of authorship in the case of a work in which the copyright has expired.

Although Article 6bis of the Berne Convention requires all signatories to protect an author's rights of attribution and integrity, independently of the author's economic rights, Congress did not enact any moral rights legislation in the Berne Convention Implementation Act of 1988, taking the position that domestic law already provided adequate protection for these rights through federal copyright law and state and federal trademark and defamation laws. The correctness of this position has been widely debated.

Notwithstanding its assertion that domestic law already complied with Article 6bis, in 1990 Congress enacted a very limited form of express moral rights protection in the Visual Artists Rights Act (VARA). Codified in § 106A, VARA provides limited protection for the rights of attribution and integrity, but only for a narrow category of copyrightable works known as "works of visual art."

As defined in § 101, "works of visual art" are a subset of "pictorial, graphic, and sculptural works." The subset includes paintings, drawings, prints, sculptures, and certain photographs. All other types of copyrightable works—including literary, dramatic, and musical works, audiovisual works, sound recordings, and databases—are excluded from VARA. Posters, maps, globes, charts, technical drawings, diagrams, models, and works of applied art are ineligible. Mass-produced works are also ineligible; a work of visual art must be a work that exists only in a single copy or in a signed, numbered limited edition of 200 copies or fewer. In the case of photographic works, only works produced "for exhibition purposes" are eligible. Works made for hire, works unprotected by copyright, and works produced for purposes such as advertising or packaging are also ineligible.

Thus, the typical "work of visual art" is a work of fine art existing in a single copy or a small limited edition. The main purpose of granting moral rights protection to such works is to preserve the works for future generations. However, it will not always be easy to determine whether a particular work of art qualifies for protection as a work of visual art. For example, the First Circuit has held that VARA does not apply at all to "site-specific" artwork that is integrated with its surrounding landscape. *Phillips v. Pembroke Real Estate, Inc.,* 459 F.3d 128 (1st Cir. 2006). Other courts have struggled to distinguish between models (unprotected by VARA) and sculptures (protected) when an artist has created a three-dimensional prototype as one step in the development of a finished work.

One further limitation on works protected by VARA is largely hidden in the enacting legislation. VARA does not protect a work created prior to its effective date (June 1, 1991) if the title to that work was transferred before the effective date. The statutory language does not indicate whether transferring "title" to the work means transferring ownership of the copyright in the work or ownership of the tangible object. The legislative history implies the latter, because language in an earlier version of the bill which referred specifically to a transfer of copyright was replaced by the current language referring to a transfer of the title to the "work." Congress may have been seeking to protect the reliance interests of persons who had purchased artwork prior to VARA. If this interpretation is accurate, then VARA does not apply at all to works of art that were purchased before its effective date. On the other hand, persons who acquired copyright interests in works of visual art prior to VARA also had reliance interests worthy of protection. The correct interpretation of "title" remains unresolved.

VARA gives the author of a work of visual art several exclusive moral rights, which are independent of the § 106 rights, and which remain with the author even after the § 106 rights have been assigned. Like the § 106 rights, however, moral rights under VARA remain subject to the fair use provisions of § 107. (See § 10.2 below.)

One of these rights is the attribution right. The author of a work of visual art has the exclusive right to claim authorship of the work, and to prevent the use of his or her name in connection with a work of visual art created by another, or even in connection with his own work if it has been modified in a way that would be prejudicial to his or her honor reputation.

VARA also grants a right of integrity to the author of a work of visual art, permitting the author to prevent any *intentional* distortion, mutilation, or other modification of the work "that would be prejudicial to his or her honor or reputation." Ambiguously, this provision goes on to state that "any intentional distortion, mutilation, or modification of that work is a violation of that right." This drafting error makes it unclear whether the artist must prove only that the modification was intentional, or that it was both intentional and prejudicial. Congress may have intended to apply two different standards, depending on whether the artist was seeking to enjoin a modification, or seeking to recover damages after the modification occurred; even if this is the case, it is unclear whether the more demanding standard (requiring proof that the alteration was both intentional and prejudicial) was intended to apply to the action for injunctive relief or the action for damages. This ambiguity remains unresolved.

The integrity provision is ambiguous in another respect as well. Although the general language of the provision indicates that modifications must be *intentional* to violate the right of integrity, one of the exceptions states that this right is not violated by a modification that results from the passage of time or the inherent nature of the materials, or by a modification that results from conservation or public presentation (such as lighting and placement) unless it is caused by *gross negligence*. Because the legislative history supports the view that Congress intended to provide a remedy only for *intentional* modifications, creating liability for gross negligence in preservation activities seems inconsistent with treating only *intentional* acts as actionable outside of the preservation context.

If the work of visual art is one "of recognized stature," then VARA gives the author the additional right to prevent "any destruction" of the work. The author need not prove that the destruction was, or would be, prejudicial to his or her honor and reputation. Because the statute goes on to state that this right is violated by "any *intentional or grossly negligent*" destruction of the work, it is unclear whether liability could ever arise where the destruction is neither intentional nor caused by gross negligence. The statute also specifies that the right to prevent destruction is *not* violated where the destruction results from conservation or public presentation (such as light and placement) in the absence of gross negligence. It is possible that Congress intended to apply one standard to artists seeking injunctive relief in order to *prevent* destruction of their work, and a different standard to artists seeking a damages remedy *after* the destruction has occurred. Even if that was Congress's intent, it remains unclear which remedy—injunctive relief or damages—requires the artist to meet the higher standard (by establishing intentional or grossly negligent destruction, rather than destruction regardless of fault). As a practical matter, of course, in any situation where an artist has the opportunity to seek injunctive relief, the imminent destruction is likely to be intentional or grossly negligent rather than merely negligent or accidental. Where an artist seeks damages after the destruction has occurred, however, it makes a significant difference if the artist must prove that the destruction was caused by gross negligence rather than mere negligence or accident.

The statute does not define the terms "prejudicial to . . . honor or reputation" and "work of recognized stature." This is left to case-by-case determination, and courts have found expert testimony to be helpful. In the case of works of recognized stature, VARA's legislative history indicates that, while there is no per se rule, it is likely that *any* modification to such a work will be prejudicial to the artist's honor or reputation.

According to the enacting legislation, VARA does not apply to any destruction or modification of a work which took place before VARA's effective date.

In contrast, with respect to violations of the attribution right, VARA appears to permit injunctive relief regardless of when the non-attribution or misattribution commenced. The availability of damages for pre-VARA attribution violations is doubtful, however.

The moral rights set forth in VARA do not apply to any reproduction or use of a work of visual art in connection with a work made for hire or any other category of copyrighted works excluded from the definition of a "work of visual art." (Such uses, of course, would have to be licensed by the copyright owner.)

Due to peculiarities of drafting, there are two—or possibly three—different measures for the term of moral rights protection. Determining which measure applies depends on three factors: (1) the date on which the work of visual art was created; (2) whether the author has retained title to the work; and (3) whether the work is a joint work. If the work was created on or after June 1, 1991 (VARA's effective date), the rights endure only for the life of the author. If the work was created before this date, and the title to the work had not been transferred by the author as of that date, the moral rights endure for the entire copyright term. (While the statute is silent on who inherits the moral rights after the author's death, the legislative history implies that state inheritance laws will apply; however, where the renewal copyright of a pre–1978 work vested in a party other than the author under § 304(a)(1)(C) (see § 5.1 above), it is not clear whether Congress intended the moral right to vest in the same party.) However, in the case of a joint work, § 106A states that moral rights "shall endure for a term consisting of the life of the last surviving author." All terms run to the end of the calendar year in which they would expire.

The duration provisions are problematic in several respects. First, Congress articulated no policy reason for giving a longer term of moral rights protection to pre-VARA works than to works created after VARA's enactment; the differential treatment apparently results from inattentive drafting.

The special durational rule for joint works is also ambiguous. As noted earlier, this rule provides that moral rights "shall endure for a term consisting of the life of the last surviving author." Taken literally, this means that the moral rights in a joint work that was created after 1977 will always expire 70 years before the copyright in that work expires, because the copyright term does not end until 70 years after the death of the last surviving author. Although this is consistent with the general rule for duration of moral rights in *post*-VARA works, it is not consistent with the general rule for *pre*-VARA works; as noted above, moral rights in pre-VARA works endure until the copyright expires. The legislative history does not suggest that Congress intended to give pre-VARA joint works a shorter moral rights term than pre-VARA works of sole authorship. More likely, the intent of this language was simply to clarify that, for both pre- and post-VARA joint works, the "life of the author" refers to the life of the last surviving author. Under this interpretation, the moral rights term for all pre-VARA works would be coextensive with the copyright term.

Moral rights under VARA are not assignable, but they are waivable. To be enforceable, a waiver must be express, written, and signed by the author, and must specifically identify the work and the uses to which the waiver applies. In the case of a joint work, a waiver by one author binds all of the authors. However, the legislative history indicates that the waiving joint author must account to the other joint authors for any compensation received in exchange for the waiver.

Because moral rights are independent of copyright and independent of ownership of the physical object, a transfer of any interest in the copyright, or of the physical object, does not assign or waive moral rights. Similarly, a moral rights waiver has no effect on ownership of the copyright or the physical object.

According to § 501, a violation of any of the exclusive rights under § 106A is subject to the same civil remedies as an infringement of copyright, but criminal penalties do not apply. Thus, potential remedies include injunctive relief, actual or statutory damages, costs, and attorney's fees. (See Chapter 11 on Remedies.) Copyright registration is not a prerequisite to obtaining relief under § 106A.

Despite the broad language of § 501, however, it is not entirely clear whether, and under what circumstances, Congress intended to make the full array of civil remedies available for every actual or threatened moral rights violation. As noted earlier, for example, inconsistent language in the provisions addressing the right of integrity may suggest that, with respect to this right, Congress intended to make injunctive relief more readily available than damages. Furthermore, the attribution provisions recognize only a "right to prevent" non-attribution or misattribution of authorship. In contrast, the integrity provisions not only describe a "right to prevent" modification or destruction of a work, but also describe certain conduct as "a violation of that right." This can be read to suggest that only injunctive relief is available for violations of the attribution right, while the full array of remedies is available for violations of the integrity right. These ambiguities remain unresolved.

Where a work of visual art has been physically incorporated into a building, the moral rights of the artist are limited, in order to protect the interests of the owner of the building. These limitations are set out in § 113(d) of the 1976 Act, discussed in § 8.6 below.

Although a number of states also provide moral rights protection, VARA preempts enforcement of these laws under some circumstances. VARA preempts a state law only if (1) the state law applies to a "work of visual art" that is protected by § 106A, and (2) the right granted by the state law is "equivalent" to one of the rights conferred by § 106A. (The determination of what laws are "equivalent" awaits case-by-case determination.) Moreover, even if both of these conditions are satisfied, VARA does not preempt a cause of action that arises "from undertakings commenced before" VARA's effective date, nor does it apply to activities "violating legal or equitable rights which extend beyond the life of the author." 17 U.S.C. § 301(f). The latter provision is ambiguous in several respects. If VARA does not preempt state moral rights that extend beyond the life of the author, this could mean that VARA does not preempt those rights at all, or it could mean that VARA preempts them only during the author's lifetime. Furthermore, because § 106A protects pre-VARA works for their entire copyright term—meaning, for works created between January 1, 1978, and June 1, 1991, for 70 years after the author's death—then moral rights violations that take place during the post-mortem copyright term would not be subject to preemption at all with respect to these works, and could therefore be actionable under both state and federal law. Finally, because § 106A does not protect artwork that was purchased before VARA's effective date, states are free to extend their own moral rights protection to such works.

Because § 301 states that "all legal or equitable rights" equivalent to the § 106A rights are "governed exclusively" by VARA, it has been suggested that VARA also preempts application of other federal statutes—such as § 43(a) of the Lanham Act— that could otherwise be invoked to protect the rights of attribution or integrity in works of visual art. No court has addressed this question.

§ 7.9 Exclusive Rights of Live Musical Performers

Laws recognizing the rights of performers to prevent unauthorized copying or broadcast of their live performances have traditionally been the domain of state law—for example, laws protecting the right of publicity. Federal copyright law has not recognized such rights, because it applies only to works that have been fixed in a tangible medium of expression.

In the Uruguay Round Agreements Act of 1994("URAA"), Congress enacted the first federal statute expressly granting performers exclusive rights in their live performances, in an effort to comply with the requirements of the treaty now known as the WTO Agreement—specifically, the Trade–Related Aspects of Intellectual Property Rights ("TRIPS") provisions of that agreement.

Codified at 17 U.S.C. § 1101 (with a corresponding criminal provision at 18 U.S.C. § 2319A), this "anti-bootlegging" provision applies only to live *musical* performances. The statute creates a cause of action against any person who, without the consent of the performers, takes any of the following actions:

(1) fixes the sounds, or sounds and images, of a live musical performance in a copy or phonorecord, or reproduces copies or phonorecords of such a performance from an unauthorized fixation;

(2) transmits or otherwise communicates to the public the sounds, or sounds and images, of a live musical performance; or

(3) distributes, offers to distribute, sells, offers to sell, rents, offers to rent, or traffics in any copy or phonorecord fixed as described in paragraph (1), regardless of whether the fixations occurred in the United States.

One who undertakes any of these actions without the performers' consent is subject to the full array of copyright remedies—injunctions, actual or statutory damages, impounding or destruction of infringing articles, costs, and attorney's fees. (See Chapter 11 on Remedies.)

Although § 1101 applies only to acts that take place on or after its enactment date (December 8, 1994), the statute does not provide for expiration of a performer's rights. Thus, for example, if an unauthorized recording took place in 1950 (well before § 1101's enactment), a reproduction or distribution of that recording at any time in the future will still be actionable. Furthermore, even when the performers are no longer living, the fact that § 1101 does not provide for expiration of the rights at death suggests that the performers' heirs can bring a post-mortem action.

Section 1101 does not preempt any cause of action under state law. Thus, a plaintiff can pursue a state law right of publicity or unfair competition claim in addition to, or instead of, a § 1101 claim. Although federal courts have exclusive jurisdiction over § 1101 actions, state law claims could ordinarily be combined in the same action through pendent jurisdiction.

There are many ambiguities in § 1101, and these have not been resolved through litigation. For example: What is a "live musical performance"? Is it only the specific portion of a performance during which music is performed live? If the performance consists predominantly of non-musical elements, does a brief interlude of live music transform the entire performance into a live musical performance, or can liability be avoided by turning off the recording device only during the live music portion?

Also, no details are provided for avoiding liability by obtaining the performers' consent. For example: Must the consent be in writing? If there are multiple performers, how many must consent? If a consent by one or more performers is binding on the others, are the consenting performers required to account to the nonconsenting performers for any consideration they received? Can the performers assign their § 1101 rights—for example, to a record company or a management company?

Congress's failure to specify a limited term for § 1101 rights adds a further complication, because courts must determine who inherits a deceased performer's postmortem rights. Most likely, this would be determined under state inheritance laws. Especially where multiple performers were involved, the postmortem § 1101 rights may be divided among a large number of heirs, raising the question of how many heirs must consent to an act of reproduction or distribution in order for a potential defendant to avoid liability.

The prohibition against transmitting or otherwise communicating "the sounds or sounds and images of a live musical performance" is also unclear. Does it apply only to a transmission that takes place during the live performance? Or would it also apply to a defendant who transmits or publicly communicates the sounds of an unauthorized recording of an unfixed performance?

A possible answer to this question is found in a portion of the legislative history that addresses yet another ambiguity in the statute—whether or not § 1101 is subject to the fair use exception. While not expressly invoking fair use, the legislative history suggests that at least some activities should be exempt:

> It is intended that the legislation will not apply in cases where First Amendment principles are implicated, such as where small portions of an unauthorized fixation of a sound recording are used without permission in a news broadcast or for other purposes of comment or criticism.

By reverse implication, this passage suggests that, in the absence of First Amendment concerns, § 1101 is violated not only when a live performance is transmitted, but also when an unauthorized fixation of such a performance is transmitted. If this interpretation is correct, this raises the additional question of whether § 1101 would be violated by broadcasting an unauthorized recording that was fixed before the statute was enacted. The answer would appear to be yes, by analogy to the trafficking provision: If the statute applies to trafficking in a pre-enactment recording, then surely it applies to broadcasting such a recording as well.

Despite its placement in Title 17, § 1101 is not, strictly speaking, a copyright statute, because live performances are not fixed in a tangible medium of expression, and therefore do not qualify as "Writings" under the Copyright Clause of the Constitution. Furthermore, because the statute appears to protect a performer's right in perpetuity, it does not conform to the "limited Times" requirement of the Copyright Clause. The legislative history of § 1101 specifically invokes Congress's authority under the Commerce Clause. Nonetheless, courts and commentators have questioned the constitutionality of § 1101, raising the question whether Congress should be permitted to invoke its Commerce Clause power in order to enact copyright-like protection that exceeds Congress's powers under the Copyright Clause.

§ 7.10   Vessel Hull Design Protection Act

Under the "useful articles" analysis (see § 2.4 above), boat hulls are unlikely to qualify for copyright protection because their functional and artistic aspects are intertwined. After the Supreme Court held that a state law prohibiting the copying of boat hull designs was unenforceable due to federal preemption in *Bonito Boats, Inc. v. Thunder*

Craft Boats, Inc., 489 U.S. 141 (1989) (see Chapter 13 below), Congress enacted sui generis legislation protecting such designs. Although the legislation was enacted as part of the DMCA, and is codified in Chapter 13 of Title 17, it operates independently of the copyright statutes (and thus without regard to the useful articles doctrine), providing the creator of an original boat hull design with the exclusive right for 10 years to make, import, sell, or distribute products embodying that design, and provides a full array of infringement remedies (subject to limited exemptions) against one who copies the design with knowledge that it is a protected design. Protection is lost if the design is not registered within two years of being made public.

§ 7.11   Semiconductor Chip Protection Act

The Semiconductor Chip Protection Act of 1984 (SCPA) created sui generis protection for the design of semiconductor chips, due to concerns that these designs were difficult to create, easy to copy, and likely to be unprotectible under copyright law because of the useful articles doctrine. Codified in Title 17, the SCPA creates a system for registering original semiconductor chip designs, and gives the registrant of the design the exclusive right, for a 10–year period, to reproduce the design and to distribute or import products embodying that design. The SCPA uses the "substantial similarity" standard of copyright law to determine when a design is infringing, and exempts copying for the purpose of reverse engineering.

CHAPTER 8

LIMITATIONS ON EXCLUSIVE RIGHTS

In addition to the broad and indefinite fair use defense of § 107 (see Chapter 10), the exclusive rights of copyright owners are subject to a large number of more narrowly-defined exceptions and statutory licenses. These are found in §§ 108–122 and in the Audio Home Recording Act, found in §§ 1001–10.

§ 8.1 Reproduction and Distribution by Libraries and Archives

Under § 108, libraries and archives may take advantage of a limited exception to the reproduction and distribution rights where necessary to maintain and preserve their collections. Copying that exceeds the scope of this exception may give rise to infringement liability, unless it constitutes fair use under § 107.

In general, the § 108 reproduction and distribution privileges do not apply to musical, pictorial, graphic, or sculptural works, or to motion pictures or other audiovisual works (other than those dealing with news). There are significant exceptions to this rule, however, as noted in the discussion below.

The general rule of § 108(a) permits libraries and archives, and their employees, to make and distribute no more than one copy or phonorecord of a work, provided that:

(1) these actions are not undertaken for direct or indirect commercial advantage;

(2) the collections are either open to the public or available to researchers doing research in a specific field regardless of whether they are affiliated with the library or archive itself; and

(3) the copy or phonorecord that is made and/or distributed includes a copyright notice or, if no such notice can be found on the work, a legend stating that the work may be protected by copyright.

The general rule of § 108(a) is subject to several exceptions. In the case of *unpublished* works, the reproduction and distribution privileges granted by § 108 permit the making of up to three copies or phonorecords of a work, if it is duplicated solely for preservation, security, or deposit for research use in another library or archive meeting the qualifications described above, and provided that (1) the copy or phonorecord being reproduced is currently in the library or archive's collection, and (2) any digital reproduction remains on the premises of the library or archive. In the case of *published* works, the § 108 reproduction privilege applies to up to three copies or phonorecords of a work if it is duplicated solely for purposes of replacing damaged or missing items or if the existing format has become obsolete, and provided that (1) the library or archive has, after a reasonable effort, determined that an unused replacement cannot be obtained at a fair price, and (2) any digital reproduction remains on the premises of the library or archive. The general rule excluding musical, pictorial, graphic, and sculptural works, motion pictures, and other audiovisual works from the § 108 privilege does not apply to these preservation/replacement/obsolescence privileges.

The § 108 privileges also apply to certain copies made at the request of users. In this context, § 108 applies to (1) a copy made from the collection of the library or archive that receives the user request, or from another library or archive, of a single contribution to a copyrighted collective work; (2) a copy or phonorecord of a "small part" of any other copyrighted work; and (3) an entire copyrighted work, or a substantial part of it, if the work is in the collection of the library or archive receiving the request, or another library or archive, and, after reasonable investigation, it is determined that a copy or phonorecord of the work cannot be obtained at a fair price. All three of these privileges are subject to three additional limitations: (1) the copy or phonorecord must become the user's property; (2) the library or archive must have no notice that the user has a purpose other than research, (3) the library or archive must prominently display to users a copyright warning that meets the requirements of the Register of Copyrights. The general rule excluding pictorial and graphic works from the § 108 privilege does not apply to pictorial or graphic works that are adjuncts to material covered by the privileges for user requests. Although the user request privileges do not apply to most audiovisual works, § 108(f)(3) creates a narrow exception, stating that nothing in § 108 limits the reproduction and distribution by lending, by a library or archive, of "a limited number of copies and excerpts" of an audiovisual news program, as long as the general requirements of § 108(a) are satisfied.

The § 108 privileges apply to multiple instances of copying the same material if those occasions are "isolated and unrelated." They do not apply if the library or archive, or its employee, either:

(1) knows, or has reason to believe, that it is engaging in the "related or concerted" reproduction or distribution of multiple copies or phonorecords of the same material, on one occasion or over a period of time, either for the aggregate use of individuals or for separate use by members of a group; or

(2) engages in systematic reproduction or distribution of copies or phonorecords of individual contributions to collective works or small portions of other copyrighted works, except in the case of interlibrary arrangements that do not have the purpose or effect of causing the receiving library or archive to accumulate aggregate quantities which substitute for a subscription to or purchase of such a work.

The rules that apply to copying by library or archive employees in response to user requests do not apply to unsupervised self-service copying by patrons. However, libraries can generally avoid infringement liability arising from self-service copying if their copying equipment displays a copyright warning notice.

When Congress added 20 years to subsisting copyrights in the 1998 CTEA, it also added a new privilege to § 108, applicable only during the last 20 years of the copyright term for a published work. This privilege permits a library or archive (including any nonprofit educational institution functioning as such) to reproduce, distribute, display, or perform in facsimile or digital form a copy or phonorecord of such published work, or portions thereof, for preservation or research purposes, if, after reasonable investigation, the library or archive determines that *none* of the following conditions apply:

(1) the work is subject to normal commercial exploitation;

(2) a copy or phonorecord of the work can be obtained at a reasonable price; or

(3) the copyright owner or its agent provides notice pursuant to copyright regulations that either of the above conditions applies.

The general rule excluding musical, pictorial, graphic, and sculptural works, motion pictures, and other audiovisual works from the scope of § 108 does not apply to the CTEA privilege.

§ 8.2   The First Sale Rule

Under the first sale rule of § 109, certain exclusive rights of the copyright owner may terminate with respect to a particular copy or phonorecord of a work that has been lawfully made and sold. This principle is sometimes referred to as the *exhaustion of rights*.

The first sale rule applies only to copies or phonorecords that have been "lawfully made under this title," a reference to Title 17—*i.e.,* the copyright statutes. Thus, the first sale rule does not apply to infringing copies or phonorecords. Furthermore, as discussed below, the first sale rule does not apply to copies or phonorecords made outside the United States, even if they were made with the consent of the copyright owner.

A.   Sale or Other Disposition

If a copy or phonorecord of a work has been lawfully made under Title 17, then, as a general rule, the owner of that particular copy or phonorecord is entitled to sell or otherwise dispose of it—*e.g.,* by lending it or giving it away. In other words, the copyright owner's exclusive right of public distribution under § 106(3) has been exhausted with respect to that particular copy. Thus, for example, lawfully made books and CDs may be re-sold in secondhand stores or on Internet auction sites. As discussed below, with the exception of sound recordings and computer software, the first sale rule even permits the commercial rental of lawfully made copies and phonorecords. Thus, for example, a company (such as Blockbuster or Netflix) may purchase motion picture DVDs and rent them to the public for commercial gain without the consent of the copyright owner, provided that the DVDs were lawfully made under Title 17.

The requirement that the copy or phonorecord in question be "lawfully made" under Title 17 means that the copy or phonorecord must have been made in the United States. In *Quality King Distributors, Inc. v. L'anza Research International, Inc.*, 523 U.S. 135 (1998), the Supreme Court held that the first sale rule permitted a defendant to re-import into the United States copies that had been lawfully made in the United States but exported for sale abroad before being re-imported without the copyright owner's consent. The court distinguished between copies lawfully made under Title 17 (that is, in the United States) and copies lawfully made under foreign law (that is, outside the United States). For a copy or phonorecord to be lawfully made under Title 17, it must have been made in the United States, because Title 17 has no extraterritorial application. If a copy or phonorecord is made in Germany, then regardless of whether it was made with the consent of the German copyright owner, the first sale rule will not permit its importation into the United States without the consent of the United States copyright owner (even if that person is also the German copyright owner). The *Quality King* decision thus implicitly resolved a circuit split over the question whether copies lawfully made *outside* the United States can be imported without the consent of the United States copyright owner; after *Quality King,* the answer is no.

The recording and software industries lobbied successfully for an exception to the first sale rule, persuading Congress that the commercial rental of phonorecords and computer software was contributing to widespread unauthorized copying. The resulting exception prevents the commercial rental of phonorecords and most computer software without the consent of the copyright owner (which, in the case of phonorecords, would include the owner of the sound recording copyright as well as the owners of the copyrights in any musical works embodied therein). This exception, found in § 109(b), prohibits the owner or possessor of a phonorecord or a copy of a computer program from disposing of that phonorecord or computer program by any act or practice "in the nature of" rental, lease, or lending, for the purpose of direct or indirect commercial advantage. The "in the nature of" language covers rentals disguised as sales—for example, where a retailer allows a customer to return opened software or phonorecords in exchange for a "restocking" or similar fee.

It is unclear whether the § 109(b) commercial rental prohibition applies to sound recordings of works other than musical works, such as audiobooks. Although the statute indicates that the prohibition applies to "phonorecords" of "sound recordings," and § 101 defines these terms to include recordings of any kind of sound, the Sixth Circuit held, in a 2–1 decision, that Congress intended the commercial rental prohibition to apply only to sound recordings of musical works; under this interpretation, the first sale rule permits commercial rental of audiobooks. *Brilliance Audio, Inc. v. Haights Cross Communications, Inc.*, 474 F.3d 365 (6th Cir. 2007). No other circuit has addressed this question.

Because the rental prohibition is limited to rental, lease or lending for the purpose of direct or indirect commercial advantage, noncommercial lending is permitted. Thus, for example, one person may lend a phonorecord to another person at no charge.

The prohibitions contained in § 109(b) do not apply to certain activities of nonprofit libraries and nonprofit educational institutions. Specifically, the prohibition against the rental, lease or lending of phonorecords does not apply to nonprofit lending by such entities, even if a fee is charged. Also, if a nonprofit educational institution transfers possession of a lawfully made copy of a computer program to another such institution, or to faculty, staff, or students, this will not be treated as rental, lease or lending for direct or indirect commercial purposes. Finally, the § 109(b) prohibition does not apply to the nonprofit lending of a computer program by a nonprofit library, if each copy bears the copyright warning prescribed by the Register of Copyrights at 37 C.F.R. § 201.24.

The prohibition against rental, lease, or lending of computer programs does not apply to video games or to programs which are embodied in machines or products and which cannot be copied during ordinary operation of the machine or product (for example, programs included in automobiles).

Commercial rental, lease, or lending of phonorecords or computer programs in violation of § 109(b) constitutes copyright infringement subject to the full array of civil remedies, but it is not a criminal offense.

B. Public Display

In § 109(c), the first sale rule permits certain public displays of lawfully made copies of copyrighted works. Specifically, notwithstanding the copyright owner's exclusive public display right under § 106(5), the first sale rule permits the owner of a copy that was lawfully made under Title 17, or any person acting under that owner's authority, to display that copy publicly, either directly or by the projection of no more than one image at a time, to persons present at the place where the copy is located. Thus, for example, the owner of a copyrighted painting may permit a museum to display that painting. In contrast, the transmission of images of that painting, on television or via the Internet, will not be protected by § 109(c), because the images will be seen by viewers who are not physically present where the painting is located. In the case of a copy that was not lawfully made under Title 17 (either an infringing copy or a copy that was made outside the United States, whether or not lawfully), § 109(c) does not authorize any public displays.

C. Coin–Operated Audiovisual Games

The first sale rule also creates an exemption from the exclusive public performance and public display rights (§ 106(4) and § 106(5), respectively) in the case of electronic audiovisual games intended for use in coin-operated equipment (*i.e.*, arcade games). If a copy of the game was lawfully made under Title 17, then the owner of that copy may publicly perform or display it in coin-operated equipment. However, this privilege does not apply to a copyrighted work incorporated in the game if the copyright owner of that work is not also the copyright owner of the game.

§ 8.3 Exempt Performances and Displays

The § 110 exemptions pertain specifically to public performances and displays. Many of the exemptions are limited to nondramatic works. Some, though not all, of the exemptions pertain to nonprofit activities.

A. Exemptions for Nonprofit Activities

Under the 1909 Act, nonprofit performances of musical works and nondramatic literary works were exempt from infringement liability. While the 1976 Act no longer provides a blanket exemption for such nonprofit activities, many of the exemptions contained in § 110 are in fact limited to nonprofit activities.

1. *Classroom Teaching*

Although the performance or display of a copyrighted work in a classroom teaching situation is considered a public performance or display, in most cases it will be exempt under § 110(1). This exemption applies to performances or displays by students or teachers in the course of face-to-face teaching activities of a nonprofit educational institution in a classroom or similar place devoted to instruction. However, in the case of audiovisual works such as motion pictures (or the individual images thereof), the exemption will not apply if the performance or display uses a copy that was not lawfully made under Title 17, *and* the person responsible for the performance knew or had reason to believe that the copy was not lawfully made.

2. *Distance Learning*

In the Technology, Education, and Copyright Harmonization (TEACH) Act of 2002, Congress expanded the scope of the original § 110(2) exception in the 1976 Act (for certain instructional broadcasting activities) in order to encompass the expanded range of activities encompassed by modern distance learning. In effect, the TEACH Act applies the classroom teaching exemption of § 110(1) to distance learning. With some exceptions, § 110(2) permits the performance of a nondramatic literary or musical work, or reasonable portions of any other work, and the display of a work in an amount comparable to what is typically displayed in a classroom session, in the context of a qualifying transmission.

To qualify, the performance or display in question (1) must be made under the supervision of an instructor in a class session offered as a regular part of the instructional activities of a governmental body or an accredited nonprofit educational institution, and (2) must be directly related, and of material assistance, to the teaching content of the transmission.

The transmission must be limited to enrolled students or to government employees acting within their official duties, and the institution must establish and disseminate appropriate copyright policies. In the case of digital transmissions, the institution must apply technological measures to prevent recipients from retaining or further disseminating the material, and must not interfere with the technological measures used by copyright owners to prevent such retention or dissemination.

The exemption does not apply if (1) the copyrighted work in question was produced or marketed primarily for performance or display as part of an instructional activity transmitted via digital networks, or (2) the institution or governmental body making the transmission uses a copy or phonorecord that was not lawfully made and acquired under Title 17, *and* knew or had reason to believe that it was not lawfully made and acquired.

3. *Religious, Charitable, and Other Nonprofit Organizations*

Section 110(3) exempts the display of a work, or the performance of a nondramatic literary or musical work, or a dramatic-musical work of a religious nature, during worship services.

Section 110(4) exempts the performance of a nondramatic literary or musical work, not in the course of a transmission to the public, with no purpose of commercial advantage, and with no compensation paid to participants or organizers, provided that either (1) there is no admission charge, or (2) the proceeds in excess of reasonable costs are used exclusively for educational, religious, or charitable purposes, and not for private gain. However, this exemption does not apply if, prior to the performance, the copyright owner serves a notice of objection that complies with the statute.

Section 110(10) exempts the performance of a nondramatic literary or musical work during a social function of a nonprofit veterans' or fraternal organization open to invitees but not to the general public, if the proceeds in excess of reasonable costs are used for charitable purposes and not for private gain. Social functions of college fraternities and sororities are not covered by the exemption unless they are held solely to raise funds for a specific charitable purpose.

Section 110(6) exempts the performance of a nondramatic musical work by a governmental body, or a nonprofit agricultural or horticultural organization, at its annual agricultural or horticultural fair or exhibition. However, where the performance is by a concessionaire or other person at the venue, the exemption applies only to the governmental body or nonprofit organization, and not to the concessionaire or other person engaging in the performance.

4. *Performances for Persons with Disabilities*

Section 110(8) exempts the performance of a non-dramatic literary work in certain transmissions (made through facilities of a type specified in the statute) which are directed to blind or other handicapped persons who cannot read normal printed material, or to deaf or other handicapped persons who cannot hear the aural signals accompanying a visual transmission, if the performance is made without any purpose of commercial advantage.

Section 110(9) exempts the one-time performance of a dramatic literary work published at least ten years before the performance, in a transmission (made through a facility of a type specified in the statute) that is directed to blind or other handicapped persons who cannot read normal printed material, if the performance is made without any purpose of commercial advantage. The exemption will not apply to more than one performance of the same work by the same performers or the same organization.

B. Exemptions Applicable to For–Profit Activities

Section 110 includes three exemptions that apply even to for-profit activities. Two of these allow broadcasts incorporating public displays or performances of copyrighted works to be received in places that are open to the public, including commercial establishments, but only under the specific circumstances discussed below. The third for-profit exemption permits the manufacture, sale, and use of editing technology that permits consumers to alter the performance of a motion picture.

1. *Broadcasts Received in Public Places*

The first of the for-profit exemptions, § 110(5), today consists of two exemptions, found in subsections (A) and (B). Section 110(5)(A), also known as the "homestyle" exception, permits transmission of a performance or display of a work by public reception of that transmission on a single receiving apparatus of a kind commonly used on private homes, unless (1) a direct charge is made to see or hear the transmission, or (2) the transmission thus received is further transmitted to the public. A sports bar, for example, can rely on this exemption to show televised sporting events for its customers. The exemption permits the bar to show each such broadcast only on a single television set. Although, in a typical sports bar situation, copyright owners often raise no objections if a broadcast is shown simultaneously on several screens, they would be within their legal rights to do so. Outside of the typical sports bar scenario, some copyright owners have recently become more assertive about enforcing their rights against establishments that exceed the homestyle limitation, as evidenced by the NFL's annual enforcement efforts against Las Vegas casinos hosting Super Bowl parties.

The meaning of the "further transmission" clause in § 110(5)(A) has never been clear. Some courts have concluded that further transmission occurs, and the exception is therefore unavailable, when the receiving device is in a different room from the speakers; however, the Seventh Circuit rejected this interpretation in *Broadcast Music, Inc. v. Claire's Boutiques, Inc.*, 949 F.2d 1482, 1495 (7th Cir. 1991), stating that a further transmission "must entail the use of some device or process that expands the normal limits of the receiver's capabilities."

When § 110(5) was first enacted in the 1976 Act, the homestyle exemption applied to all copyrighted works, including nondramatic musical works. The intent of the provision was to permit operators of stores, restaurants, and other public establishments to turn on a radio or television for the incidental enjoyment of customers or employees in the store. For example, a retail store might have a radio playing in the background, or a bar might show a televised sporting event.

In 1998, however, the statute was amended, partly in response to concerns that the scope of the exemption was unclear, and partly in response to lobbying pressure from the hospitality industry. Courts had taken conflicting approaches to determining what kinds of establishments (*e.g.*, franchises versus independent stores) were eligible for the exception, and what kinds of apparatus were "commonly used in private homes" (a question of fact, which can be difficult to resolve due to the constant evolution of home entertainment technology). In the 1998 amendments, the original homestyle exemption was redesignated § 110(5)(A), and a new provision, § 110(5)(B), was added. The 1998 amendments preserved the original language of the homestyle exemption in § 110(5)(A), adding only the introductory phrase "[e]xcept as provided in subparagraph (B)." As discussed below, subparagraph (B) takes the form of a safe harbor which is more detailed than the original homestyle exemption.

As a threshold matter, it is not entirely clear whether the new subsection (B) safe harbor is limited to performances or displays of nondramatic musical works *alone*, or whether it encompasses all transmissions that incorporate such performances or displays, regardless of whether other works are also performed or displayed in the transmission. The safe harbor applies specifically to "a transmission or retransmission embodying a performance or display of a nondramatic musical work." (The reference to a "display" here seems to be a drafting error, since there is not much demand for displays of lyrics or musical notations during television broadcasts.) This language could mean that the safe harbor exempts the establishment from infringement liability only with respect to the nondramatic musical work itself. Alternatively, it could be interpreted more broadly, exempting the establishment from infringement liability with respect to all works that are performed or displayed in the course of the transmission. For example, a broadcast of the Super Bowl includes nondramatic musical works as well as the game itself and the accompanying commentary (and commercials, although it is unlikely that any advertiser would object to its ads being seen in a public place). It is unclear whether the safe harbor applies to the entire Super Bowl broadcast, or only to the specific musical works that are performed during that broadcast. In the latter case, the defendant could invoke the safe harbor only with respect to the nondramatic musical works, and would have to try to qualify under subsection (A)—the original homestyle exemption—to avoid liability for infringing the copyright in the broadcast of the game and the accompanying commentary.

A transmission embodying a performance or display of a nondramatic musical work will qualify for the § 110(5)(B) exemption only if (1) it was intended to be received by the general public, and (2) it was originated by an FCC-licensed radio or television broadcast station or, in the case of an audiovisual transmission, by a cable system or satellite carrier.

The new exemption is also limited to "establishments." Section 101 defines an "establishment" as a place of business open to the public for the primary purpose of selling goods or services in which the majority of space is devoted to that purpose. Because this definition seems to be limited to commercial enterprises, it is unclear whether a noncommercial venue such as a church or public recreation center can take advantage of § 110(5)(B).

Whether or not a particular establishment qualifies for the subsection (B) exemption depends on the type and size of establishment where the broadcast is being received, as well as the type of receiving equipment that it uses. The exemption distinguishes between two types of establishments—(1) food service and drinking establishments, and (2) all others. Each type of establishment is then further subdivided according to size, with only the larger establishments being subject to specific limitations as the nature of their receiving apparatus.

In the case of a food service or drinking establishment, the subsection (B) exemption applies to any establishment with less than 3,750 gross square feet (excluding parking), regardless of the nature of the receiving apparatus. In the case of an establishment other than a food service or drinking establishment, this square footage must be less than 2,000 gross square feet.

Larger establishments wishing to invoke the § 110(5)(B) exemption must limit their receiving apparatus. A food service or drinking establishment that is 3,750 square feet or larger, or any other business that is 2,000 square feet or larger, may use no more than six loudspeakers for audio performances (with no more than four speakers in any one room), and no more than four audiovisual devices for an audiovisual performance (with no screen size greater than 55 inches diagonally, and no more than one such device in each room).

The new exemption for nondramatic musical works is more precise than the original homestyle exemption, but it is in many respects much broader as well. It has been estimated that more than 70% of bars and restaurants in the United States qualify for the exemption. Despite a ruling by the World Trade Organization (WTO) that § 110(5)(B) violates the United States' treaty obligations under the TRIPS provisions of the WTO Agreement by creating too large an exemption, there has been no effort to narrow the scope of this provision.

It should be noted that the § 110(5) exemption (both parts (A) and (B)) is limited to broadcast transmissions. Some establishments that would qualify for the § 110(5)(B) exception choose not utilize it, opting instead to pay for a commercial music service that provides content more tailored for their needs.

Congress's retention of the original homestyle exemption in § 110(5)(A) even after enactment of the more specific provisions of § 110(5)(B) created an ambiguity that has yet to be resolved: Does § 110(5)(A) still have any application to nondramatic musical works, or does it now apply only to other types of copyrighted works? This question becomes relevant if an establishment fails to meet the requirements of § 110(5)(B) for its performances of nondramatic musical works. If § 110(5)(B) is merely a safe harbor, then the establishment could, in theory, argue that it still qualifies under § 110(5)(A). But if § 110(5)(B) is meant to define the limits of the exemption for nondramatic musical works, then there should be no recourse to § 110(5)(A). Alternatively, there could be situations in which a broadcast of a nondramatic musical work is publicly performed but not by an "establishment"—for example, if an individual plays a loud radio on the beach, in a park or public street, or on public transportation, or if a church, school, or public recreation center hosts a Super Bowl party (since the Super Bowl broadcast includes musical performances). While the latter scenarios raise the theoretical question of whether § 110(5)(A) applies, they are unlikely to be tested in court.

2. Vendors of Audiovisual Devices

Under § 110(7), a retail store may publicly perform a nondramatic musical work for the sole purpose of promoting the sale of copies or phonorecords of that work or of the devices utilized in the performance (*e.g.,* stereo equipment). No admission may be charged, and the performance must be limited to the immediate area where the sale is occurring.

3. Editing Private Motion Picture Performances

The § 110(11) exemption affects both the non-profit activities of consumer households and the for-profit activities of vendors that supply consumers with certain types of motion picture editing technology.

Congress enacted § 110(11) when vendors began to make and distribute software that enabled consumers to edit the performance of motion picture DVDs in order to eliminate nudity, violence, offensive language, and other objectionable material. Although the editing in question did not permanently alter the DVDs, conflicting case law made it unclear whether merely editing the performance was sufficient to infringe the copyright owner's exclusive right to create derivative works. (See § 7.3 above.) To resolve this issue, § 110(11) permits consumers to edit a performance of a motion picture within their private household by "making imperceptible ... limited portions" of the performance, provided that they are using an authorized copy of the motion picture.

Section 110(11) also affects for-profit activities, because it permits the creation and distribution of computer programs or other technology that make this consumer editing possible, provided that the technology is designed and marketed for use in private households, and that it does not create a fixed copy of the altered version of the motion picture.

§ 8.4   Secondary Transmissions of Television Broadcasts

According to § 101, a public performance or display occurs when a work is transmitted either (1) to a place open to the public or where members of the public are gathered, or (2) to members of the public by any device or process, whether the members of the public receive the transmission at the same place or different places, and at the same time or at different times.

What are the rights of the copyright owner when this initial transmission is received and simultaneously retransmitted by the recipient? In addressing this question, the statutes refer to the initial transmission to the public as the *primary transmis-*

sion; the retransmission is referred to as a *secondary transmission*.

Although the statutes do not expressly state that a simultaneous secondary transmission is a public performance separate and apart from the underlying primary transmission, this conclusion may reasonably be inferred from a number of statutory provisions. For example, while the § 110(5) exemption permits many radio and television broadcasts in bars, restaurants, and retail establishments, the exemption does not apply if the broadcast is "further transmitted to the public."

Section 111 is another provision which suggests, by reverse implication, that simultaneous secondary transmissions ordinarily require the consent of the copyright owner. Specifically, § 111 describes a number of circumstances in which simultaneous secondary transmissions *do not* infringe the exclusive rights of public performance and display. Additional exceptions are set forth in §§ 119 and 122 (see § 8.12 below). Some of these involve outright exemptions, while others involve statutory licenses.

Under § 111(a), a simultaneous secondary transmission does not infringe if:

(1) it consists entirely of FCC-licensed broadcasts, transmitted within the local service area of the broadcast station to the private lodgings of guests or residents of a hotel, apartment house, or similar establishment, by the management of the establishment, and not by a cable system, provided that no direct

charge is made to see or hear the secondary transmission; or

(2) it falls within the instructional activities exemption of § 110(2); or

(3) the carrier has no control over the content or selection of the primary transmission or over the recipients of the secondary transmission, and its activities with respect to the latter consist solely of providing wires, cables, or other communications channels for the use of others (but this exemption applies only to the carrier, and not to other parties involved in the transmission); or

(4) it is made by a satellite carrier pursuant to a statutory license under § 119 (see § 8.12 below); or

(5) it is made by a government body or nonprofit organization, and not by a cable system, with no purpose of commercial advantage, and with no charge to the recipients beyond the cost of operating the secondary transmission service.

In contrast, § 111(b) provides that simultaneous secondary transmissions to the public are actionable as infringing public performances or displays if the primary transmission was not made for reception by the public at large. An exception applies only if *all* the following conditions are met:

(1) the primary transmission was by an FCC-licensed broadcast station;

(2) the secondary transmission is required by the FCC; and

(3) the secondary transmitter does not alter the signal of the primary transmitter.

Simultaneous secondary transmissions by cable systems to the public are subject to statutory licensing under §§ 111(c) and (d) when the underlying primary transmission is made by an FCC-licensed broadcast station and the secondary transmission is permitted by FCC rules.

Under § 111(c), simultaneous secondary transmissions by a cable system to the public are actionable as infringing public performances or displays in the following cases:

(1) willful or repeated secondary transmission of a primary transmission from an FCC-licensed broadcast station where either the secondary transmission is not permissible under FCC rules, or the cable system has failed to comply with the statutory licensing procedures of § 111(d);

(2) secondary transmission of a primary transmission from an FCC-licensed broadcast station, if the content of the program, or of any commercial advertising or station announcements in the primary transmission, is willfully altered by the cable system (subject to a narrow exception for market research); and

(3) certain secondary transmissions where the primary transmission is from a broadcast station licensed by Canada or Mexico.

Nonsimultaneous secondary transmissions. For the most part, the exemptions and statutory licensing provisions described above for secondary transmissions are limited to simultaneous secondary transmissions. However, §§ 111(e) and (f) set forth the conditions under which these privileges can apply to nonsimultaneous secondary transmissions by cable systems in Alaska, Hawaii, and certain U.S. territories. In general, these conditions are designed to ensure that the cable system does not alter the primary transmission, does not retransmit it more than once, and does not retain or duplicate copies of the program.

§ 8.5   Ephemeral Recordings

Section 112 limits the exclusive right of reproduction by permitting certain reproductions of transmissions embodying public performances or displays. A transmission program that is recorded pursuant § 112 may not be protected as a derivative work without the express consent of the owners of copyright in the preexisting works embodied in the program.

Section 112(a) applies only to a lawful transmission of a copyrighted work, or to a broadcast performance of a sound recording in a digital format on a nonsubscription basis by an FCC-licensed radio or television station. Unlike the other provisions in § 112, subsection (a) applies only to copyrighted works *other than* motion pictures and other audiovisual works. This exception permits the making of no more than one copy or phonorecord of a particular transmission program embodying a public performance or display or a work, if *all* of the following conditions are met:

(1) the copy or phonorecord is retained and used only by the transmitting organization, and is not further reproduced;

(2) the copy or phonorecord is used only for the transmitting organization's own transmissions within its local service area, or for archival purposes; and

(3) unless used only for archival purposes, the copy or phonorecord is destroyed within six months of the program's first transmission.

If the transmitting organization cannot make a copy or phonorecord due to the copyright owner's technological protection measures, and the copyright owner does not provide reasonable assistance, the transmitting organization will be immune from anticircumvention liability under § 1201(a)(1) for making such copies or phonorecords (see Chapter 12).

Section 112(b) applies to a governmental body or other nonprofit organization engaged in a lawful transmission under § 110(2) or § 114(a). This provision allows the making of up to 30 copies or phonorecords of a particular transmission program, if these are not further reproduced, and if all are destroyed (except for one archival copy or phonorecord) within seven years of the first transmission.

Section 112(f), a second provision dealing with educational transmissions under § 110(2), was added in 2002 to complement the distance learning provisions of § 110(2) that were introduced by the TEACH Act. Section 112(f) permits a governmental body or other nonprofit education to copy a work that embodies a performance or display to be used for making transmissions authorized by § 110(2). (However, works in analog form may not be converted to digital form unless no digital version is available to the institution or the digital version that is available is subject to technological protection measures preventing its use under § 110(2)). The copies or phonorecords made under § 112(f) may be retained and used only by the organization that made them, may be used only for transmissions authorized under § 110(2), and may not be further reproduced.

Section 112(c) permits a governmental body or other nonprofit organization to distribute one copy or phonorecord of a particular transmission program embodying a performance of a nondramatic musical work of a religious nature, or a sound recording of such a work, if all of the following conditions are met:

    (1) there is no direct or indirect charge for making or distributing the copies or phonorecords;

    (2) none of the copies or phonorecords is used for any further performances of the work; and

(3) all of the copies or phonorecords (except for a single archival copy or phonorecord) are destroyed within one year of the first transmission.

Section 112(d) permits a governmental body or other nonprofit organization that is lawfully performing a work in a transmission under § 110(8) (performances for persons with disabilities) to make up to ten copies or phonorecords of the performance, and to permit those copies to be used by any governmental body or nonprofit organization entitled to transmit a performance of the work under § 110(8), if all of the following conditions are met:

(1) the copies or phonorecords are retained and used only by a governmental body or nonprofit organization entitled to transmit a performance of the work under § 110(8), and are not further reproduced;

(2) the copies or phonorecords are used only for transmissions under § 110(8) or for archival purposes; and

(3) the governmental body or nonprofit organization permitting use of such copies or phonorecords does not charge for such use.

In the case of digital transmissions of sound recordings that are authorized by either § 114(d)(1)(C)(iv) (transmissions to businesses) or § 114(f) (transmissions under a statutory license) (see § 8.7 below), § 112(e) creates a statutory license to make a phonorecord of the sound recording. The license applies only if (1) phonorecords of the sound recording have been distributed to the public under the authority of the copyright owner, or the copyright owner authorizes the transmitting entity to transmit the sound recording; *and* (2) the transmitting entity makes the phonorecord from a phonorecord that was lawfully made and acquired under the authority of the copyright owner. In addition to these requirements, all of the following conditions must be met:

(1) the phonorecord is retained and used solely by the transmitting organization, and no further phonorecords are made from it;

(2) the phonorecord is used only for transmissions originating in the United States under a § 114(f) statutory license or pursuant to § 114(d)(1)(C)(iv); and

(3) the phonorecord is destroyed within six months from the first transmission (unless preserved solely for archival purposes).

In the absence of negotiated agreements between copyright owners and transmitting organizations, the royalty rates and terms for the statutory license will be determined in proceedings before administrative law judges known as the Copyright Royalty Judges, who will also establish requirements for providing notice to the copyright owners of the sound recordings that are utilized under a statutory license, and for maintaining records of such use. Where a sound recording is protected by technological measures that prevent reproduction, the copyright owner must provide reasonable assistance to the transmitting organization in making phonorecord; otherwise, the transmitting organization will be immune from liability under the anticircumvention provisions of § 1201(a)(1) (see Chapter 13) for reproducing the sound recording.

§ 8.6 Reproduction of Pictorial, Graphic, and Sculptural Works

In the case of pictorial, graphic, and sculptural works, the exclusive reproduction right is subject to several limitations.

Section 113(b) provides that ownership of copyright in a work that depicts a useful article does not give the copyright owner any rights with respect to the useful article so depicted, except to the extent that such rights would have been recognized under pre–1978 law. Thus, the owner of the copyright in a technical drawing of a machine cannot prevent others from constructing the machine from the drawing.

Where a copyrighted work is lawfully reproduced in useful articles offered to the public, § 113(c) provides that the copyright owner may not prevent the making, distribution or display of pictures or photographs of the useful articles in advertisements or commentaries relating to those articles, or in news reports.

Under § 113(d), several limitations apply to the moral rights granted to the author of a work of visual art under § 106A (see § 7.8 above) when that work has been incorporated into a building:

If removing the work from the building will destroy or otherwise modify the work within the meaning of § 106A, then the author's right to prevent modification and/or destruction of the work will not apply if the author consented to installation of the work either (1) before VARA's effective date (June 1, 1991), or (2) in a written instrument (signed by the author and the building's owner) which specifies that installation of the work may subject it to destruction, distortion, mutilation, or other modification by reason of its removal.

If a building's owner wishes to remove a work of visual art that is a part of the building, and which can be removed without destroying or otherwise modifying the work within the meaning of § 106A, ordinarily the author's right to prevent modification and/or destruction of the work will apply. However, those rights will not apply if either (1) the owner has made a diligent good faith attempt (as defined in the statute) to notify the author of the owner's intended action, but without success, or (2) the owner provided such a notice in writing and the author failed to arrange for the work's removal within 90 days after receiving the notice.

§ 8.7 Limitations on Exclusive Rights in Sound Recordings

The rights of the owner of copyright in a sound recording are subject to several significant limitations. This is because, when Congress extended copyright protection to sound recordings in the

1971 Sound Recording Act, its only concern was to prevent unauthorized copying and distribution.

A. Section 114(a): No General Public Performance Right

Unlike the owner of a copyright in a musical work, the owner of the copyright in a sound recording does not enjoy an exclusive public performance right under § 106(4). When a copyrighted sound recording is publicly performed—for example, in a club or on the radio—the record company that owns the copyright in that sound recording is not entitled to collect any public performance royalties. In contrast, the owners of copyright in any of the musical compositions embodied in that sound recording will receive performance royalties collected by their representative organizations (ASCAP, BMI, or SESAC). The only public performance right available for sound recordings is the digital audio transmission right under § 106(6) (see § 7.7 above).

B. Section 114(b): Limits on Reproduction and Adaptation Rights

Under § 114(b), both the exclusive reproduction right and the exclusive right to create derivative works are defined more narrowly with respect to sound recordings than with respect to any other class of copyrighted work. The reproduction right is limited to the right to recapture the actual sounds fixed in the recording. It does not apply to an independent fixation of sounds, no matter how closely they resemble the sounds in the original recording. In other words, a close imitation—a "soundalike" recording—is not an infringing reproduction of a sound recording, even if a listener would be unable to distinguish the soundalike recording from the original. Similarly, the exclusive right to create derivative works is, in the case of sound recordings, limited to the creation of derivative works that incorporate actual sounds from the original recording; mere imitation of those sounds does not implicate the exclusive rights of the copyright owner. Thus, for either of these exclusive rights to be implicated, some or all of the sounds fixed in the original recording must have been replicated through mechanical or electronic means, rather than independently re-created.

In addition, the exclusive rights to reproduce, publicly distribute, and create derivative works do not apply to sound recordings included in educational television and radio programs distributed or transmitted by public broadcasting entities, provided that the broadcasting entities do not commercially distribute copies or phonorecords of those programs to the public.

C.   Sections 114(d)-(j): Limits on Digital Audio Transmission Right

Although § 106(6) confers on the owner of a sound recording copyright the exclusive right to perform the sound recording by means of a digital audio transmission, §§ 114(d)-(j) impose significant limits on the scope of that right, in the form of exemptions and statutory licensing provisions.

First, many kinds of audio transmissions are completely *exempt* from the public performance right of § 106(6). In general, the exemptions apply to non-subscription, non-interactive transmission services, because these are comparable to traditional radio; thus, the exemptions preserve the longstanding relationship between record companies and traditional radio broadcasters. *Interactive* services, in contrast, are never exempt from the § 106(6) right, because listeners who can choose which sound recording will be transmitted at any given time are more likely to be engaged in unauthorized recording.

Exempt transmissions include, *inter alia*, the following non-interactive services: (1) purely *analog* transmissions; (2) *nonsubscription* transmissions, whether digital or analog, by FCC-licensed terrestrial broadcast stations (in other words, traditional radio broadcasters); (3) transmissions strictly within business establishments; and (4) transmissions to business establishments for use in the ordinary course of business (subject to certain additional limitations). This last exemption is designed to exempt background music services.

Second, many non-exempt digital subscription transmissions of sound recordings are subject to *statutory licensing*. Statutory licensing is also available for certain *non*subscription digital audio transmissions, such as Internet radio, which fall outside of the exempt categories because they do not originate from FCC-licensed terrestrial broadcast stations. In both cases, statutory licensing is available only if the transmission services (1) are not interactive, (2) do not announce in advance which recordings will be transmitted, and (3) comply with certain statutory limits (the "sound recording performance complement") on the number of tracks from the same artist, phonorecord, or compilation that can be played within a designated time period.

Interactive digital audio services are neither exempt from § 106(6) nor eligible for statutory licensing. Thus, the owner of the sound recording copyright has the exclusive right to make or authorize such transmissions. Authorization must be obtained through voluntarily negotiated license agreements. However, in order to prevent record companies from exercising too much control over the market for interactive services, § 114(d) imposes some limitations on the extent to which a copyright owner can grant *exclusive* licenses for § 106(6) rights.

Neither § 106(6) nor its limitations have any effect on the copyright in any *musical work* embodied in a sound recording. Thus, even if a public performance of a sound recording falls within one of the exemptions listed in § 114(d), this "exempt" performance of the sound recording may still be an infringing performance of any musical composition performed in that recording if a public performance license has not been obtained from the copyright owner of that musical composition. For example, a background music service that is exempt under § 114(d) will still have to obtain the appropriate blanket licenses from ASCAP, BMI, and/or SESAC in order to publicly perform copyrighted musical compositions.

The rules for statutory licensing are set forth in § 114(f). In general terms, the statute authorizes representatives of record companies and digital transmission services to establish royalty rates through voluntary negotiation. Rates that are not voluntarily negotiated will be determined by Copyright Royalty Judges. Rates are redetermined every five years.

Section 114(g) dictates how the statutory licensing royalties must be allocated. The largest shares go to the owner of the performance right in the recording (usually a record company), who receives 50%, and the artist(s) featured on the recording (45%). The remaining 5% is split between two funds that must be distributed to all nonfeatured recording artists who have performed on sound recordings.

Where statutory licensing does not apply (for example, in the case of interactive services), § 114 does not dictate how the royalties from nonexempt digital audio performance licenses must be distributed; any payments to the recording artists who perform on the sound recording are determined by the terms of the contract between the artist and the record company.

Cooperation among copyright owners and users is permitted in negotiations for statutory licenses under § 114(f), notwithstanding antitrust laws. However, the antitrust exemption does not apply to negotiation of other licenses under § 106(6), such as interactive licenses.

The compulsory licensing rules for digital phonorecord deliveries (see § 8.8 below) do not apply to any exempt transmissions under § 114(d)(1).

§ 8.8 Compulsory License for Nondramatic Musical Works

In the case of nondramatic musical works (see § 2.2 above), the exclusive rights of reproduction and public distribution are limited by the compulsory licensing provisions of § 115. The mechanical compulsory license applies only to mechanical licenses—that is, licenses to record and distribute musical compositions on phonorecords (*e.g.*, records, tapes and CDs). As discussed below, the compulsory licensing provisions have now been extended to encompass digital delivery of sound recordings as well.

A. Mechanical Compulsory Licenses

The mechanical compulsory license applies to a musical composition only after it has been recorded on phonorecords which have been distributed to the public in the United States under the authority of the copyright owner. Once this prerequisite has been satisfied, any person may, by complying with the conditions of § 115, obtain a compulsory license to make and distribute phonorecords of the same musical composition.

A person may obtain a compulsory license to record a musical composition only if his or her primary purpose in making phonorecords of the work is to distribute them to the public for private use (including by means of digital phonorecord delivery). Thus, for example, a compulsory license does not permit the public performance of a musical composition, or the recording of that composition as part of the sounds accompanying a motion picture.

The holder of a compulsory license is permitted to arrange the musical composition to the extent necessary to conform it to the performer's style or manner of interpretation. However, the arrangement may not change the "basic melody or fundamental character" of the composition, and is not protected as a derivative work.

The procedure for utilizing a compulsory license involves serving notice on the owner of the copyright in the musical composition, or upon the Copyright Office if there is insufficient information to locate the copyright owner. The form and content of the notice is dictated by regulations issued by the Register of Copyrights. If the owner of the musical composition can be identified through the public records of the Copyright Office, then the licensee must pay the owner a royalty (2-3/4 cents per work, or one half of one cent per minute of playing time, whichever is larger) for each record made and distributed. Additional royalties are, in theory, payable for any acts of rental, lease, or lending that should occur, although no regulations implementing this provision have ever been enacted because record companies have consistently refused to authorize such activities ever since the enactment of the Record Rental Amendment of 1984 (allowing record companies to prohibit record rentals).

In practice, the mechanical compulsory license is rarely used, because parties typically enter negotiated licenses at rates lower than the compulsory licensing rate. The practical effect of the compulsory license, then, is to establish a ceiling for negotiated mechanical royalties.

A person seeking to duplicate a copyrighted sound recording (rather than independently re-creating the sounds of the recording) may use a compulsory license to reproduce and distribute the copyrighted musical compositions included in that recording only if (1) the existing sound recording was fixed lawfully, and (2) the duplication of the sound recording is authorized by its copyright owner or, if the sound recording was fixed before February 15, 1972 (the date on which sound recordings first became eligible for federal copyright protection), by a person who made that recording either under an express license from the owner of the copyright in the musical work or pursuant to a compulsory license to record that composition.

The compulsory licensing provisions were originally included in the 1909 Act in response to concerns that the making of phonorecords (which, in those days, consisted of player piano rolls) might become a monopoly controlled by a single company. Although the continuing need for this provision was doubtful, it was retained in modified form in the 1976 Act. In the 1990s, however, it quickly became clear that the manufacturing of phonorecords for public distribution was being displaced by digital deliveries of sound recordings. This necessitated adapting the compulsory license to digital transmissions, as discussed below.

B. Digital Phonorecord Deliveries

In the Digital Performance Right in Sound Recordings Act of 1995, Congress revised the compulsory licensing provisions to make them applicable to digital phonorecord deliveries. These revisions are reflected in §§ 115(c)(3) and 115(d). A digital phonorecord delivery is defined in § 115(d) as the delivery of a phonorecord by digital transmission of a sound recording that results in a reproduction of that phonorecord by or for a recipient of the transmission—in common terms, a music download. A digital phonorecord delivery may or may not involve a public performance.

The definition of digital phonorecord deliveries *excludes* real-time, non-interactive subscription transmissions of sound recordings in which neither the transmitted sound recording nor the musical work is reproduced in order to make the sound recording audible. For purposes of the § 115 compulsory license, a transmission of the latter sort is a public performance, but not a reproduction, and therefore is not covered by the compulsory licensing provisions. (As a public performance via digital subscription transmission, of course, it will generate public performance royalties with respect to both the musical work and the sound recording, as discussed in § 8.7 above).

In general, the rules governing the mechanical compulsory license apply equally to the digital compulsory license. As discussed below, the main differences are: (1) royalties are determined differently, (2) the compulsory licensee can be any party engaged in lawful digital phonorecord deliveries, and thus need not be the actual maker of the sound recording, and (3) a digital phonorecord delivery must be accompanied by certain information encoded in that sound recording by the copyright owner.

Since 1998, royalties under the compulsory license for digital phonorecord deliveries have been determined differently from royalties under the mechanical compulsory license. The rates and other terms of the digital delivery royalties are determined, and periodically adjusted, by Copyright Royalty Judges acting as arbitrators. With one exception, however, the Copyright Royalty Judges are required to give effect to agreements resulting from voluntary negotiations (whether or not through agents) between the copyright owners of nondramatic musical works and the parties seeking compulsory licenses.

The one exception applies to a category of musical compositions commonly known as "controlled compositions." A controlled composition clause is a provision in a recording contract between a musician/songwriter and his or her record company in which the musician/songwriter agrees to accept a mechanical royalty rate below the statutory compulsory license rate. (Such provisions are common, because the record company typically has the greater bargaining power in negotiating the initial recording contract.) Unlike other voluntarily negotiated royalty agreements for digital phonorecord deliveries, any controlled composition clauses entered into after June 22, 1995 will not be given effect in the royalty-setting process. In contrast, if the musician/songwriter separately negotiates a digital delivery royalty after the recording has been made, the Copyright Royalty Judges must defer to this voluntary negotiated rate.

In setting the terms and rates for compulsory licensing of digital phonorecord deliveries, Copyright Royalty Judges are required to distinguish between (1) digital phonorecord deliveries in general, and (2) those in which "the reproduction or distribution of a phonorecord is incidental to the transmission which constitutes the digital phonorecord delivery." Section 115 does not dictate how this distinction should be made, or what impact it should have on the royalty rates and terms. Nor have these issues been addressed by regulations. As an interim and partial solution, the Recording Industry Association of America (RIAA), the National Music Publishers Association (NMPA) and the Harry Fox Agency have entered an agreement under which musical compositions are licensed for Internet subscription services. These nonexclusive licenses apply to all reproduction and distribution rights for delivery of on-demand real-time music streaming as well as limited downloads (that is, digital deliveries that allow the recipient to retain a copy of the sound recording only for a limited time or allow the recipient to play the recording only a limited number of times).

The second difference between the mechanical compulsory license and the digital compulsory license is that the latter can be applied to digital deliveries of sound recordings by a party other than the owner of the copyright in the sound recording. A party other than the copyright owner of a sound recording may provide digital deliveries of phonorecords of that sound recording only if (1) the copyright owner of the sound recording authorizes the digital deliveries and (2) either the copyright owner of the sound recording, or the party making the digital deliveries, has obtained a compulsory license or a negotiated license from the copyright owner of the musical composition to engage in digital phonorecord deliveries embodying the musical composition. In other words, the compulsory licensee need not be the record company that made the sound recording that embodies the licensed composition; it can, in effect, be a retailer of digital phonorecord deliveries. However, as a condition of utilizing the compulsory license, the digital retailer must have obtained the record company's consent to distribute the copyrighted sound recording.

Unless a digital phonorecord delivery has been authorized by the copyright owner of the sound recording, and a compulsory or negotiated license has been obtained from the owner(s) of the copyright in the musical work(s) embodied therein, the digital phonorecord delivery will be actionable as an infringement. However, if the owner of the copyright in a sound recording—that is, a record company—authorizes a third party's digital phonorecord delivery of that sound recording, but this authorization does not include a license for digital delivery of the musical work embodied in the recording (because the record company may not itself have the authority to grant such a license), then the record company will not be liable for the third party's infringement of that musical work by digital phonorecord delivery, because it is the responsibility of the third party to obtain that license.

A third difference between the mechanical compulsory license and the digital compulsory license is that a digital phonorecord delivery permitted under a compulsory license must be accompanied by the information, if any, encoded in that sound recording which identifies the title of the sound recording, the featured recording artist, and related information, including information about the underlying musical work(s) and the author(s) thereof.

The compulsory licensing rules for digital phonorecord deliveries do not apply to any exempt transmissions under § 114(d)(1).

Section 1008 of the Audio Home Recording Act, which grants a limited right to copy sound recordings for personal use, and to supply equipment for such copying, is not overridden by the compulsory licensing rules for digital phonorecord deliveries. As discussed in § 8.15 below, § 1008 permits consumers to copy sound recordings for noncommercial use, and has been interpreted as inapplicable to copies that reside on computer storage media. It also exempts the manufacturers of certain types of copying equipment and media used in these consumer copying activities. It does not exempt parties that provide digital phonorecord deliveries.

§ 8.9 The Jukebox Compulsory License

The "jukebox" exception of § 116, applicable only to nondramatic musical works embodied in phonorecords, calls for Copyright Royalty Judges to establish the terms and rates of royalty payments to the owner of musical compositions when those works are performed on "coin-operated phonorecord players." However, negotiated licensing agreements between jukebox operators and copyright owners take precedence over determinations by the Copyright Royalty Judges.

§ 8.10 Copying Computer Programs

The exclusive rights of owners of copyright in computer programs are limited by § 117(a), which permits the owner of a copy of a computer program to make, or authorize another to make, a copy or adaptation of the program, provided that one of the following two conditions is satisfied:

(1) the new copy or adaptation is created as an essential step in utilizing the software in conjunction with a machine, and is not used in any other manner; or

(2) the new copy or adaptation is for archival purposes only, and all archival copies are destroyed when continued possession of the program ceases to be rightful.

Any copy that is made pursuant to § 117(a) may be leased, sold, or otherwise transferred, together with the copy from which it was made, only as part of the lease, sale, or other transfer of all rights in the program. Adaptations are subject to a greater restriction; any adaptation prepared under § 117(a) may be transferred only with the consent of the copyright owner of the underlying program. The restriction on sales, leases, or other dispositions effectuates congressional intent that the copy or adaptation must be solely for the owner-user's internal use.

A separate copying privilege, under § 117(c), applies only in the context of computer maintenance activities.

Each of the § 117 privileges will be examined in turn.

A.   Essential Step in Utilization

The § 117(a)(1) privilege of making a copy of a computer program as an essential step in its utilization recognizes that loading a program into the memory of a computer in order to run the program involves the creation of a copy which would otherwise implicate the copyright owner's exclusive reproduction right under § 106(1). The privilege of adapting a computer program in order to utilize it recognizes that software must sometimes be modified for use in a specific machine, and that such modifications might otherwise implicate the copyright owner's exclusive adaptation right under § 106(2).

In some respects, courts have interpreted the "utilization" concept broadly. For example, in *Vault Corp. v. Quaid Software Ltd.*, 847 F.2d 255 (5th Cir. 1988), the utilization privilege was applied to loading copy-protection software into a computer's memory in order to reverse-engineer the software and, ultimately, to create a program that could defeat the copy protection.

B. Archival Copying

The archival exemption of § 117(a)(2) permits the owner of a copy of software to copy or adapt it for archival purposes, provided that the archival copies are destroyed when continued possession of the software ceases to be rightful. For the exemption to apply, some courts have held that the owner's original copy of the software must be susceptible to damage by "mechanical or electrical failure," and have not permitted archival copying where the original copy was susceptible only to physical damage or erasure. *See, e.g., Micro–Sparc, Inc. v. Amtype Corp.*, 592 F.Supp. 33 (D. Mass. 1984); *Atari, Inc. v. JS & A Group, Inc.*, 597 F.Supp. 5 (N.D. Ill. 1983). Other courts have interpreted § 117 more literally, allowing archival copying to guard against any conceivable risk. *See, e.g., Vault Corp. v. Quaid Software Ltd.*, 847 F.2d 255 (5th Cir. 1988).

C. Computer Maintenance

Because of case law which had interpreted § 117(a) as inapplicable to licensees of software (based on the dubious assumption that licensees do not truly "own" a copy of their software), Congress found it necessary in 1998 to clarify that persons engaged in computer maintenance or repair are permitted to make copies of software where the copying is caused solely by activating a machine that contains an authorized copy of the software; this privilege applies even where the computers containing the software have been leased rather than purchased. The new copy may be used for no purpose other than the repair or maintenance activity, and must be destroyed immediately after the activity is completed. Where the copy exists only in the temporary memory (RAM) of the computer, it is "destroyed" when the machine is turned off.

Note that this provision, § 117(c), implicitly concedes that loading copyrighted material into the temporary memory (RAM) of a computer constitutes the making of a copy within the meaning of § 106(1), a conclusion that is not apparent from other provisions of the Copyright Act. (*See* § 2.1 and § 7.2 above.)

Owners of copyright in computer programs may attempt to use shrinkwrap licenses to negate the § 117 exemptions (as well as other statutory limitations on their exclusive rights). As discussed in Chapter 13, such contractual provisions will be upheld only if their enforcement is not preempted by federal copyright law. *See, e.g., Vault Corp. v. Quaid Software Ltd.*, 847 F.2d 255, 270 (5th Cir. 1988) (holding that enforcement of shrinkwrap license was preempted).

§ 8.11   Public Broadcasting Compulsory License

The § 118 compulsory license applies to performances or displays of published nondramatic musical works and published pictorial, graphic, and sculptural works in the course of transmissions made by public broadcasting entities. It also applies to the production of such transmission programs, and to their reproduction and distribution in copies or phonorecords, by a nonprofit institution solely for the purpose of such transmissions. In addition, § 118 allows a governmental body or nonprofit institution to copy such programs simultaneously with their transmission, and, for no more than seven days after the transmission date, to perform or display the contents of such programs in face-to-face teaching activities covered by § 110(1), after which the copies must be destroyed.

Where an activity qualifies under § 118, the copyright owners of the works being performed or displayed are entitled to a royalty, the rates and terms of which are determined by the Copyright Royalty Judges. If any copyright owners enter into voluntarily negotiated licensing agreements with public broadcasting entities, and copies of those agreements are submitted in compliance with § 118(b)(2), then the negotiated licenses will be given effect in lieu of any determinations by the Copyright Royalty Judges.

Except to the extent allowed by § 107 (the fair use provision), § 118 does not permit (1) the unauthorized dramatization of a nondramatic musical work, (2) the production of a transmission program that is drawn to a substantial extent from a published compilation of pictorial, graphic, or sculptural works, or (3) the unauthorized use of any portion of an audiovisual work.

§ 8.12   Compulsory Licenses for Satellite Retransmissions of Television Broadcasts

Whereas exemptions and compulsory licensing provisions for cable television systems were included in § 111 of the original 1976 Act (see § 8.4 above), not until later did satellite television emerge as another means of expanding public access to television programming, especially for regions not served by cable systems. In order to place satellite services on an equal footing with cable systems, Congress expanded the scheme of exemptions and compulsory licenses to include satellite systems by adding § 119 in the Satellite Home Viewer Act of 1988. Originally scheduled to expire in 1994, § 119 has been extended several times, most recently through the end of 2009. If a satellite carrier fails to satisfy the requirements of § 119, then its retransmissions of copyrighted television broadcasts will constitute infringement of the exclusive rights of public display and/or public performance. Because § 119 has become increasingly complex as a result of multiple amendments since 1988, only the major provisions are summarized here.

A satellite carrier must satisfy several requirements to qualify for a compulsory license to retransmit the signals of network stations and/or superstations. In the case of a superstation (which is a television station other than a network station), the satellite carrier's retransmission must be made to the public either for private home viewing or for viewing in a commercial establishment, and the carrier must impose a direct or indirect charge either on each subscriber or on a distributor that contracts with the subscribers, must pay the compulsory licensing fee and comply with certain information reporting requirements, must not unlawfully discriminate against any of its downstream distributors (for example, in terms of pricing structure or access to programming), and must not willfully alter the superstation's signal (for example, by removing or replacing the commercials). In the case of a network station (meaning a station owned or operated by, or affiliated with, a United States television network, or a noncommercial educational broadcast station), the satellite carrier must meet these same requirements, except that the retransmission to the public must be only for private home viewing, the direct or indirect charge must be imposed on subscribers only, the carrier must submit its subscriber list to each network and must retransmit the network's programming only to "unserved households" in the United States, and the retransmission cannot include the signals of more than two network stations per day for each television network (subject to exceptions) and, in general, cannot include retransmission of an analog signal from a distant network station that is affiliated with the same network as a local network station whose analog signal the carrier is also retransmitting to the subscribing household (subject to grandfathering provisions). The term "unserved household" has a complex definition, but refers primarily to a household that, with respect to a particular television network, cannot receive a signal of sufficient intensity (as defined by statute) from a network station affiliated with that network through a conventional rooftop antenna.

Satellite carriers, distributors, and copyright owners may establish royalty rates for the § 119 license through voluntary negotiation; in the absence of voluntary agreement, the rates will be determined by Copyright Royalty Judges. Each carrier must submit its royalty payments to the Register of Copyrights, who then distributes the royalties among the copyright owners who submit timely claims indicating that their works were included in the satellite carrier's secondary transmissions.

A satellite carrier that fails to comply with the requirements of § 119 will be liable for infringement only if (1) in the case of signal alterations, the alteration is willful, or (2) in the case of failure to comply with the payment or reporting requirements, or retransmission of a network station transmission to a party other than an unserved household, the retransmissions are willful and re-peated. The full range of infringement remedies applies (see Chapter 11), except that special limita-tions on damages apply in the case of network signal retransmissions to parties other than un-served households.

In contrast to § 119, the statutory license under § 122 allows satellite carriers to retransmit the signals of *local* television broadcast stations. In addition, the § 122 license is royalty-free, and ap-plies without regard to whether the subscriber is in an unserved household. To take advantage of § 122, the satellite carrier must impose a charge on its subscribers or distributors, and must provide sub-scriber lists to the network affiliated with any net-work station whose signals it retransmits.

Willful alterations of a broadcast of copyrighted material, or willful and repeated retransmissions to the local market of a television station without complying with the requirements of § 122, will sub-ject the satellite carrier to the full array of remedies for copyright infringement with respect to the per-formance or display of copyrighted content con-tained in the retransmitted broadcasts.

§ 8.13 Limits on Exclusive Rights in Archi-tectural Works

Section 120(a) limits the exclusive rights of those who own copyrights in architectural works by pro-viding that, after such a work has been constructed, the copyright owner does not have the right to prevent the making, distribution, or public display of "pictures, paintings, photographs, or other pictorial representations of the work," provided that the building embodying the work is located in, or ordinarily visible from, a public place. The quoted language implies that this exception is limited to two-dimensional static representations, and would not apply to scale models, sculptures, or other three-dimensional objects, or to audiovisual representations, such as the use of the building in the background of a motion picture. The examples of permissible uses given in the legislative history include photographs and posters, as well as "scholarly books on architecture." The legislative history notes that "these uses do not interfere with the normal exploitation of architectural works," and serve "an important public purpose."

The § 120(a) privilege is clearly not limited to noncommercial activities. Thus, the privilege would extend to the commercial sale of postcards or posters depicting copyrighted buildings. Although the only books mentioned in the legislative history are "scholarly books on architecture," nothing in the statute or legislative history suggests that the privilege is not equally applicable to non-scholarly books. If the privilege applies to books, then presumably it applies also to other two-dimensional derivative works, such as calendars, since these do not interfere with the normal exploitation of an architectural work.

A different limitation is imposed by § 120(b), which provides that, notwithstanding the copyright owner's exclusive adaptation right under § 106(2), the owner of a building embodying a copyrighted architectural work is free to alter or destroy the building, or to authorize others to do so.

§ 8.14   Exceptions for Persons with Disabilities

Section 121 allows certain nonprofit or government entities to reproduce and/or distribute copies or phonorecords of previously published nondramatic literary works in specialized formats exclusively for use by blind persons or other persons with disabilities. Specialized formats include braille, audio, or digital text, as well as large print formats in the case of instructional materials.

To qualify for the exemption, the nonprofit or government entity must have a primary mission to provide specialized services related to training, education, or adaptive reading or information access needs of blind or disabled persons.

Copies or phonorecords reproduced and/or distributed under this provision must bear a notice that further reproduction or distribution in a non-specialized format is an infringement, and must bear a copyright notice identifying the copyright owner and the date of the original publication.

Section 121 does not apply to certain types of standardized tests and related testing material, or to computer programs (except for those portions that contain text displayed to users, such as descriptions of pictorial works).

§ 8.15   The Audio Home Recording Act

When digital recording media for sound recordings first became widely available, record companies became concerned that consumers' ability to make digital copies of sound recordings would lead to widespread unauthorized copying, thereby hurting record sales. In response to this concern, in 1992 Congress enacted the Audio Home Recording Act (AHRA), 17 U.S.C. §§ 1001–10.

The AHRA represents a compromise between the interests of record companies and the manufacturers of digital recording equipment and media (such as blank CDs and digital audio tapes). Section 1008 forecloses any infringement action "based on the manufacture, importation, or distribution of a digital audio recording device, a digital audio recording medium, an analog recording device, or an analog recording medium, or based on the noncommercial use by a consumer of such a device or medium for making digital musical recordings or analog musical recordings." In return for protecting consumers and manufacturers from liability for noncommercial copying of musical recordings, § 1003 imposes a royalty on each digital audio recording device or medium distributed in the United States. In addition, § 1002 provides that each digital audio recording or interface device made, imported, or distributed in the United States must incorporate copy controls which prevent the making of second-generation copies—in other words, copies of copies. Noncompliance with either the royalty or the copy control provisions is actionable under § 1009; remedies include injunctions, actual or statutory damages, costs, and attorney's fees, as well as the impounding, remedial modification, and/or destruction of the offending devices and recordings.

Although the AHRA resolved the conflict between record companies and manufacturers of copying equipment at the time it was enacted, due to changes in technology it has far less significance today. In 1999, the Ninth Circuit held that the Rio, a portable device which played mp3 recordings downloaded by a computer from the Internet, was not a "digital audio recording device" as defined in the AHRA; accordingly, the Rio did not have to incorporate the copy controls required by § 1002. *Recording Industry Ass'n of America v. Diamond Multimedia Systems, Inc.,* 180 F.3d 1072 (9th Cir. 1999). Because no other courts have ruled to the contrary, the use of computers to download musical recordings, and the use of portable mp3 players to play those recordings, are now understood to fall outside the scope of the AHRA. The distributors of computers and mp3 players therefore do not have to comply with the royalty or copy control requirements of the AHRA. On the other hand, the makers of these devices, and the consumers who use these devices to copy and play musical recordings, cannot claim immunity from infringement liability under § 1008. As a result, record companies and music publishers are free to pursue infringement claims against consumers who make unauthorized downloads of musical recordings, and against parties that induce or knowingly facilitate such downloads. *See, e.g.*, *Metro–Goldwyn–Mayer Studios, Inc. v. Grokster, Ltd.*, 545 U.S. 913 (2005); *A & M Records v. Napster, Inc.*, 239 F.3d 1004 (9th Cir. 2001).

CHAPTER 9

INFRINGEMENT

§ 9.1 Prima Facie Case

Copyright infringement occurs when a party engages in any of the following activities:

(1) violates any of the exclusive rights of the copyright owner as provided in §§ 106–122;

(2) violates the author's moral rights under § 106A; or

(3) imports copies or phonorecords into the United States in violation of § 602.

17 U.S.C. § 501(a).

To establish a prima facie case of infringement of any of the exclusive rights set forth in §§ 106 and 602, the plaintiff must demonstrate (1) *ownership* of the right asserted and (2) *unauthorized appropriation* by the defendant of a material amount of the plaintiff's copyrighted expression. Only after the plaintiff has established a prima facie case of infringement does the burden shift to the defendant to establish an affirmative defense.

There is little case law addressing the elements of a prima facie case of infringement under § 106A. At minimum, however, the plaintiff must establish that he or she is the author or joint author of the work in question, that the work is a "work of visual art" as defined in § 101, and that the defendant has engaged in one of the activities proscribed by the moral rights provisions of § 106A. If the alleged violation is destruction of the work, the plaintiff must also establish that it is a "work of recognized stature."

The remainder of this chapter addresses infringement under §§ 106 and 602.

§ 9.2 Ownership

Because registration is a prerequisite to bringing an infringement claim for a United States work (see Chapter 4), ordinarily a plaintiff will rely on the registration certificate to establish ownership of a valid copyright. If the copyright in a work was registered before or within five years of first publication, then the registration certificate is prima facie evidence that the copyright is valid and that the person named on the certificate is the owner. If registration is obtained more than five years after publication, then the evidentiary weight of that certificate is left to the court's discretion. A plaintiff who is not named on the registration certificate must produce a chain of title establishing that person's status as owner or exclusive licensee of the rights allegedly infringed. The defendant, in turn, may submit evidence to rebut the presumption of ownership and validity. If the Copyright Office has refused to register the copyright, then the plaintiff can proceed with the infringement action if notice thereof is served on the Register of Copyrights. The court will then determine whether the plaintiff has a valid copyright in the work, under the standards discussed in Chapter 2.

For purposes of an infringement action, the plaintiff must have been either the assignee or the exclusive licensee of the particular rights alleged to have been infringed, *at the time* of the infringement. In certain situations, however, other parties have standing to sue. For more on standing, see § 9.5 below.

§ 9.3   Unauthorized Appropriation

In some cases, the accused infringer does not dispute using the plaintiff's work, but argues that the manner of use did not constitute infringement. For example, a store that plays radio broadcasts of music for its customers may concede that it is publicly performing copyrighted works, but may argue that the public performance is permitted by § 110(5), one of the statutory limitations on the public performance right.

In other cases, however, the infringement dispute focuses on whether the defendant's activity utilized the plaintiff's work at all, or whether the defendant's work is non-infringing because it was an independent creation or was copied from a work other than the plaintiff's. In these cases, an infringement claim may not be predicated solely on the fact that the plaintiff's and defendant's works are similar. The plaintiff must also establish that the similarities result from the defendant actually copying the plaintiff's work, and not from parallel independent creation or copying from another source. (Copyright law differs from patent law in this respect, because liability for patent infringement can arise through independent creation.) Therefore, to prove unauthorized appropriation of copyrighted material, the plaintiff must establish (1) that copying occurred, and (2) that the copying involved *improper appropriation* of copyrightable expression. *See Arnstein v. Porter,* 154 F.2d 464 (2d Cir. 1946).

A. Proof of Copying

Copying is a question of fact, and may be established through direct or circumstantial evidence. Direct evidence includes admissions, testimony of witnesses who observed the copying, or a "paper trail" of documentary evidence demonstrating that the defendant used the plaintiff's work as source material. Because direct evidence is typically unavailable, most plaintiffs rely on circumstantial evidence. To raise an inference of copying through circumstantial evidence, the plaintiff must establish that (1) the defendant had access to the plaintiff's work, and (2) there is substantial similarity (also known as "probative similarity") between the plaintiff's and defendant's works. *See Arnstein v. Porter, supra.* The plaintiff need not prove knowledge or intent.

Access may be established in many ways. In some cases, a plaintiff can prove that the defendant actually possessed a copy of the work, or that the work was performed or displayed for the defendant. In other cases, access may be inferred from the widespread availability of the work—for example, where a book has been published and made available through bookstores and libraries, where a song has been recorded and played on the radio, or where a motion picture has been theatrically released or performed on television. Many situations fall between these two extremes; in these cases, the plaintiff must establish that the defendant could have had access through some plausible chain of events. For example, the plaintiff may establish that the defendant had dealings with a third party that possessed a copy of the plaintiff's work.

Access may be established even where the defendant has no recollection of encountering the plaintiff's work. This is common, for example, in cases of unconscious copying, where a defendant may have heard the plaintiff's music or read the plaintiff's book (or heard the book read aloud) at some point in the past, but no longer recalls the event.

If access is established, then the trier of fact must determine whether the similarities between the works are sufficient to support the inference of copying. To assist the trier of fact, courts will generally permit expert testimony on the degree of similarity. Where the infringement claim is based on unauthorized creation of a derivative work, the defendant's work does not have to resemble the plaintiff's work in its entirety, because, by definition, a derivative work *incorporates* but does not exactly duplicate the underlying work.

At this stage of the prima facie case, some, but not all, circuits divide the analysis of similarity into two tests: (1) an extrinsic test, which is an objective analysis that identifies similarities between discrete concrete elements of each work (such as plot, setting, character, and dialogue), and (2) an intrinsic test, which is a subjective analysis of whether, from the perspective of the average reasonable observer, the works have a substantially similar overall concept and feel. *See Shaw v. Lindheim*, 919 F.2d 1353 (9th Cir. 1990). Courts which follow this approach will generally consider expert testimony under the extrinsic test, but not under the intrinsic test, and will grant a summary judgment for the defendant if the extrinsic test is not satisfied.

The degree of similarity required to prove copying varies, depending on the extent to which access has been established. In general, the weaker the evidence of access, the greater the degree of similarity necessary to establish a prima facie case of copying. Even where there is no evidence of access, plaintiffs can still establish copying by demonstrating "striking similarity" between the works. Striking similarity has been defined as a degree of similarity great enough to preclude coincidence, independent creation, or use of a common source. Striking similarity may be established, for example, where two works contain the same unusual errors or other idiosyncrasies.

If the plaintiff proves sufficient access and similarity to raise an inference of copying, the defendant may rebut that inference by providing proof of independent creation, either by establishing that the defendant's work was original, or that the defendant copied from a source other than the plaintiff's copyrighted work.

B. Improper Appropriation

If the trier of fact determines that the defendant in fact copied the plaintiff's work, the plaintiff must still prove that the copying amounted to *improper appropriation*. This, too, is a question of fact. The appropriation is improper only if it consists of a material amount of copyrighted expression. Thus, if the copying consists only of facts, general ideas, and unoriginal expression, there is no illicit copying because there is no improper appropriation; in other words, the defendant copied from the plaintiff, but did not infringe the plaintiff's copyright. Also, if only a *de minimis* amount of copyrighted expression was copied, there is no infringement; however, there is no clear rule as to what constitutes a *de minimis* amount of improperly appropriated expression, and courts have been willing to treat a small amount of copying as material provided that it is qualitatively significant. Courts will grant summary judgment for the defendant if the only material similarities between the works consist of uncopyrightable elements of the plaintiff's work.

1. *Literal and Nonliteral Similarity*

Infringement claims based on literal (or verbatim) similarity are typically easier to evaluate than claims based on nonliteral similarity. Literal or verbatim similarity arises when the defendant copies highly specific elements of expression, such as actual words, numbers, musical phrases, software code, visual images, recorded sounds, and so forth. Nonliteral similarity—sometimes called "comprehensive nonliteral similarity"—is based on copying more abstract elements such as plot, character, structure, sequence, and organization. Because these elements are one level removed from the literal expression, they come closer to the ill-defined line that distinguishes copyrightable expression from uncopyrightable ideas under § 102. (See Chapter 2.)

Rather than a "line" at all, the idea/expression dichotomy is probably better envisioned as a spectrum. An infringement claim based on a close paraphrase of a novel would probably be safely on the "expression" side of the spectrum, whereas a claim based on general similarities in plot or character would fall more on the "idea" end of the spectrum and thus would probably fail to support a finding of infringement. Thus, even if a plaintiff owns a valid copyright and proves that the defendant copied from the plaintiff's work, if the defendant's copying was nonliteral then the plaintiff will still have to persuade the court that the defendant copied protected expression rather than merely ideas. Claims of nonliteral infringement arise frequently in infringement suits involving works of fiction and computer software.

Generally speaking, the more creative a work is, the more likely it is that its copyright owner will succeed in an infringement claim based on nonliteral similarity. If a work is only minimally creative—

such as a database—the plaintiff will typically need to demonstrate near-verbatim copying (also called "bodily appropriation") in order to establish improper appropriation. This is one consequence of the difference between a strong copyright and a "thin" copyright.

In cases alleging infringement based on nonliteral similarity, courts sometimes invoke the concepts of *merger* and *scene a faire*. As discussed in § 2.5 above, the merger doctrine denies copyright protection when expression is so closely intertwined with an idea that protecting the expression would prevent others from copying the idea. The scene a faire doctrine applies to a nonliteral element of expression that is typical for a genre. For example, in a film about Nazi Germany, it is commonplace to see a depiction of a Nazi salute or a scene in a German beer hall. Although the exact depiction of these elements in the film may be copyrightable, anything short of a verbatim copy of such an element is likely to be non-infringing because the idea of including that element is so unoriginal.

2. *Computer Software*

In the specific context of computer software, many courts have adopted a three-step abstraction/filtration/comparison test for assessing nonliteral similarity, as formulated by the Second Circuit in *Computer Associates Int'l, Inc. v. Altai, Inc.*, 982 F.2d 693 (2d Cir. 1992), and some courts have applied this standard to claims of literal similarity as well. (Indeed, some courts have expanded the test to copyrighted works other than software.)

In the *abstraction* stage, the court identifies the structure and organization of the program at different levels of abstraction, from its highest level of abstraction (the ultimate function of the program) to the lower levels (the sequence of instructions within each module of the program).

In the *filtration* stage, the structural components at each level of abstraction are identified and characterized according to whether they consist of: (1) unprotectible ideas, (2) elements dictated by considerations of efficiency (in which case merger is likely to apply), (3) elements required by factors external to the program, such as compatibility with hardware or other programs (in which case they are likely to be treated as unoriginal under the "scene a faire" doctrine), (4) elements taken from the public domain, or (5) copyrightable expression (reflecting creative choices as to selection and arrangement of programming elements).

Finally, in the *comparison* stage, the court compares the plaintiff's program with the defendant's, to determine whether any of the plaintiff's copyrightable expression was copied, and whether the copied expression was an important aspect of the plaintiff's overall program (so as to preclude liability for *de minimis* copying).

Although a number of courts have endorsed the *Altai* approach to analyzing software copyrights, and no court has developed a more workable approach, it is widely agreed that infringement analysis is especially difficult in the case of computer software because the copyright regime is fundamentally ill-suited to software. However, Congress is not expected to develop an alternative regime in the near future.

§ 9.4   Secondary Liability

Concepts of secondary liability for copyright infringement are well-established in the case law, even though they are not expressly recognized in the copyright statutes. Two types of secondary liability have been recognized—contributory and vicarious. Both doctrines permit a defendant to be found liable for infringement even though the defendant did not personally engage in one of the infringing activities described in §§ 106 and 602. To date, courts have not addressed the possibility of secondary liability for moral rights violations under § 106A.

Liability for contributory or vicarious infringement will arise only when there has been an underlying act of direct infringement. However, the plaintiff need not file suit against the direct infringer in order to proceed against the contributory or vicarious infringer.

A.   Contributory Infringement

The classic formulation of contributory copyright infringement was articulated by the Second Circuit in *Gershwin Publishing Corp. v. Columbia Artists Management, Inc.*, 443 F.2d 1159, 1162 (2d Cir.

1971): "One who, with knowledge of the infringing activity, induces, causes or materially contributes to the infringing conduct of another, may be held liable as a 'contributory' infringer." Although the copyright statutes do not expressly recognize the concept of contributory infringement, some courts have found a statutory basis for contributory infringement in the exclusive rights listed in § 106, which expressly grants the copyright owner the exclusive right "to authorize" the exercise of those rights.

Under the *Gershwin* standard, contributory liability may arise from merely providing the means, facilities, or site for an infringing activity with knowledge that the activity is taking place. Thus, for example, a video rental store which permits customers to view its videos in the store is contributorily liable for those infringing public performances. *Columbia Pictures Indus., Inc. v. Aveco, Inc.*, 800 F.2d 59 (3d Cir. 1986). A flea market operator may be contributorily liable for sales of infringing merchandise by vendors to whom it rents space and provides support services; in *Fonovisa, Inc. v. Cherry Auction, Inc.*, 76 F.3d 259 (9th Cir. 1996), the Ninth Circuit held that a flea market operator was contributorily liable because, with knowledge of the infringing activities, it supplied space, customers, advertising, and support services to the infringing vendors. However, in *Perfect 10, Inc. v. Visa International Service Ass'n*, 494 F.3d 788 (9th Cir. 2007), the Ninth Circuit refused to hold a credit card processing service contributorily liable for continuing to process credit card payments despite having knowledge that the payments were going to websites that provided access to infringing material. Merely processing payments did not, in the court's view, "materially contribute" to the infringing activity, because processing the payments did not assist in copying, displaying, or distributing the copyrighted materials, nor did it assist users in locating those materials.

Lower courts have held that the knowledge requirement for contributory liability is satisfied where a defendant was "willfully blind" to the infringing conduct—meaning that there was sufficient evidence of infringing activity that the defendant *reasonably should have known* of the direct infringement. In other words, the defendant must "know or have reason to know" of the infringing activity.

The Supreme Court has modified the *Gershwin* standard in situations where a defendant's contribution to the infringing activity consists *only* of supplying a product that can be used in that activity. The concern in such cases is that, even if the supplier of the product knows that some of the purchasers are using the product in infringing activities, the consequence of holding the supplier liable may be that the supplier will no longer make the product readily available, thus depriving the public of the use of that product for non-infringing purposes. For example, while photocopiers can be used to infringe copyrights, they also have important non-infringing uses. Because of the potential social harm of driving such goods from the marketplace, the Court has found it necessary to strike a balance between the interests of copyright owners and the public interest in having access to goods that have substantial non-infringing uses.

In *Sony Corp. v. Universal City Studios, Inc.*, 464 U.S. 417 (1984), the Court addressed the standard under which Sony could be held liable for the infringing conduct of consumers that used Sony's Betamax videotape recorders to make infringing copies of television broadcasts. The Court found no precedent in copyright law for imposing liability based on a merchant's constructive knowledge that its customers may use its equipment in infringing activities. Therefore, the Court imported a concept from patent law—specifically, 35 U.S.C. § 271(c)—under which the seller of an article is not liable for third parties' infringing uses of that item unless it is unsuited for any commercial non-infringing use. Adapting that rule to the copyright context, the Court held that the mere sale of copying equipment, or other articles of commerce, does not constitute contributory copyright infringement so long as the product "is capable of commercially significant non-infringing uses." Because substantial numbers of Betamax purchasers used these devices to record television programs to watch at a later time ("time-shifting"), an activity that constituted a "fair use" of the copyrighted programs, the Court held that the Betamax was capable of substantial non-infringing uses. Accordingly, Sony's sale of these devices did not give rise to liability for contributory infringement.

In interpreting the phrase "capable of commercially significant non-infringing uses," lower courts have held that it is not sufficient to show that the product is physically capable of such uses; courts will disregard a use that is improbable, implausible, or commercially insignificant. For example, it is implausible that a consumer would purchase an expensive video game copying device when only a handful of video games are marketed with a license to copy, and those games are of poor quality and are manufactured by the maker of the copying device.

The Supreme Court next addressed the standard for contributory infringement in the context of peer-to-peer file sharing software that was widely used by consumers to locate and make infringing copies of copyrighted music and motion pictures stored on other users' computers. In *Metro–Goldwyn–Mayer Studios, Inc. v. Grokster, Ltd.*, 545 U.S. 913 (2005), the defendants argued that their role was limited to distributing the software, and that they provided no ongoing support or other services to their purchasers; thus, under *Sony*, even if they were aware of their customers' infringing activity, they could be contributorily liable only if their software had no commercially significant non-infringing uses. The Court, however, held that *Sony* did not apply, because the defendants' conduct was not limited to supplying the software with knowledge of the users' infringing activities. Instead, the defendants engaged in conduct designed to induce

these infringing activities, including actively promoting their software to former users of the infringing Napster file-sharing system, responding affirmatively to requests for help in locating and playing
copyrighted materials, and failing to take any steps
to diminish the infringing activity through filtering
tools or other mechanisms (indeed, rejecting offers
of assistance in monitoring infringement, and block-
ing access of parties attempting to engage in such
monitoring).

Because the defendants did more than simply
supply a software product, the *Grokster* Court held
that the *Sony* exception for products with substantial non-infringing uses did not apply, and the defendants were contributorily liable because they
affirmatively *induced* the infringing activity:
"[O]ne who distributes a device with the object of
promoting its use to infringe copyright, as shown
by clear expression or other affirmative steps taken
to foster infringement, is liable for the resulting
acts of infringement by third parties." In contrast,
the Court noted, liability would not arise where the
supplier of the device, knowing of the infringing
activity, simply continued to offer customers technical support or product updates, or engaged in other
activities that are ordinarily incident to product distribution. Rather, inducement involves "purposeful,
culpable expression and conduct."

B. Vicarious Liability

Vicarious liability for copyright infringement is
based on principles of respondeat superior. Thus,

for example, employers are vicariously liable for
infringing acts performed by employees who are
acting within the scope of their duties. However,
vicarious liability may arise even outside of an
employment relationship. The Second Circuit established the current standard for determining which
relationships give rise to vicarious liability for copyright infringement in *Gershwin Publishing Corp. v.
Columbia Artists Management, Inc.*, 443 F.2d 1159,
1162 (2d Cir. 1971):

> [E]ven in the absence of an employer-employee
> relationship one may be vicariously liable if he
> has the right and ability to supervise the infring-
> ing activity and also has a direct financial interest
> in such activities.

Applying this standard, courts have imposed vicarious liability on operators of entertainment venues for infringing musical performances, on operators of flea markets and similar venues for sales of
infringing merchandise by their concessionaires,
and on parent corporations for the infringing acts of
their subsidiaries. In these cases, courts have found
that the party held vicariously liable had the ability
and authority to supervise and control the activities
of the direct infringers, and also profited from the
infringing activities. These authorities also make
clear that it does not matter whether the right and
ability to supervise is actually exercised.

In contrast, courts have not imposed vicarious
liability in a typical landlord/tenant situation, on
the ground that the landlord lacks the right and
ability to supervise the tenant's infringing activi-

ties. In addition, a landlord typically does not derive greater revenue from tenants who infringe copyrights than from tenants who do not, whereas parties that have been held vicariously liable generally profit from the fact that infringing conduct is taking place, either through a share of the infringer's revenues or through other revenues that are generated by increased customer traffic (such as admissions, parking and concession fees).

On the other hand, courts have not strictly construed the requirement that the defendant's financial interest in the infringing activities be "direct"; thus, for example, the fact that sales of infringing goods at a flea market increase the flea market's customer traffic, thus boosting the operator's general revenues, is a sufficient financial benefit, even if the operator does not receive a percentage of the profits from the actual infringing sales.

In *Perfect 10, Inc. v. Visa International Service Ass'n*, 494 F.3d 788 (9th Cir. 2007), the Ninth Circuit refused to hold a credit card processing service vicariously liable for processing credit card payments to websites that provided access to infringing material. Even if the payment processing service gained a direct financial benefit from the infringing activity (a point which the court did not decide), it lacked the right and ability to supervise the infringing activity.

§ 9.5 Liability of Internet Service Providers

Under the generally applicable standards for contributory and vicarious liability, a variety of Inter-

net service providers ("ISPs") (such as access providers, search engines and online auction sites)
could face liability for the infringing activities of
their users. The Supreme Court's *Grokster* decision
(see § 9.4 above) is the leading example. An earlier
example is the *Napster* decision, where the Ninth
Circuit upheld an injunction against the Napster
file-sharing service on the grounds of both contributory and vicarious liability, finding that, with actual
knowledge of its users' infringing activities, Napster
provided its users with the means to locate and
download the infringing material, and also that
Napster had the right and ability to supervise its
users' infringing activities. Although Napster did
not derive any revenues from the infringing activities, the Ninth Circuit took a broad view of the
"direct financial benefit" requirement for vicarious
liability, agreeing with the district court that the
infringements led to increases in Napster's user
base, and that Napster's *future* revenues directly
depended on that increased user base. *A & M
Records, Inc. v. Napster, Inc.,* 239 F.3d 1004 (9th
Cir. 2001).

The Seventh Circuit, however, disagreed with
Napster's conclusion that actual knowledge of users'
infringements is sufficient to make a file-sharing
service contributorily liable. In *In re Aimster Copyright Litigation,* 334 F.3d 643 (7th Cir. 2003), the
court held a Napster-like service liable for contributory infringement because, even if the service was
capable of non-infringing uses, the defendant failed
to show that (1) the service had in fact ever been

used for such purposes, and (2) that it would have been disproportionately costly to take steps to eliminate or reduce the infringing uses.

Some courts have also held Internet service providers *directly* liable for infringing activities that utilize their services. These courts have focused on infringements of the exclusive rights of public distribution, public performance, and public display, because one or more of these acts may take place when the service provider facilitates a transmission of infringing content by a user.

As *Grokster*, *Napster*, and *Aimster* illustrate, ISPs have sometimes been active participants in their users' infringing activities. More difficult questions arise, however, when the ISP provides its services in a passive, neutral capacity, acting as a mere conduit for its users. In an influential 1995 decision, a California district court declined to hold an ISP either directly or secondarily liable for its users' infringing activities where the service provider acted purely as a passive conduit for those activities. The court expressed concern that imposing liability in such circumstances would burden service providers with the impracticable task of screening every piece of information passing through their systems. *See Religious Technology Center v. Netcom On–Line Communication Services, Inc.*, 907 F.Supp. 1361 (N.D. Cal. 1995).

In order to provide greater certainty for Internet service providers, the 1998 Digital Millenium Copyright Act (DMCA) added safe harbor provisions for such service providers in § 512. These provisions are discussed in Chapter 12. The safe harbors do not provide complete immunity. Instead, service providers seeking to qualify for the safe harbors must comply with a number of requirements, including taking appropriate action when they receive notice of infringing activity by their users. Section 512 represents an attempt to shield ISPs from infringement liability when they act purely as passive conduits, unless they fail to take appropriate corrective action once they learn of infringing conduct. It remains unsettled, however, whether § 512 completely supplants the "passive conduit" defense of *Netcom*.

§ 9.6   Procedural Aspects

A.   Registration as Prerequisite to Suit

Subject to three exceptions, an action for infringement of a copyright may not be instituted until the copyright has been registered or preregistered under § 411. (See § 4.2 above.) If the copyright owner has submitted a properly executed application to the register the work, but registration has been refused, the plaintiff may still file an infringement action if notice thereof is served on the Register of Copyrights. The latter has the option to become a party to the action with respect to the issue of registrability. The infringement action may proceed even if the Register of Copyrights opts not to participate. In either case, the court will determine whether the work is entitled to registration.

Because one requirement of copyright registration is the deposit of a copy of the work, a plaintiff who no longer has access to a copy of his or her work may be unable to register the work, and thus may be barred from pursuing an infringement action.

Actions under § 106A(a) are one exception to the general rule of § 411 that a work must be registered as a prerequisite to an infringement action. An author seeking to bring suit for violation of his or her right of attribution or integrity in a work of visual art need not register the copyright in that work in order to enforce these rights, because authors may enforce these rights even if they no longer own an interest in the copyright.

A second exception applies to works of foreign origin. Under § 411, the registration prerequisite to infringement actions applies only to a "United States work." That term is defined in § 101 to *exclude* (1) works that were first published outside of the United States and which have one or more foreign authors, (2) unpublished works that have one or more foreign authors, and (3) pictorial, graphic, or sculptural works incorporated in buildings or structures located outside the United States. The owner of an interest in such non-United States works may bring an action for copyright infringement even if the copyright has not been registered. This exception to the general rule reflects the United States' obligations, under the Berne Convention and the TRIPs provisions of the WTO Agreement (incorporating Berne), to impose no formalities as a condition to copyright protection for works originating in treaty countries.

The third exception applies to an action for infringement of a live broadcast, such as the Super Bowl. Under § 101 (definition of "fixed"), a live broadcast is protected by copyright only if it is fixed in a tangible medium of expression during its transmission. Section 411(b) provides that an action for infringement of such a work can be instituted only if the plaintiff serves notice on the infringer at least 48 hours *before* the fixation (that is, 48 hours before the live broadcast). The notice must specify the work as well as the time and source of its first transmission, and must declare the plaintiff's intent to secure copyright in the work. In addition, the plaintiff must register the work within three months of its first transmission (unless the work is not a "United States work").

B. Standing

In order to have standing to bring a cause of action for copyright infringement, the plaintiff must generally be the legal or beneficial owner of the exclusive right at the time that the right is infringed. 17 U.S.C. § 501(b). The legal owner of an exclusive right may be the author or joint author of the work, or any party that acquired an interest in the copyright through an assignment or exclusive license (*i.e.*, a "transfer," as defined in § 101).

The statutes do not define the "beneficial owner" of an exclusive right, but the House Report explains that this term includes an author who has transferred his or her copyright "in exchange for percentage royalties based on sales or license fees." This suggests that the beneficial owner must be one whose consideration for the copyright transfer depends on the extent to which the transferee's exclusive rights can be protected.

By allowing an infringement action to be brought by the owner or exclusive licensee of the particular right that has been infringed, § 501(b) reflects the 1976 Act's rejection of the rule of "indivisibility" of copyright ownership. (Prior to the 1976 Act, an infringement action could be brought only by the owner of the entire copyright interest in a work.) For the protection of other parties holding or claiming interests in the infringed work, however, § 501(b) provides that the court may require a plaintiff to serve written notice on any such parties whose interests might be affected by a decision in the case, and that the court may require joinder, and must permit intervention, of any person claiming an interest in the copyright.

A copyright transferee cannot bring suit for any acts of infringement that ended before the transfer took place. In other words, a fully accrued cause of action for infringement cannot be assigned. Only the party that owned the exclusive right at the time of infringement (or a party that was a beneficial owner at that time) can bring the cause of action.

In contrast to a transferee, a non-exclusive licensee does not have standing to bring an infringement action, because such a licensee does not have the right to exclude others from exercising the rights of the copyright owner.

Sections 501(c)-(f) provide several exceptions to the general rule that only a legal or beneficial owner of an exclusive right can bring an action for infringement of that right. As discussed below, these exceptions apply only to the public performance or display of a copyrighted work by a cable system in a secondary transmission that violates § 111(c) (see § 8.4 above), or by a satellite carrier in a secondary transmission that violates § 119(a)(5) (see § 8.12 above).

In the case of an infringement by a cable system under § 111(c), an action may be brought by any television broadcast station that holds a copyright or other license to perform or transmit the same version of the work if the unauthorized secondary transmission occurs within the broadcast station's local service area. 17 U.S.C. § 501(c). If the infringement involves unauthorized alteration of the broadcast, then actions may also be brought by (i) the primary transmitter whose transmission was altered, and (ii) any broadcast station within whose local service area the secondary transmission occurs (regardless of whether that broadcast station was licensed to carry the primary transmission). 17 U.S.C. § 501(d).

In the case of an infringement by a satellite carrier, if the infringement occurs under § 119(a)(5), then an action may be brought by any network station that holds a copyright or other license to transmit or perform the same version of that work if the secondary transmission occurs within the network station's local service area, 17 U.S.C. § 501(e); if the infringement occurs under § 122, then an action may be brought by any television broadcast station that holds a copyright or other license to transmit or perform the same version of that work if the secondary transmission occurs within the station's local market, *id.* § 501(f)(1).

C. Exclusive Jurisdiction

Federal district courts have exclusive jurisdiction over actions arising under the federal copyright statutes, and appeals are heard in the regional federal courts of appeal.

D. Right to a Jury

Where a copyright plaintiff seeks only equitable remedies for infringement—injunctive relief, seizure or destruction, attorneys' fees, or declaratory relief—neither party is entitled to a jury trial. In contrast, if the plaintiff seeks actual damages, profits, or statutory damages, the Seventh Amendment entitles either the plaintiff or the defendant to demand a trial by jury.

CHAPTER 10

DEFENSES

§ 10.1 Overview

In addition to the statutory limitations on the exclusive rights of the copyright owner, there are a number of affirmative defenses to copyright infringement. Several of these defenses have been codified. These include the judicially-created defense of fair use, now codified in § 107 of the 1976 Act, the statute of limitations under § 507, and innocent infringement under § 406(a). The other affirmative defenses are judicially-created and not yet codified. These include copyright misuse, laches, estoppel, unclean hands, abandonment, and Eleventh Amendment immunity. Finally, there is an open question as to the extent to which the First Amendment itself can be a defense to copyright infringement.

§ 10.2 Fair Use

The fair use defense began as a judge-made doctrine, but was codified by Congress in § 107 of the 1976 Act. Congress stated that its intent in codifying fair use was "to restate the present judicial doctrine of fair use, not to change, narrow, or enlarge it in any way." H.R. Rep. No. 94–1476, at 66 (1976). While the case law preceding codification

293

is therefore still relevant, nonetheless the most influential fair use precedents today are those based on § 107.

Unlike the limitations on the exclusive rights of copyright owners in §§ 108–122, the Supreme Court has held that fair use is an affirmative defense. *Harper & Row Publishers, Inc. v. Nation Enterprises,* 471 U.S. 539, 561 (1985); *Campbell v. Acuff–Rose Music,* 510 U.S. 569 (1994). Accordingly, the defendant bears the burden of persuasion regarding fair use, but need raise the defense only after the plaintiff has established a prima facie case of infringement.

The fair use analysis offers no bright-line tests and no per se rules. Both Congress and the Supreme Court have described fair use as an "equitable rule of reason." *See, e.g., Sony Corp. v. Universal City Studios, Inc.,* 464 U.S. 417, 448 & n. 31 (1984) (quoting H.R. Rep. No. 94–1476, at 65–66). Thus, every case turns on its specific facts, and requires courts to balance a variety of factors. This makes the fair use defense flexible, but can also make its likelihood of success difficult to predict in specific cases.

Section 107 provides a non-exhaustive list of factors for a court to consider in determining whether a particular use is fair:

> In determining whether the use made of a work in any particular case is a fair use the factors to be considered shall include—

    (1) the purpose and character of the use, including whether such use is of a commercial nature or is for nonprofit educational purposes;

    (2) the nature of the copyrighted work;

    (3) the amount and substantiality of the portion used in relation to the copyrighted work as a whole; and

    (4) the effect of the use upon the potential market for or value of the copyrighted work.

While a court is required to consider these four factors, it is not precluded from considering any other relevant factors, such as whether the defendant acted in bad faith.

Fair use is a mixed question of law and fact. The district court engages in factfinding with respect to each of the fair use factors, but its ultimate conclusion after weighing all of the factors against one another is a question of law.

Fair use is a defense to claims of infringement under § 106 as well as moral rights violations under § 106A. However, it has not succeeded as a defense to violations of the Digital Millennium Copyright Act (DMCA), *see* Chapter 12, and its application to bootlegging claims under § 1101 has yet to be determined.

A. Purpose and Character of the Use

In what is often referred to as its "preamble," § 107 specifically lists certain purposes for which the use of a copyrighted work may be fair; these include "purposes such as criticism, comment, news reporting, teaching (including multiple copies for classroom use), scholarship, or research." However, the fact that a particular activity fits within one of these categories does not establish that the activity is fair use per se, and in fact many activities that fit within these categories are not fair use. This is because § 107 indicates only that the "fair use" of a work for one of these purposes is not an infringement. For example, while copying materials for classroom teaching purposes is specifically mentioned in the preamble of § 107, the legislative history incorporates a highly restrictive set of guidelines for educational copying. Although these are presented as the "minimum" rather than "maximum" amount of permissible copying—in other words, a safe harbor—it is not clear how much they may be exceeded without incurring liability.

Section 107 indicates that the inquiry into the purpose and character of the use "includes whether such use is of a commercial nature or is for nonprofit educational purposes." By using the term "includes," Congress indicated that courts are not restricted to considering these two characteristics, but should conduct a broad inquiry into the purpose and character of the activity. In practice, courts analyzing the purpose and character of the defendant's use often focus on the extent to which the activity is or is not (1) transformative and (2) commercial. In general, the more transformative the use, the more likely it is a fair use. The more commercial the use, the more likely it will be found to infringe. However, neither commerciality nor transformativeness is, by itself, dispositive.

Although dicta in the Supreme Court's *Sony* decision indicated that "every commercial use of copyrighted material is presumptively an unfair exploitation," *Sony*, 464 U.S. at 451, the Supreme Court unequivocally repudiated that position in *Campbell v. Acuff–Rose*, where it held that the commerciality of the defendant's activity is "only one element of the first factor enquiry into its purpose and character," and noted that even those activities specifically mentioned in the preamble of § 107, such as news reporting, comment, and criticism, are often conducted for profit. The importance of commerciality, therefore, varies with context. "The use, for example, of a copyrighted work to advertise a product, even in a parody, will be entitled to less indulgence under the first factor of the fair use enquiry, than the sale of a parody for its own sake, let alone one performed a single time by students in school." *Campbell*, 510 U.S. at 585.

The "transformativeness" aspect of the first fair use factor inquires whether the defendant's work merely serves the same function as the original work, "or instead adds something new, with a further purpose or different character, altering the first with new expression, meaning or message." *Campbell*, 510 U.S. at 579. Transformative uses are favored as a matter of public policy:

[T]he goal of copyright, to promote science and the arts, is generally furthered by the creation of transformative works. Such works thus lie at the heart of the fair use doctrine's guarantee of breathing space within the confines of copyright, and the more transformative the new work, the less will be the significance of other factors, like commercialism, that may weigh against a finding of fair use.

Id. Thus, for example, in *Campbell*, the Court weighed the commercial purpose of the defendant's musical parody, on the one hand, against its transformative character as well as the defendant's purpose of commenting critically on the plaintiff's work.

In the Internet context, courts have found transformative uses where search engines produce thumbnail images that enable their users to locate full-sized images on third party websites; these courts note that, without such thumbnails, searching for an image on the Internet would be extremely difficult.

Although transformative uses are favored in the fair use analysis, some activities will qualify as fair use even though they are relatively or completely nontransformative. For example, photocopying of printed materials for teaching purposes can qualify as fair use, even though there is little or no transformative aspect to the copying itself (the only arguably transformative aspect of the activity being the teacher's classroom commentary and any editing of the materials). Similarly, in *Sony Corp. v.*

Universal City Studios, the Supreme Court held that fair use permitted individuals to copy television broadcasts in order to view them at more convenient times; the Court emphasized the noncommercial aspect of this "time shifting" activity, even though the activity was clearly nontransformative. These nontransformative uses are considered fair because they are noncommercial; in contrast, it is difficult for an activity to qualify as fair use if it is both nontransformative and commercial (for example, making and selling copies of a work for commercial gain).

B. Nature of the Copyrighted Work

Fair use is more difficult to establish for some copyrighted works than for others. Some works receive greater protection against infringement, because, as the Supreme Court noted in *Campbell*, 510 U.S. at 586, they are "closer to the core of intended copyright protection than others."

If a plaintiff's work is highly creative, this will generally weigh against a finding of fair use. Thus, for example, where the plaintiff's work is a musical composition, a poem, a work of art, a fictional work, or a motion picture or musical sound recording, the defendant will generally have to make a strong showing under the other fair use factors in order to prevail. However, because the nature of the copyrighted work is just one factor in the fair use analysis, unauthorized uses of highly creative works will sometimes qualify as fair. This is especially true in the context of parodies. Because parodies, by their very nature, tend to target highly creative works, in this context the creative nature of the targeted work receives little weight in the fair use analysis. For example, in *Suntrust Bank v. Houghton Mifflin Co.*, 268 F.3d 1257 (11th Cir. 2001), the appellate court applied the fair use factors to overturn a preliminary injunction against a parodic retelling of "Gone with the Wind," and in the *Campbell* case, the Supreme Court held that the highly creative nature of the song "Pretty Woman" did not foreclose treating a parody of that song as fair use.

Where a work is less creative, the scope of fair use tends to be broader. "The law generally recognizes a greater need to disseminate factual works than works of fiction or fantasy." *Harper & Row Publishers v. Nation Enterprises*, 471 U.S. 539, 563 (1985). Because protected expression and unprotected facts are intertwined in factual works, the latter are considered to have "thinner" copyrights than more creative works, and fair use permits some protected expression to be copied in order to allow the facts to be disseminated. However, the amount of expression which may be copied will vary, depending on the nature of the work:

> [E]ven within the field of fact works, there are gradations as to the relative proportion of fact and fancy. One may move from sparsely embellished maps and directories to elegantly written biography. The extent to which one must permit expressive language to be copied, in order to assure dissemination of the underlying facts, will thus vary from case to case.

Id. (quoting Gorman, *Fact or Fancy? The Implications for Copyright*, 29 J. Copyright Soc. 560, 561 (1982)).

For example, in *Harper & Row* the defendant's magazine appropriated verbatim expression from Gerald Ford's soon-to-be-published memoir. In the Supreme Court's view, it was permissible for the defendant to copy phrasing that was "so integral to the idea expressed as to be inseparable from it," but when the defendant copied "subjective descriptions and portraits of public figures whose power lies in the author's individualized expression," the defendant's copying could not be justified by the importance of the underlying facts: "Such use, focusing on the most expressive elements of the work, exceeds that necessary to disseminate the facts." 471 U.S. at 563–64.

In determining the degree of protection to extend to a work, some courts have considered not only the level of creativity in the work but also whether the work represents a "substantial investment of time and labor . . . in anticipation of a financial return." *See, e.g., Wall Data Inc. v. Los Angeles County Sheriff's Dept.,* 447 F.3d 769, 780 (9th Cir. 2006). Although this approach has not been tested at the Supreme Court, and is arguably inconsistent with the views the Court expressed in *Harper & Row, supra,* as well as the Court's rejection of the "sweat of the brow" theory in *Feist Publications v. Rural Telephone Service,* 499 U.S. 340 (1991) (see Chapter 2), the Ninth Circuit applied it in *Wall Data* to hold that the second fair use factor favored the plaintiff in a case involving software which enabled a personal computer using one operating system to access data stored on computers using different operating systems.

In *Harper & Row,* the Supreme Court held that "the fact that a work is unpublished is a critical element of its 'nature,'" and, thus, "the scope of fair use is narrower with respect to unpublished works." Subsequent rulings in the Second Circuit appeared to interpret this language as imposing a per se rule that fair use does not apply to unpublished works. Responding to these concerns, in 1992 Congress amended § 107 to provide that "[t]he fact that a work is unpublished shall not itself bar a finding of fair use if such finding is made upon consideration" of all of the fair use factors. Although Congress clearly rejected the per se rule suggested by the Second Circuit rulings, the legislative history of the 1992 amendment expressly reaffirms the Supreme Court's statement in *Harper & Row* that, for purposes of the second statutory factor, the unpublished nature of the work is a " 'key, though not necessarily determinative' factor tending to negate a defense of fair use." H.R. Report 102–836, 102d Cong., 2d Sess. (1992), 1992 U.S.C.C.A.N 2553, 2561 (quoting *Harper & Row*, 471 U.S. at 554).

C. Amount and Substantiality of the Portion Used

Section 107 also requires courts to consider the amount and substantiality of the portion of the copyrighted work that was used relative to that work as a whole.

Where a work is copied in its entirety, this generally weighs against fair use. However, copying a work in its entirety is not per se unfair. In *Sony,* for example, the Supreme Court held that fair use permitted individuals to copy entire television broadcasts for viewing at more convenient times, because the activity was noncommercial and there was insufficient evidence that such "time-shifting" would harm the market for the copyrighted works.

Where only portions of a work are copied, the "amount and substantiality" of what was copied will generally be assessed both quantitatively and qualitatively. The qualitative measure was crucial in *Harper & Row.* Here, the defendant's news story appropriated only about 300 words from a full-length book. Although by any quantitative measure this taking was insubstantial, the Court held that it was qualitatively significant, because those passages were among the most powerful passages in the book, going to the "heart" of the plaintiff's work. It was also important that the verbatim copying constituted a substantial portion of the *infringing* work; the Court saw this as further evidence of the qualitative value of the copied expression.

Qualitative analysis was also important in the "amount and substantiality" analysis in *Campbell.* Although the defendants in that case copied only the opening musical phrase and a few words from the original lyrics, the Court acknowledged that these could be characterized as the "heart" of the plaintiff's work.

However, in determining whether the defendant used too much of a plaintiff's work, courts also consider the purpose of the copying. The same amount of copying may be considered reasonable for some purposes, but excessive for others.

Because the essence of parody is imitation for the purpose of criticism, in general a greater degree of copying is tolerated in a parodic context than in many other contexts. In the case of parody, it is well-settled that a parodist may copy at least enough protected expression to "conjure up" the targeted work—that is, at least enough to enable the audience to recognize which work or works are being parodied. Moreover, the Supreme Court made clear in *Campbell* that the "conjure up" standard establishes the minimum, and not the maximum, amount of copying permitted in the case of parody. In some cases, even copying that goes to the "heart" of the original may be reasonable in light of the defendant's parodic purpose; thus, the question whether a parody involves excessive copying must be determined in light of the parodic purpose and character of the defendant's work, its transformative elements, and its potential for serving as a market substitute for the original. In some cases, the amount of the copying may be found to exceed what is necessary to achieve the legitimate purpose of the parody; for example, in a pre-*Campbell* case which nonetheless applied the same principles, the Ninth Circuit found that a defendant had copied more than was necessary to conjure up the plaintiff's well-known cartoon characters even in light of the parodic purpose of the copying. The court therefore rejected the claim of fair use. *Walt Disney Productions v. Air Pirates,* 581 F.2d 751 (9th Cir. 1978).

D. Market Effect

In assessing the effect of the defendant's activities on the market for the copyrighted work, the "market" in question includes not only the market for the original work but also the markets for existing or potential derivatives of that work. For example, an unauthorized film adaptation of a novel may not displace demand for the novel itself— indeed, it may even increase that demand—but it is very likely to displace demand for an authorized film adaptation. Similarly, an unauthorized translation of a book from Japanese into English will have little effect on the market for the original Japanese version, but may completely supplant demand for an authorized English version.

However, there is one derivative market that must be disregarded in analyzing the market effect of a defendant's work: the market for parodies of that work. In *Campbell*, the Supreme Court made clear that a copyright owner has no right to control the market for parodies of the copyrighted work, because this would allow the copyright owner to silence one of the most effect methods for criticizing the work.

The "effect" on the market that is relevant for fair use purposes is specifically the market substitution effect. In other words, the analysis of market effect asks whether the defendant's work could serve as a substitute for the plaintiff's work (or as a substitute for a derivative thereof). If so, then the fourth factor weighs against fair use. For example, a search engine's "thumbnail" images of the plaintiff's full-sized digital photographs were found not to be market substitutes for the latter, because the smaller images lost their clarity when enlarged; thus, anyone seeking the full-sized photographs would have to obtain them from the copyright owner rather than from the defendant's search engine. *Kelly v. Arriba Soft Corp.*, 336 F.3d 811 (9th Cir. 2003).

In assessing market effect, courts must "consider not only the extent of market harm caused by the particular actions of the alleged infringer, but also whether unrestricted and widespread conduct of the sort engaged in by the defendant would result in a substantially adverse impact on the potential market." *Campbell*, 510 U.S. at 590. Thus, for example, while a single instance of unauthorized downloading of a song or a motion picture will have a negligible effect on the market for authorized copies of that work, the same conduct repeated many times could significantly undermine authorized sales.

In some situations, a defendant's work may harm the market for the plaintiff's work, but in a manner that does not involve market substitution. This type of market harm does not weigh against fair use. A successful parody, for example, may cause audiences to change their opinion about the parodied work, and thus may reduce demand for the plaintiff's work. However, this injury to the plaintiff's market does not involve market substitution, and therefore is not relevant to the analysis of the fourth fair use factor. If a parody causes audiences to take a negative view of the targeted work, the harm to the market for that work is the result of the parody's criticism; thus, it is similar to the harm that would result from a devastating review. "[W]hen a lethal parody, like a scathing theater review, kills demand for the original, it does not produce a harm cognizable under the Copyright Act." *Campbell,* 510 U.S. at 591–92. Neither a parody nor a devastating review is an adequate substitute for the plaintiff's work, but both of them can significantly reduce the public's desire to have access to the work. In other words, infringement *usurps* demand, while criticism *suppresses* it. *Fisher v. Dees*, 794 F.2d 432, 438 (9th Cir. 1986).

Of course, there may be situations in which a parody is capable of causing two kinds of harm to the market for the targeted work—harm through criticism, and also harm through substitution. In such a situation, courts must engage in factfinding—and litigants must provide relevant evidence—to determine which type of harm has actually occurred. In *Campbell*, for example, while the Supreme Court held that the harm resulting from the parody's "disparagement" of the plaintiff's song was irrelevant, it remanded for further factfinding on the possibility that the defendant's rap parody could supplant demand for *authorized* rap derivatives of the plaintiff's song.

§ 10.3   Statute of Limitations

Under § 507, a civil action for copyright infringement must be commenced within three years from the date on which the claim *accrues*. In contrast, a criminal copyright proceeding must commence within five years after the cause of action *arose*.

Because the statute is silent on when an infringement claim "accrues" for purposes of civil infringement litigation, courts have reached different conclusions. The majority approach holds that a claim accrues when the copyright owner knows or has reason to know of the infringement (the "discovery rule"); under the minority view, a claim accrues when the infringing acts take place (the "injury rule"), even if the copyright owner does not discover them until later (and could not reasonably have been expected to).

Where acts of infringement continue over time, most courts hold that recovery is barred for any infringing act that accrued more than three years prior to filing the infringement suit. Under a minority view advanced by the Seventh Circuit, if a series of acts constitute a "continuing wrong," only the last act of the continuing infringement must occur within the three-year limitations period for the plaintiff to recover for all of the acts constituting the continuing wrong. In the Seventh Circuit's view, such a continuing wrong occurs where the act of copying precedes the limitations period, but copies continue to be sold within the limitations period; the plaintiff may then recover not only for the infringing sales but for the copying itself. *Taylor v. Meirick,* 712 F.2d 1112 (7th Cir. 1983). Note, however, that the *Taylor* opinion implicitly assumes that a claim accrues when the infringing act occurs, rather than when a reasonable copyright owner would have discovered it.

In some circumstances, the statute of limitations may be tolled. For example, the Seventh Circuit held in *Taylor v. Meirick* that the statute was tolled where an infringer failed to take steps to stop the infringement and recall the infringing goods, and also fraudulently concealed the infringement. In a jurisdiction which follows the injury rule for accrual, tolling by fraudulent concealment will often lead to the same result as the discovery rule.

The statute of limitations applies not only to infringement actions, but also to actions for declaration of joint copyright ownership and/or accounting of profits to a joint owner. However, courts have encountered difficulty in determining when such a claim "accrues" for purposes of § 507. Under the prevailing view, courts have held that a joint ownership claim accrues when one owner plainly and expressly repudiates the joint ownership status of another. Plain and express repudiation need not be directly communicated to the putative joint owner; it may be inferred from one party's open exploitation of the work without sending an accounting to the other party. Other courts, however, have not required plain and express repudiation, at least where the plaintiff is a putative joint *author*; under these facts, courts have held that the joint author's claim accrued as soon as the joint work was created, because the plaintiff knew or should have known of his or her joint ownership status at that time.

The statute may be tolled where circumstances beyond the joint owner's control prevent the joint owner from bringing suit within the limitations period. For example, where a joint owner's heir was unaware of her ownership claims due to fraudulent concealment by the defendants, a court held that the statute did not begin to run until she discovered her status.

In another case involving an heir's joint ownership claims, the Second Circuit treated the joint ownership claims of Hank Williams' unacknowledged daughter as accruing continuously as the work generated profits (thus adopting an approach similar to the approach used for continuing infringements). As a result, even though the limitations period began when the plaintiff first discovered that Hank Williams was her father, she was precluded only from participating in the profits that were generated outside of the limitations period; thus, she was still entitled to bring an action for her share of the most recent three years of revenues. *Stone v. Williams*, 970 F.2d 1043 (2d Cir. 1992). However, subsequent case law suggests that the reasoning of *Stone* may be limited to its unusual facts, even in the Second Circuit. *See, e.g., Merchant v. Levy*, 92 F.3d 51 (2d Cir. 1996). As a result, most joint ownership claims will be completely time-barred if they are not filed within three years of the actions constituting plain and express repudiation.

Under *Taylor v. Meirick, supra*, the common law doctrine of equitable estoppel (see § 10.6 below) applies to copyright claims if the defendant takes affirmative steps to prevent the plaintiff from filing suit within the limitations period. The plaintiff must show that he actually and reasonably relied on the defendant's conduct or representations.

§ 10.4 Innocent Intent

A narrow defense of innocent intent is recognized under § 406(a). The defense applies only with respect to copies or phonorecords that were publicly distributed by or under the authority of the copyright owner *before* the effective date of the Berne Convention Implementation Act (March 1, 1989), the legislation which prospectively eliminated the requirement of copyright notice. If the copyright notice on such a copy or phonorecord names a person who is not in fact the copyright owner, then a person who innocently infringes the work has a complete defense to an infringement claim if he or she was misled by the notice, and began the infringing undertaking in good faith under a purported transfer or license from the person named in the copyright notice, unless, before the infringing activity began, either: (1) the copyright owner registered the copyright, or (2) a document executed by the person named in the copyright notice, and showing the correct ownership of the copyright, was recorded in the Copyright Office.

§ 10.5 Laches

The circuits are split on whether laches is a viable defense to copyright infringement. Some circuits reject the laches defense, because the copyright statutes already provide an explicit statute of limitations (see § 10.3 above.) Others—including the Second and Ninth Circuits—recognize laches as a defense distinct from the statute of limitations.

Where recognized, laches provides an equitable defense to an infringement claim by a plaintiff who, with full knowledge of the infringing conduct (or of the intended infringing conduct), unreasonably delays taking action against the infringer. A defendant pleading laches must establish (1) unreasonable delay by the plaintiff, and (2) prejudice to the defendant as a result of that delay.

A successful laches defense will preclude recovery of damages for the infringing acts as to which laches applies, but not for infringing acts as to which the plaintiff acted without undue delay. In addition, laches ordinarily will not bar injunctive relief against future infringements, although a few courts have made an exception where there is unconscionable delay and severe prejudice to the defendant.

§ 10.6 Estoppel

Equitable estoppel is a well-established equitable defense to infringement. The elements of equitable estoppel are:

(1) the plaintiff knew about the infringing conduct;

(2) the plaintiff intended that its conduct would be acted upon, or acted in such a way that the defendant had a right to believe this was the plaintiff's intent;

(3) the defendant was ignorant of the true facts; and

(4) the defendant relied on the plaintiff's conduct to its detriment.

This type of estoppel has been applied, for example, where a copyright owner encouraged, facilitated, or acquiesced in the defendant's infringing activities.

Although there is little authority on the question, the prevailing view is that equitable estoppel bars actions not only for infringing conduct that took place before the infringement suit was filed, but also for prospective infringements as well. Thus, both monetary and equitable remedies would be precluded. This distinguishes equitable estoppel from an implied license, because the latter may be revoked by the filing of the infringement suit or by some earlier act communicating revocation.

A different type of estoppel, sometimes called *copyright estoppel*, applies where a copyright owner falsely represents portions of his or her work as factual or otherwise original, then later asserts copyright in that material in order to sue a copyist. The estoppel defense almost always succeeds where the copyright owner has made an *express* false representation. A closer case arises, however, where the false representation is merely implied. For example, when a story is presented as "news," a reasonable person would understand that the author represents it to be factual. But when a writer publishes a work of nonfiction, such as history, biography, or a memoir, a reasonable person might understand that some dramatic license has been taken, and thus there is a question of fact as to whether a reasonable person in the defendant's position would have understood the allegedly infringed material to be factual.

§ 10.7 Abandonment

Although there are no statutory provisions addressing abandonment of copyright, it has been recognized as a defense to infringement. Abandonment is the intentional surrender of copyright (as opposed to inadvertent forfeiture due to failure to comply with such formalities as notice and renewal, as discussed in Chapter 4). Abandonment is determined on a case-by-case basis, and while a majority of courts have held that an overt act is necessary to establish affirmative intent to abandon, there are no clear rules as to what types of acts will suffice.

§ 10.8 Copyright Misuse

The majority of circuits have recognized an affirmative defense of copyright misuse, and no circuit has rejected it. The Supreme Court has on several occasions implied its approval of the defense. *United States v. Loew's, Inc.,* 371 U.S. 38, 44–51 (1962);

United States v. Paramount Pictures, 334 U.S. 131, 157–59 (1948).

The misuse defense applies when the owner of a copyright attempts to extend its monopoly beyond the scope of the copyright grant in a manner which contravenes the public interest. A copyright owner that engages in misuse loses the right to enforce that copyright for so long as the misuse continues. *See, e.g., Practice Management Information Corp. v. American Medical Ass'n,* 121 F.3d 516, 520 & n.3 (9th Cir. 1997).

Where a plaintiff's use of its copyright violates antitrust laws, this typically will constitute copyright misuse. However, the reverse is not true; a defendant need not prove an antitrust violation to prevail on a copyright misuse defense. *Id.* at 521. Copyright misuse has been found where a software licensor required the licensee to use the licensor's hardware, *Alcatel USA, Inc. v. DGI Technologies, Inc.,* 166 F.3d 772, 794–95 (5th Cir. 1999); where a licensor prohibited the licensee from using competing products, *Practice Management, supra,* and where a software licensor prohibited its licensee from participating in the development of competing software, *Lasercomb Am., Inc. v. Reynolds,* 911 F.2d 970 (4th Cir. 1990).

Because misuse makes the copyright itself unenforceable, the misuse defense is available even to an infringement defendant that was not harmed by the misuse. For example, where the misuse arises from anticompetitive licensing restrictions such as those in *Alcatel, Practice Management,* or *Lasercomb*, the misuse defense can be raised even by a defendant who is not the plaintiff's licensee.

The copyright misuse defense is based on the established defense of patent misuse, which was recognized by the Supreme Court in *Morton Salt Co. v. G.S. Suppiger Co.*, 314 U.S. 488 (1942). Patent misuse, in turn, is based on the equitable concept of unclean hands. Copyright misuse, therefore, is an equitable defense. It is unsettled, however, whether the defense is precluded where the party raising the defense itself has unclean hands. *See Alcatel, supra.*

§ 10.9 Unclean Hands

To establish unclean hands, a defendant must demonstrate (1) that the plaintiff has engaged in inequitable conduct; (2) that this conduct directly relates to the claim asserted against the defendant; and (3) that this conduct injured the defendant. A general public injury is not sufficient; the injury must be one that specifically harms the defendant. The defense succeeds only where the copyright owner has committed a serious transgression, such as fraudulent registration or fraudulent representations to a court regarding the originality of the copyrighted work. The wrongful acts must affect the equitable relations between the parties with respect to the controversy; the defense does not apply where the copyright owner's transgression is unrelated to the merits of the controversy between the parties, such as where the content of the copyrighted work is considered obscene or immoral.

Although the doctrine of unclean hands is equitable in nature, some courts have held that a successful unclean hands defense bars not only injunctive relief, but recovery of damages as well.

§ 10.10 Eleventh Amendment

Sovereign immunity under the Eleventh Amendment prevents a state, a state agency, or a state employee acting in an official capacity from being sued in federal court for monetary damages. It operates by denying federal courts jurisdiction over such claims unless the state consents to suit.

In 1990, Congress expressly abrogated states' Eleventh Amendment immunity from copyright infringement suits by providing that, the Eleventh Amendment notwithstanding, states, state actors, and state agencies were liable for copyright infringement to the same extent as other persons, and were subject to the full array of remedies. 17 U.S.C. §§ 501(a), 511(a). However, subsequent Supreme Court decisions strongly imply that this abrogation exceeded Congress's constitutional authority, and is therefore wholly or partly invalid.

In a pair of 1999 decisions, the Supreme Court invalidated Congress's attempts to abrogate the states' Eleventh Amendment immunity to suits for false advertising under the Lanham Act and for patent infringement. *Florida Prepaid Postsecondary Educ. Expense Bd. v. College Savings Bank,* 527

U.S. 627 (1999); *College Savings Bank v. Florida Prepaid Postsecondary Educ. Expense Bd.*, 527 U.S. 666 (1999). These opinions held that, while Congress can abrogate state immunity when acting pursuant to its authority under Section 5 of the Fourteenth Amendment, Congress could not rely on this authority with respect to Lanham Act and patent infringement claims, because Congress had not been presented with evidence that states had engaged in a pattern of patent infringement or Lanham Act violations. Applying this same analysis to copyright infringement claims, the Fifth Circuit concluded that Congress similarly had not been presented with evidence of a pattern of copyright infringement by states, and accordingly its abrogation of state immunity from copyright infringement claims was not a valid exercise of its Fourteenth Amendment power. *Chavez v. Arte Publico Press*, 204 F.3d 601 (5th Cir. 2000). Several district courts have reached the same conclusion, and there is no contrary authority.

The consequence of applying the Eleventh Amendment to copyright infringement claims is that a state, state agency, or state actor cannot be sued for damages for copyright infringement, because these damages would have to be paid by the state. However, under the doctrine of *Ex Parte Young*, 209 U.S. 123 (1908), a copyright owner may obtain prospective injunctive relief against an individual state actor to prevent continued infringement. Furthermore, if a state employee commits copyright infringement outside of the scope of his or her official duties, the Eleventh Amendment does not preclude a suit for damages against the individual in his or her non-official capacity, because the damages would not be paid by the state.

Because federal courts have exclusive jurisdiction over federal copyright claims (although not over common law copyright claims), the Eleventh Amendment effectively precludes a claim for damages arising from federal copyright infringement if the infringer is a state, a state agency, or a state actor, unless the state expressly and unequivocally waives its immunity. Accordingly, arguments based on "implied waiver" are unlikely to succeed. A waiver will not be inferred, for example, by a state's registration of copyrighted works. However, analogous case law concerning patent infringement suggests that, where a state invokes federal court jurisdiction as a plaintiff, it waives its immunity with respect to compulsory counterclaims.

On several occasions, legislation has been proposed which would condition a state's enjoyment of certain intellectual property rights on waiver of its immunity to infringement claims. However, no such legislation has been enacted.

§ 10.11 First Amendment

It is unclear whether the First Amendment can serve as an independent defense to claims of copyright infringement. In general, the Supreme Court has been unreceptive to First Amendment defenses, for two reasons.

First, the Constitution itself expressly grants Congress the power to protect copyrights, and the First Amendment was adopted soon after the Copyright Clause was drafted, thus implying that the framers saw no inherent conflict. The Supreme Court has repeatedly expressed the view that the framers "intended copyright itself to be the engine of free expression" by creating an "economic incentive to create and disseminate ideas." *Harper & Row Publishers, Inc. v. Nation Enterprises*, 471 U.S. 539, 558 (1985).

Second, the Supreme Court has emphasized that copyright law itself contains substantial safeguards for First Amendment values. The most important of these are the fair use doctrine and the distinction between uncopyrightable ideas and copyrightable expression. Other such safeguards may be found in the various specific limitations on the exclusive rights of copyright owners.

However, the Court has also rejected the view that copyright laws are categorically immune from First Amendment scrutiny. In *Eldred v. Ashcroft*, 537 U.S. 186, 221 (2003), the Court expressly refused to endorse such categorical immunity, but held that First Amendment scrutiny of the CTEA's 20–year extension of subsisting copyrights in 1998 was "unnecessary" because, in light of Congress's previous extensions of the copyright term, the CTEA had not altered "the traditional contours of copyright protection."

In its post-*Eldred* decision in *Golan v. Gonzales*, 501 F.3d 1179 (10th Cir. 2007), however, the Tenth Circuit held that the restoration of copyright to works in the public domain under § 104A involved just such an alteration of the "traditional contours" of copyright protection, and should therefore be subjected to heightened scrutiny under the First Amendment.

§ 10.12   Manufacturing Clause

An obscure statutory defense that has not been litigated since the 1980s derives from the otherwise-obsolete "manufacturing clause," 17 U.S.C. § 601. Until June 1, 1986, it was generally unlawful to import copies of an English-language nondramatic literary work by a United States author unless the copies were printed in the United States or Canada. Violation of § 601 was a complete defense to an infringement claim arising from unauthorized copying or distribution of such works if the unauthorized copies were made in the United States or Canada. Although the importation prohibition expired in 1986, the defense may still be available to a defendant that copies or distributes one of these unlawfully imported works.

CHAPTER 11

REMEDIES

§ 11.1 Civil Infringement Remedies

A. Injunctions

Courts have broad discretion under § 502 to grant temporary and permanent injunctions, nationwide in scope, on such terms as they deem reasonable, in order to prevent or restrain copyright infringement. Such injunctions may be enforced by any federal court having personal jurisdiction over the defendant.

Circuits vary in their precise standards for granting a temporary (or "preliminary") injunction. Most circuits, however, consider some combination of the following factors: (1) the plaintiff's likelihood of success on the merits, (2) the possibility of irreparable harm to the plaintiff in the absence of an injunction, and (3) the balance of hardships between the parties. Several circuits also take account of the possibility of harm to third parties and/or general public interest considerations.

Although permanent injunctions have routinely been issued upon a finding of infringement, the Supreme Court has cautioned that there may be instances in which injunctive relief may properly be withheld, noting that the goals of copyright "are not always best served by automatically granting injunctive relief." *New York Times Co., Inc. v. Tasini,* 533 U.S. 483, 505 (2001). For example, in *Campbell v. Acuff–Rose Music, Inc.,* 510 U.S. 569, 578, n. 10 (1994), the Court suggested, in dicta, that injunction relief might not be appropriate in a close case in which a parodist is found to have exceeded the bounds of fair use. In *Abend v. MCA, Inc.,* 863 F.2d 1465, 1479 (9th Cir. 1988*), aff'd on other grounds sub nom. Stewart v. Abend*, 495 U.S. 207 (1990), the Ninth Circuit noted that the district court was not required to enjoin the continued exploitation of the film "Rear Window," even though the film infringed the underlying short story. The Ninth Circuit found that this case presented "special circumstances" supporting denial of injunctive relief, because (1) the defendant filmmakers had made substantial creative contributions to the derivative work, so that its success was due in large part to factors unrelated to the infringing material, (2) the plaintiff had not demonstrated irreparable harm, and (3) the public would be harmed if it were denied access to the film.

Uncertainty regarding the circumstances in which injunctive relief should be granted to prevailing copyright infringement plaintiffs has increased since the Supreme Court's decision in *eBay, Inc. v. MercExchange, L.L.C.,* 547 U.S. 388, 126 S.Ct. 1837, 1839 (2006). In *eBay*, the Court held that a patent owner is not presumptively entitled to a permanent injunction against an infringer. Rather, under traditional principles of equity, a plaintiff seeking a permanent injunction must make a four-part showing: (1) that the plaintiff has suffered an irreparable injury; (2) that remedies available at law, such as monetary damages, are inadequate to compensate for that injury; (3) that, considering the balance of hardships between the plaintiff and defendant, a remedy in equity is warranted; and (4) that the public interest would not be disserved by a permanent injunction.

These traditional principles of equity apply equally to copyright plaintiffs, yet courts in copyright cases have frequently granted injunctions without careful application of the four-factor test. Although this appears to be changing after *eBay,* it remains to be seen whether scrupulous application of these equitable principles will in practice lead to the granting of fewer injunctions. For example, several post-*eBay* decisions have held that irreparable harm can no longer be presumed solely because infringement has occurred and is likely to continue. However, courts have not yet determined what showing is necessary to establish irreparable harm, and whether that harm must flow from past infringements, from the threat of continuing infringement, or both.

The applicability of *eBay* to preliminary injunctions also remains unsettled. Arguably, courts should no longer be permitted to presume irreparable harm simply because a plaintiff has demonstrated a likelihood of success on the merits.

B. Impounding and Destruction

While an infringement action is pending, courts may order the impounding of the allegedly infringing articles. 17 U.S.C. § 503(a). Upon the entry of a final judgment or decree of infringement, courts may order the destruction or other reasonable disposition of the articles found to infringe. *Id.* § 503(b). According to the 1976 House Report, in exercising its discretion to order a "reasonable disposition" of the infringing articles, a court may order the articles to be delivered to the plaintiff, sold, or disposed of in some other way that avoids unnecessary waste and serves the ends of justice.

C. Monetary Remedies

An infringement plaintiff may recover actual damages plus any additional profits which the infringer derived from the infringing activity, plus litigation costs and, in appropriate cases, attorney's fees. In some cases, a plaintiff may elect to recover statutory damages as an alternative to actual damages and profits.

Where a defendant's actions have infringed the plaintiff's rights under both copyright and trademark law, the plaintiff may recover both copyright and trademark damages.

1. *Actual Damages and Profits*

The plaintiff may recover any actual damages suffered as a result of the infringement, as well as any profits of the infringer that are attributable to the infringing activity and which were not taken into account in calculating the actual damages. Damages and profits awards have distinct purposes; the purpose of a damages award is to compensate the copyright owner for any losses resulting from the infringement, whereas the purpose of awarding the infringer's profits to the copyright owner is to prevent the infringer from being unjustly enriched. In neither case does the award have a punitive purpose.

Actual damages represent the injury to the market value of the copyrighted work caused by the infringing activity. An estimate of actual damages based on lost sales or lost licensing fees often involves some degree of speculation, but courts will deny an award if the estimate is unduly speculative. Courts may consider expert testimony or other evidence on such matters as the decline in the fair market value of the copyrighted work or the price which the defendant would have had to pay in order to obtain a license for its use. The copyright owner must also establish, with reasonable probability, that the infringing conduct was the cause of its loss.

In order to avoid unjust enrichment of the infringer, a copyright owner may recover, in addition to actual damages, all of the infringer's profits that are attributable to the infringement, except to the extent that those profits are duplicative of the actual damages awarded. Where the copyright owner's damages arising from lost sales are the result of sales which were diverted to the infringer, for example, an award of damages for the lost sales and profits from the diverted sales would be duplicative.

The plaintiff must show a causal relationship between the infringement and the profits which is not unduly speculative. However, profits may include non-monetary gains, such as enhanced goodwill and market recognition, if sufficient causation can be established.

In establishing the infringer's profits, the copyright owner need only submit proof of the infringer's gross revenue resulting from the infringement. The burden then shifts to the infringer to prove the amount of any expenses and the elements of profit that were attributable to factors other than the use of infringing material, such as the infringer's own contributions to an infringing derivative work. Expenses which may be deducted from the profits award do not include expenses which the infringer incurred primarily to make the infringement more difficult to discover. Courts generally permit deduction of overhead expenses to the extent that they can be allocated to the infringing activity, but the infringer bears the burden of demonstrating that its allocation is reasonable. In the case of infringements that are willful, conscious, or deliberate, some courts apply heightened scrutiny to the overhead allocation, or deny the overhead deduction altogether. A number of courts have allowed infringers to deduct income taxes paid on their infringement profits, but the deduction for taxes may be disallowed by some courts where the infringement is willful, conscious or deliberate.

Although a copyright owner may not bring an action under federal copyright law for acts of infringement which take place overseas (because federal copyright laws have no extraterritorial effect), if a domestic act of infringement gives rise to foreign profits for the infringer, the copyright owner may recover those foreign profits. For example, if an infringing copy of a film is made in the United States and publicly performed abroad, the copyright owner may recover the infringer's profits from the foreign performances, regardless of whether the foreign performances themselves would be considered infringing under the law of the country where they took place. *See Sheldon v. Metro–Goldwyn Pictures Corp.,* 106 F.2d 45, 52 (2d Cir. 1939), *aff'd,* 309 U.S. 390 (1940). Although authority is scant, it appears that no corresponding rule exists for actual damages; thus, if a copyright owner suffers actual damages in its overseas operations, it may not recover those items of damages even if they flow from a domestic act of infringement. *See Los Angeles News Service v. Reuters Television Int'l, Ltd.,* 340 F.3d 926, 927–31 (9th Cir. 2003).

2. *Statutory Damages*

In some cases, a successful infringement plaintiff may elect to recover statutory damages under § 504(c) instead of actual damages and profits.

The availability of statutory damages is governed by § 412, which provides that, subject to three exceptions, a prevailing plaintiff may *not* recover statutory damages (1) in the case of an unpublished work, if the infringement commenced before the effective date of copyright registration, or (2) in the case of a published work, if the infringement commenced after first publication and before the effective date of registration, unless registration is made within three months after first publication. The three exceptions are:

(1) an action for violations of authors' rights under § 106A(a);

(2) an action for infringement of a live broadcast, where the requirements of § 411(b) have been satisfied; and

(3) an action for infringement of a work that was preregistered under § 408(f) before the infringement commenced, *provided* that the effective date of registration is no later than the *earlier* of three months after the first publication of the work or one month after the copyright owner learns of the infringement.

With respect to works in which copyright has been restored under § 104A (see § 5.9 above), for purposes of an award of statutory damages under § 412, infringement by a reliance party is deemed to have commenced before registration if actions that would have constituted infringement had the restored work been subject to copyright commenced before the date of restoration. 17 U.S.C. § 104A(d)(4).

When statutory damages are available with respect to an infringed work, the plaintiff can make the election at any time before the entry of final judgment. The election can be made for any or all of the eligible works. Once the election has been made with respect to a given work, it applies to all infringements involved in the action with respect to that work for which any single infringer is individually liable or for which any two or more infringers are jointly and severally liable. In contrast, if a single work is infringed by multiple infringers who are not jointly and severally liable, but who are joined as defendants in the same action, statutory damages may be awarded separately against each defendant for each infringed work.

Under the Seventh Amendment, an infringement defendant has the right to a jury trial on all issues related to an award of statutory damages, including the amount of damages, because monetary damages are a legal rather than equitable remedy. *Feltner v. Columbia Pictures Television, Inc.,* 523 U.S. 340 (1998). Thus, even though the language of § 504 indicates that the amount of statutory damages is left to the court's discretion, this determination must be made by a jury, or the award of statutory damages will be reversed as unconstitutional.

For each infringed work, the general rule of § 504(c) authorizes statutory damages of $750 to $30,000. Within this range, the statute states that the amount shall be determined "as the court considers just." As a result of the *Feltner* decision, however, defendants are now entitled to have this determination made by a jury; thus, the language referring to the "court" in both the statute and its legislative history must be read as applying to the jury in cases where the defendant elects to have a jury assess statutory damages.

In determining the amount of statutory damages to award for each work, the 1976 House Report provides that a court may take account of any evidence concerning actual damages or profits. In certain circumstances, awards outside of the $750–$30,000 range are permitted. Specifically, where the plaintiff establishes that the infringement was willful, the court has the discretion to award up to $150,000 per work. In contrast, if the defendant establishes that he or she was not aware, and had no reason to believe, that his or her actions were infringing, the court may reduce the statutory damages award to no less than $200 per work. This "innocent infringement" defense is unavailable, however, if the defendant had access to a copy or phonorecord of the work that displayed a copyright notice. 17 U.S.C. §§ 401(d), 402(d). Because Congress contemplated that these discretionary judgments would be made by a judge rather than a jury, and Congress has not yet amended § 504 to take account of *Feltner*, it is uncertain how these discretionary determinations will operate in cases where the defendant elects to submit the statutory damages question to a jury, and it is likely that jury awards of statutory damages will be somewhat unpredictable and inconsistent.

For an infringement to be considered "willful" for purposes of enhancing the statutory damages award, the defendant must know that its conduct is infringing. After *Feltner,* if a defendant elects to submit the statutory damages question to a jury, the determination of willfulness for this purpose will also be made by the jury. However, as amended in 2004, § 504(c)(3)(A) provides that a rebuttable presumption of willfulness applies if the infringer, or a person acting in concert with the infringer, knowingly provided materially false information to a domain name registration authority in registering, maintaining, or renewing a domain name (as defined in the Lanham Act, 15 U.S.C. § 1127) that was used in connection with the infringement. Although Congress enacted this presumption post-*Feltner*, the rule of *Feltner* still applies; thus, the defendant is entitled to a jury determination on the question whether the presumption has been rebutted.

A plaintiff is entitled to receive a single award of statutory damages, in an amount falling within the statutory limits, for all infringements involved in the cause of action with respect to any single work for which any one infringer is liable individually or for which two or more infringers are jointly and severally liable. Thus, only one award will be made for each infringed work, regardless of the number of infringing acts with respect to that work, and regardless of whether those infringing acts were separate, isolated, or in a related series. If four separate works are infringed, then four awards of statutory damages will be granted, with each award falling within the statutorily permitted range. Thus, in the absence of willfulness, each award could be for $750 to $30,000, for a total award of $3,000 to $120,000.

For the sole purpose of statutory damages awards, § 504(c)(1) provides that all the parts of a compilation or derivative work are considered one work. This rule has occasioned some confusion. For example, where several works in a compilation have different copyright owners, courts have permitted a separate statutory damages award to each owner, but where each work in the compilation has the same owner, courts have granted only a single award. Courts have also held that each episode of a television series is considered a separate work. However, courts have not yet reached a consensus on whether multiple works covered by a single registration may be eligible for multiple statutory damages awards. In such cases, some courts will grant a separate award of statutory damages for each infringed work that has "independent economic value"—for example, where an infringer copied multiple photographs covered by a single registration.

The limitation of statutory damages to one award per work infringed also raises interpretative problems where a single work is the subject of multiple infringing acts. Where a defendant makes multiple copies of a single work, and then distributes those copies, ordinarily this warrants a single statutory damages award, because only one work has been infringed. However, the question is more complicated where the defendant makes multiple copies over an extended period of time, or where the defendant engages in several different infringing activities with respect to the same work—for example, copying the work, then using the copy to create a derivative work, then making multiple copies of the derivative work, and then publicly performing and/or publicly distributing the unauthorized derivative work. Section 504(c)(1) states that a court may grant only one award of statutory damages for "all infringements involved in the action, with respect to any one work, for which any one infringer is liable individually." The 1976 House Report confirms that only one award is authorized per infringed work, regardless of the number of infringements. H.R. Rep. No. 94–1476, at 161. Some early decisions under the 1976 Act failed to give effect to this restriction, and granted multiple awards where a single defendant committed multiple infringements of a single work, as was previously required by § 101(b) the 1909 Act. More recent decisions, however, have rejected this "multiplicity doctrine" in favor of strict adherence to the statutory language. *See, e.g., Venegas–Hernandez v. Sonolux Records*, 370 F.3d 183 (1st Cir. 2004). With the demise of the multiplicity doctrine, some plaintiffs may still be able to multiply their statutory damages awards by filing separate lawsuits for different infringements of the same work, although the cost of this strategy may be prohibitive.

Statutory damages are not available in cases where the infringer believed, and had reasonable grounds to believe, that his or her use of the copyrighted work was a fair use under § 107, *provided* that the infringer was either: (1) a nonprofit educational institution, library, or archive, or an employee or agent thereof, that infringed by reproducing the work, or (2) a nonprofit public broadcasting entity (or a person engaged in the activities of such an entity) which infringed by performing a published nondramatic literary work, or by reproducing a transmission embodying a performance of such a work, as a regular part of the entity's nonprofit activities. The 1976 House Report, *supra*, notes that the burden of disproving the infringer's good faith in this situation rests on the plaintiff. After *Feltner*, a defendant is entitled to have a jury decide the question of whether the defendant believed, reasonably and in good faith, that its actions constituted fair use.

3. *Innocent Infringement*

Section 405(b) bars an award for actual or statutory damages only under the following circumstances: The defendant must have relied upon an authorized copy or phonorecord from which copyright notice was omitted, and which was publicly distributed by authority of the copyright owner before the effective date of the Berne Convention Implementation Act (March 1, 1989), which prospectively eliminated the copyright notice requirement. Actual and statutory damages are precluded only with respect to infringing acts which took place *before* the defendant received actual notice that the work was registered under § 408, and only if the defendant proves that he or she was misled by the omission of notice.

Section 405(b) gives the court the option to allow or disallow an award of the infringer's profits arising from the infringement. The court may also enjoin the continuation of the infringing activity, or may require the defendant to pay the copyright owner a reasonable license fee (as determined by the court) in order to continue the infringing activity.

4. Penalty for Wrongful Invocation of § 110(5)

Where an infringer invokes the § 110(5) exemption (see § 8.3.B.1 above) without having reasonable grounds to believe that its use of the copyrighted work was exempt under that provision, § 504(d) entitles the plaintiff to recover not only the monetary damages that are otherwise available under § 504(a)-(c), but also an additional award equal to twice the licensing fee that the defendant should have paid the plaintiff for the use of that work during the preceding period of up to three years.

5. Costs and Attorney's Fees

Although § 505 gives courts discretion to award costs and/or attorney's fees, the scope of that discretion is somewhat broader with respect to costs than with respect to attorney's fees.

Courts have discretion under § 505 to allow recovery of full costs by or against any party other than the United States or an officer thereof. Unlike attorney's fees, costs may be recovered regardless of whether the infringement preceded the effective date of copyright registration. Although nothing in § 505 expressly precludes awarding costs to the losing party, courts historically have awarded costs only to the prevailing party under this provision.

In contrast to the provision on costs, the attorney's fee provision in § 505 gives courts discretion to award a reasonable attorney's fee *only* to the prevailing party. As discussed below, the availability of attorney's fees under § 505 is subject to limitations imposed by § 412 as well as limitations imposed by the Supreme Court.

Under § 412, an award of attorney's fees is subject to the same limitations that apply to an award of statutory damages. Thus, subject to three exceptions, § 412 provides that a prevailing plaintiff may *not* recover attorney's fees (1) in the case of an unpublished work, if the infringement commenced before the effective date of copyright registration, or (2) in the case of a published work, if the infringement commenced after first publication and before the effective date of registration, unless registration is made within three months after first publication. The three exceptions are:

(1) an action for violations of authors' rights under § 106A(a);

(2) an action for infringement of a live broadcast, where the requirements of § 411(b) have been satisfied; and

(3) an action for infringement of a work that was preregistered under § 408(f) before the infringement commenced, *provided* that the effective date of registration is no later than the *earlier* of three months after the first publica-

tion of the work or one month after the copyright owner learns of the infringement.

With respect to foreign works in which copyright has been restored under § 104A (see § 5.9 above), for purposes of attorney's fees an infringement by a reliance party is deemed to have commenced before registration if actions that would have constituted infringement had the restored work been subject to copyright commenced before the date of restoration. 17 U.S.C. § 104A(d)(4).

Although § 505 leaves it to the court's discretion to determine whether a prevailing party is entitled to recover an attorney's fee (assuming that the requirements of § 412 are satisfied), that discretion is not unbounded. In *Fogerty v. Fantasy, Inc.*, 510 U.S. 517 (1994), the Supreme Court held that (1) attorney's fees are not to be awarded automatically to a prevailing party, and (2) prevailing plaintiffs and defendants should be treated even-handedly. The Court therefore rejected the "dual standard" which several circuits had previously applied, under which attorney's fees were routinely awarded to a prevailing plaintiff (in the absence of special circumstances), but were awarded to a prevailing defendant only upon a showing of bad faith or frivolousness on the part of the plaintiff.

In adopting the even-handed approach, the Supreme Court did not prescribe specific standards for awarding attorney's fees. The Court acknowledged that "there is no precise rule or formula for making these determinations," but noted that courts should exercise their discretion in light of the purposes of copyright law. In particular, the Court endorsed consideration of the following non-exclusive factors, provided that they are faithful to the purposes of the Copyright Act and are applied evenhandedly to plaintiffs and defendants: "frivolousness, motivation, objective unreasonableness (both in the factual and in the legal components of the case) and the need in particular circumstances to advance considerations of compensation and deterrence." *Id.* at 534 & n.19. In general, the federal courts have adhered to this guidance. A number of decisions have awarded attorney's fees based on the opponent's abusive litigation tactics. Where the litigation involves particularly novel or difficult questions of law, or where both parties have acted in bad faith, it is likely that no attorney's fees will be awarded to either party. A court's failure to explain its decision on attorney's fees has been treated as an abuse of discretion.

Determining a "Reasonable" Attorney's Fee. The statutes offer no guidance for determining what constitutes a "reasonable" attorney's fee. The amount that a court considers reasonable may differ from the actual attorney costs incurred. Although the amount of the award is left to the broad discretion of the district court, it is generally understood that it should reflect the reasonable value of the services rendered with respect to the copyright claims. In determining what is reasonable, courts may consider such factors as the amount of work necessary, the amount of work actually performed, the level of skill employed, the amounts of money involved, the results achieved, and the prevailing rates charged by lawyers of similar skill and experience in the community. The amount that is actually billed is relevant, but not conclusive, evidence of what is reasonable. Where litigation involves both copyright claims and non-copyright claims, it has been held to be an abuse of discretion for a district court not to require production of billing records or not to make a reasonable effort to determine which expenses are related to the copyright claims.

Determining Which Party Has Prevailed. In some cases, it is not easy to identify the "prevailing" party for purposes of awarding costs and/or attorney's fees under § 505. For example, an infringement plaintiff may prevail on some, but not all, of its infringement claims, or may prevail against some, but not all, defendants. Alternatively, a party may prevail on a combination of copyright and non-copyright claims, raising the question of what portion of the costs and attorney's fees should be allocated to the copyright claims. Neither the statutes nor the Supreme Court provides guidance in these circumstances, thus leaving such questions to the broad discretion of the courts. In exercising their discretion, courts will generally consider whether a party prevailed on a significant issue in the litigation that achieves some of the benefits that the party sought in bringing suit. Where a significant portion of attorney's fees is related to non-copyright claims, the award of attorney's fees is likely to be reduced accordingly. Where the fee award is based on bad faith conduct in litigation, the recovery may be limited to the costs incurred as a result of that bad faith conduct.

6. *Prejudgment Interest*

Although the copyright statutes are silent on prejudgment interest, several courts have held that the statutes permit an award of prejudgment interest, and that such an award is appropriate where it would effectuate the legislative goals of providing adequate compensation to the copyright owner, deterring infringement, and preventing infringers from being unjustly enriched.

7. *Remedies Against the United States*

In an action for copyright infringement against the United States, or against an agent or contractor acting on behalf of the United States, the normal infringement remedies are not available. Instead, the copyright plaintiff is limited to an action for reasonable compensation (including the minimum statutory damages under § 504(c)), which must be brought in the Court of Federal Claims. Injunctive relief is not available. A three-year statute of limitations applies. 28 U.S.C. § 1498(b).

§ 11.2 Criminal Penalties for Copyright Infringement

Under § 506, copyright infringement is subject to criminal prosecution only if it was willful, and only if it was committed:

(A) for purposes of commercial advantage or private financial gain (§ 506(a)(1)(A));

(B) by the reproduction or distribution (including by electronic means), during any 180–day period, of one or more copyrighted works, with a total retail value of more than $1,000 (§ 506(a)(1)(B)); or

(C) by distribution of a work being prepared for commercial distribution, by making it available on a computer network accessible to the public, if the infringer knew or should have known that the work was intended for commercial distribution (§ 506(a)(1)(C)).

As used in § 506(a)(1)(A), "financial gain" includes "receipt, or expectation of receipt, of anything of value, including the receipt of other copyrighted works." 17 U.S.C. § 101.

As used in § 506(a)(1)(C), the term "work being prepared for commercial distribution" includes the following:

(A) a computer program, musical work, motion picture or other audiovisual work, or sound recording, if at the time of the unauthorized distribution, the copyright owner has a reasonable expectation of commercial distribution, and the copies or phonorecords of the work have not been commercially distributed; or

(B) a motion picture, if at the time of the unauthorized distribution, the motion picture has been made available for viewing in a motion picture exhibition facility, and has not been made available in copies for sale to the general public in the United States in a format intended to permit viewing outside a motion picture exhibition facility.

17 U.S.C. § 506(a)(3).

The penalties for criminal copyright infringement are set forth in 18 U.S.C. § 2319, which prescribes the imposition of a prison term, a fine, or both, as follows:

For infringement under § 506(a)(1)(A): Up to ten years in prison (up to five years for a first offense), for reproducing or distributing, within a 180–day period, at least ten copies or phonorecords of one or more copyrighted works having a total retail value greater than $2,500; up to one year in prison in any other case. A statutory fine may be imposed instead of, or in addition to, the prison sentence.

For infringement under § 506(a)(1)(B): Up to six years in prison (up to three years for a first offense), for reproducing or distributing ten or more copies or phonorecords of one or more copyrighted works having a total retail value of $2,500 or more; up to one year in prison for reproducing or distributing one or more copies or phonorecords of one or more copyrighted works having a total retail value of more than $1,000. A statutory fine may be imposed instead of, or in addition to, the prison sentence.

For infringement under § 506(a)(1)(C): Up to six years in prison (up to three years for a first offense), or up to ten years in prison (up to five years for a first offense) if the offense was committed for commercial advantage or private financial gain (as defined above). A statutory fine may be imposed instead of, or in addition to, the prison sentence.

In each case, the amount of the statutory fine is governed by 18 U.S.C. § 3571, which specifies only the maximum fine which may be imposed. As a general rule, the maximum fines are $250,000 for individuals, and $500,000 for organizations. In the alternative, however, if the defendant derives a pecuniary gain from the infringement, or the copyright owner suffers a pecuniary loss, § 3571(d) allows the court to fine the infringer up to twice the infringer's gross gain or up to twice the copyright owner's gross loss.

In addition to the penalties set forth above, § 506 requires a court to order the forfeiture and destruction or other disposition of the infringing articles as well as any implements, devices, or equipment used in their production.

Section 506 also provides penalties for certain actions not involving infringement. A fine of up to $2,500 applies to: (1) any person who fraudulently places a false copyright notice on any article or who publicly distributes, or imports for public distribution, any such article, (2) any person who fraudulently alters or removes a notice of copyright, and

(3) any person who knowingly makes a false representation of material fact in an application for copyright registration or in any written statement filed in connection therewith.

Section 506 does not apply to infringements of moral rights under § 106A(a).

§ 11.3 Criminal Penalties for Music Bootlegging

A different criminal provision, 18 U.S.C. § 2319A, applies to violations of the anti-bootlegging statute, 17 U.S.C. § 1101. Criminal penalties apply only if the violator acts knowingly and for purposes of commercial advantage or private financial gain (as defined in § 101). Penalties include up to ten years in prison (five years for a first offense) and/or a fine up to the maximum allowed by 18 U.S.C. § 3571(d). In addition, a court must order the forfeiture and destruction of all copies, phonorecords, and other infringing items, and may also, in its discretion, order the forfeiture and destruction of any other equipment used in making the copies or phonorecords, taking account of the extent to which that equipment was used in the violations.

§ 11.4 Civil Remedies and Criminal Penalties for Counterfeit Labelling

Criminal penalties may also be imposed against one who knowingly traffics in (1) counterfeit or illicit labels that are used, or designed to be used, in connection with copies or phonorecords or in connection with their documentation or packaging, or (2) counterfeit documentation or packaging for copies or phonorecords. 18 U.S.C. § 2318. A "counterfeit label" is defined as one that appears to be genuine but is not; an "illicit label" is defined as one that is genuine but is being used in a manner not authorized by the copyright owner. For § 2318 to apply, the offense must be committed under one of the following circumstances:

(1) the offense is committed within U.S. jurisdiction;

(2) the mail or a facility of interstate commerce is used or intended to be used in the offense;

(3) the counterfeit or illicit label is used in connection with a phonorecord of a copyrighted sound recording or copyrighted musical work, a copy of a copyrighted computer program, a copy of a copyrighted motion picture or other audiovisual work, a copy of a literary, pictorial, graphic, or sculptural work, a work of visual art, or copyrighted documentation or packaging; or

(4) the counterfeited documentation or packaging is copyrighted.

Penalties under § 2318 include a fine (within the guidelines of 18 U.S.C. § 3571(d)) or imprisonment for up to five years, or both. In addition, the court *must* order the forfeiture and destruction or other disposition of all counterfeit or illicit labels and all articles to which they have been affixed or were intended to be affixed, together with any equipment, device, or material used to produce those labels.

A copyright owner may also bring a civil action under § 2318. Remedies include injunctions, impounding, attorneys fees, costs, and either actual damages and profits (provided that these are not duplicative) or statutory damages (ranging from $2,500 to $25,000 per violation). Damages may be trebled if the defendant commits another violation within three years after the entry of final judgment. A three-year statute of limitations applies to any civil action under § 2318.

§ 11.5   Criminal Penalties for Motion Picture Bootlegging

The criminal provisions of 18 U.S.C. § 2319B apply to any person who knowingly uses or attempts to use an audiovisual recording device to transmit or copy a copyrighted motion picture or other audiovisual work, or any portion thereof, from a performance of that work in a motion picture exhibition facility. Penalties include up to six years in prison (up to three years for a first offense), and/or a fine (under the guidelines of 18 U.S.C. § 3571(d)). In addition, the court *must* order the forfeiture and destruction or other disposition of all unauthorized copies and any recording devices or other equipment used in connection with the offense.

CHAPTER 12

DIGITAL MILLENNIUM COPYRIGHT ACT

§ 12.1 Overview

The Digital Millennium Copyright Act of 1998 ("DMCA") revised the 1976 Act by adding three sets of complex rules, accompanied by civil remedies and criminal penalties, designed to address concerns of copyright owners and Internet service providers arising from the growth of the Internet and the resulting increase in unauthorized copying and distribution of copyrighted works. The rules codified in § 512 define a set of safe harbors which enable Internet service providers (ISPs) to limit their liability for the infringing activities of their users. The rules codified at § 1201 prohibit the circumvention of technological devices that copyright owners use to protect their digitized works from unauthorized access and copying. The rules codified at § 1202 prohibit the falsifying or unauthorized alteration or removal of certain copyright information attached to or accompanying a copyrighted work.

§ 12.2 Liability of ISPs

The DMCA added § 512 to the copyright statutes, providing a detailed set of rules addressing the liability of ISPs for the infringing activities of their users. The new rules create a set of safe harbors for ISPs that meet the statutory requirements.

The legislative history of § 512 indicates Congress's approval of the 1995 district court decision in *Religious Technology Center v. Netcom On–Line Communication Services,* 907 F.Supp. 1361 (N.D. Cal. 1995), which refused to hold an ISP liable for the infringing activities of its users because the ISP's role consisted entirely of serving as a passive conduit for the transmissions of its users, without in any way inducing, influencing, encouraging, or selecting among their infringing activities. (See § 9.5 above.) Although § 512 reflects the spirit of *Netcom,* its scope is far broader than the activities at issue in that case. Rather than simply codifying *Netcom,* § 512 creates a new set of safe harbors designed to enable ISPs to determine with greater certainty which of their activities will be categorically immune from liability. The statute and its legislative history give no indication that *failure* to qualify for a safe harbor will automatically make an ISP liable for infringement. Indeed, § 512(*l*) states that failure to qualify for a safe harbor "shall not bear adversely" on any other defense raised by the ISP. Thus, the ISP will be subject to the otherwise applicable legal standards for determining liability for direct, contributory, and vicarious infringement—standards which are not always clearly defined, and which are still evolving in the courts. (See §§ 9.3–9.4 above.)

The conditions for satisfying the § 512 safe harbors differ according to the activity at issue. Four main activities are addressed—transmissions under § 512(a), system caching under § 512(b), storing of material at a user's direction under § 512(c), and providing information location tools under § 512(d). Each of these activities is discussed in Part B below.

A. Eligibility

Only a "service provider" is eligible for the § 512 safe harbors. However, this term is given a narrower meaning in § 512(a) (dealing with transmissions) than in the rest of the statute. For purposes of § 512(a), the term "service provider" refers *only* to an entity that offers transmission, routing, or providing of connections for digital online communications of material chosen by a user, between points specified by a user, without modification of the user's material. For purposes of the rest of § 512, the term includes not only these entities, but *also* any provider of online services or network access, or an operator of facilities therefore.

In addition to meeting the definition of a "service provider," the ISP must meet several other conditions under § 512(i) in order to qualify for any of the safe harbors. First, it must adopt, "reasonably implement," and inform users of a policy under which it will, "in appropriate circumstances," terminate service to users who are "repeat infringers." (Each of the quoted phrases, however, presents challenging issues of interpretation which have yet to be resolved.) Second, it must accommodate and not interfere with "standard technical measures" that copyright owners use to identify or protect their copyrighted works, if these have been developed through a multi-industry standard-setting process and are neither nondiscriminatory nor overly burdensome to service providers.

B. Safe Harbor Requirements

Even if an ISP qualifies as a "service provider" and meets the general eligibility requirements of § 512(i), it must still satisfy the conditions for the specific safe harbor it seeks to invoke. There are four general safe harbors, and one enhancement for higher education institutions, each with its own set of conditions. The safe harbors apply to transitory digital network communications (§ 512(a)), intermediate and transient system caching (§ 512(b)), storage of information on systems or networks at the direction of users (§ 512(c)), provision of information location tools (§ 512(d)), and the activities of nonprofit higher education institutions that also act as service providers (§ 512(e)). The specific requirements of each safe harbor are discussed below.

1. *Transitory Digital Network Communications*

The § 512(a) safe harbor protects a service provider (as defined under the narrower of the two definitions in Part A above) from infringement liability that might otherwise arise as a result of transmitting material through a system which it controls or operates, or as a result of the intermediate and transient storage of such material in the course of those transmissions.

For the § 512(a) safe harbor to apply, all of the following conditions must be met:

(1) the transmission must be initiated by the user, not the service provider;

(2) the transmission must be carried out through an automatic technical process in which the service provider does not select the material;

(3) the service provider must not select the recipients, except as an automatic response to another person's request;

(4) if the service provider makes a copy of the material in the course of temporary storage, the copy must not be maintained on the system in a manner that is ordinarily accessible to anyone other than the anticipated recipients or that is ordinarily accessible to the anticipated recipients for longer than is necessary to complete the transmission; and

(5) the material must be transmitted through the system without modification.

In determining whether the "automatic technical process" requirement under (2) is satisfied, courts should assess whether the ISP plays a purely passive role as in *Netcom*.

2. Caching

The § 512(b) safe harbor protects a service provider (as defined under the broader of the two definitions in Part A above) from liability for infringement arising from the intermediate and temporary storage of material on its system, but only if all of the following requirements are met:

(1) the material must be made available online by a person (*i.e.,* the content provider) other than the service provider;

(2) the material must be transmitted from the content provider through the system to another person at the latter's direction;

(3) the storage must be carried out through an automatic technical process for the purpose of making the material available to subsequent users who, after the transmission described above, ask the content provider for access to the material;

(4) the material must be transmitted to the subsequent users without modification;

(5) the service provider must comply with rules concerning refreshing, reloading, or other updating of the material when specified by the content provider in accordance with industry standard data communications protocol for the system, unless those rules are used by the content provider to prevent or unreasonably impair the intermediate storage of the material;

(6) the service provider must not interfere with the ability of technology associated with the material to give the content provider the

same information he or she would have obtained by sending the material directly to the subsequent users, unless that technology (a) interferes with the performance of the provider's system or with the intermediate storage of the material, (b) is inconsistent with industry standard communications protocols, or (c) extracts additional information from the service provider's system;

(7) if the content provider imposes any conditions on a user's access to the material (*e.g.,* payment or use of a password), the service provider must make the material accessible only to users who meet those conditions; and

(8) if the content provider makes the material available online without the consent of the copyright owner, then the service provider must, upon receiving a notice of claimed infringement (if the notice meets the statutory standards discussed in Part C below), promptly remove or disable access to the material. However, this requirement applies only if the infringing material has already been removed or disabled from the originating site (or if a court has so ordered), and if the notice of infringement states this fact.

Note that the caching safe harbor, like the § 512(a) transmission safe harbor, requires the ISP to use an "automatic technical process" for caching; as in § 512(a), this requirement invokes the standard articulated in *Netcom*.

3. *Information Storage*

The § 512(c) safe harbor protects a service provider (as defined under the broader definition above) from liability arising from storage, at a user's direction, of material that resides on the service provider's system, but only if all of the following conditions are met:

(1) the service provider must not have actual knowledge of the infringing activity, and must not be aware of facts or circumstances that make the infringing activity apparent, or upon obtaining such knowledge or awareness, must promptly remove or disable access to the infringing material;

(2) if the service provider has the right and ability to control the infringing activity, then the service provider must not derive a direct financial benefit from that activity; and

(3) upon receiving a notice of claimed infringement (if that notice meets the statutory standards discussed in Part C below), the service provider must promptly remove or disable access to the infringing material; and

(4) the service provider must have published on its website the name and contact information of the agent it has designated to receive notices of claimed infringement, and must have provided this information also to the Register of Copyrights, which maintains a public directory of these agents.

4. *Information Location Tools*

The § 512(d) safe harbor protects a service provider (under the broader definition in Part A above) from liability for infringement claims that arise from referring or linking users to an online location that contains infringing material or infringing activity, if the referring or linking uses information location tools such as a directory, index, reference, pointer, or hypertext link. This safe harbor applies only if all of the following conditions are met:

(1) the service provider must not have actual knowledge that the material or activity is infringing, and must not be aware of facts or circumstances that make the infringing activity apparent, or upon obtaining such knowledge or awareness, must promptly remove or disable access to the material;

(2) if the service provider has the right and ability to control the infringing activity, then the service provider must not derive a direct financial benefit from that activity; and

(3) upon receiving a notice of claimed infringement (if that notice meets the statutory standards discussed in Part C below), the service provider must promptly remove or disable access to the infringing material.

5. *Nonprofit Higher Education Institutions*

Rather than being a separate safe harbor, § 512(e) is an enhancement of the other four safe harbors that applies only to nonprofit higher education institutions. In broad terms, § 512(e) applies a second layer of protection to such institutions when they act as ISPs. It accomplishes this by defining the circumstances under which a teaching or research employee's conduct or knowledge will *not* be attributed to the institution, thus overriding traditional principles of respondeat superior. Section 512(e) thus recognizes that, under the principle of academic freedom, universities typically cannot control or supervise the activities of their teaching or research employees to the same degree that employee conduct is typically controlled or supervised by non-educational institutions.

If the conditions of subsection (e) are met, then when an individual who is a faculty member or graduate student employee of such an institution is performing a teaching or research function, he or she will be considered a person other than the institution for purposes of the safe harbors for transitory communications (§ 512(a)) and caching (§ 512(b)). Furthermore, for purposes of the safe harbors for storage (§ 512(c)) and information location tools (§ 512(d)), that individual's knowledge or awareness of his or her infringing activities will not be attributed to the institution.

The enhanced protections of § 512(e) apply only if all of the following requirements are met:

    (1) the individual's infringing activities must not involve providing online access to instructional materials that are or were required or

recommended, within the preceding three years, for a course taught at the institution by the same individual;

(2) the institution must not, within the preceding three years, have received more than two non-fraudulent notifications (meeting the requirements discussed in Part C below) of claimed infringement by that individual; and

(3) the institution must provide its users with information that describes and promotes compliance with federal copyright law.

C. Notice of Infringement

As noted above, the safe harbors of §§ 512(b), (c) and (d) require ISPs to promptly remove or disable access to infringing material upon receiving a notice of claimed infringement. These provisions are often referred to as the "notice and take-down provisions." For a notice of infringement to trigger the ISP's obligation to remove or disable access to the infringing material under any these provisions, the notice must meet the requirements of § 512(c)(3), which provides that the notice must be in writing, and must:

(1) bear the physical or electronic signature of a person authorized to act on behalf of the owner of the exclusive right that is allegedly infringed;

(2) identify the infringed work (or a representative listing if multiple works are involved);

(3) identify the infringing material that is to be removed or access to which is to be disabled, and must provide information reasonably sufficient to enable the service provider to locate that material;

(4) provide information reasonably sufficient to enable the service provider to contact the complaining party;

(5) state the complaining party's good faith belief that use of the material is not authorized by the copyright owner, its agent, or the law; and

(6) state that the information in the notice is accurate and, under penalty of perjury, that the complaining party is authorized to act on behalf of the owner of the exclusive right that is allegedly infringed.

In the case of §§ 512(c) and (d), a notice that fails to substantially comply with all of these requirements will *not* be considered in determining whether the ISP had actual knowledge of the infringement or was aware of facts or circumstances making the infringement apparent, subject to one exception: If the notice is noncompliant only because it lacks the required signature, statement of good faith belief, and/or statement under penalty of perjury (that is, if the notice *at least* clearly identifies the infringed work as well as the infringing material and its location, and provides the complaining party's contact information), then the ISP must promptly attempt to contact the complaining party or take other reasonable steps to assist the latter in bringing the notice into substantial compliance. If the ISP fails to take this step, then the noncompliant notice will be treated as sufficient to trigger the § 512(c) take-down obligation.

In the case of the § 512(d) safe harbor, the notice requirement is also modified in one other respect. Instead of identifying the infringing material and its location, the notice must identify the reference or link that is to be removed or disabled, and must provide information reasonably sufficient to enable the service provider to locate that reference or link.

D.   Actionable Misrepresentations

Section 512(f) creates a cause of action against anyone who, in connection with § 512, knowingly materially misrepresents that material or activity is infringing, or that material or activity was removed or disabled by mistake or misidentification. Such a person is liable for any damages, including costs and attorneys' fees, incurred by the alleged infringer, by a copyright owner or licensee, or by a service provider who is injured as a result of the service provider relying on such misrepresentation in removing or disabling access to infringing material or activities, or in replacing the removed material or restoring access to it.

E.   Effect of Safe Harbor Protection

If an ISP qualifies for any of the safe harbors, it will not be liable for any monetary relief as a result of the infringing activity on its system. This exempts the ISP from liability for damages, costs, attorneys' fees, or any other form of monetary payment.

In addition, the ISP will not be subject to injunctive or other equitable relief as a result of the infringing activity on its system, subject to several limitations. Under the § 512(b), (c) and (d) safe harbors, a court may grant injunctive relief only in one or more of the following forms:

(1) an order restraining the service provider from providing access to infringing material or activity residing at a particular online site on the provider's system;

(2) an order requiring the service provider to terminate the account of a specific infringing user; or

(3) such other injunctive relief as necessary to prevent infringement of the specified material at a particular online location, if such relief is the least burdensome to the service provider among comparably effective forms of relief.

Under the § 512(a) safe harbor, a court may grant injunctive relief only in one or both of the following forms:

(1) an order requiring the service provider to terminate the account of a specific infringing user; or

(2) an order requiring the service provider to take reasonable steps, specified in the order, to block access to a specific online location outside the United States.

Furthermore, in considering injunctive relief under *any* of the safe harbors, courts are required to consider the following:

(1) whether the injunction, alone or together with other such injunctions issued against the same service provider, would significantly burden the provider or the operation of its system;

(2) the harm which the copyright owner will suffer in the digital network environment if the infringement is not restrained;

(3) whether implementing the injunction will be technically feasible and effective, and whether it would interfere with access to noninfringing material at other online locations; and

(4) whether other less burdensome means of restraining the infringement would be comparably effective.

If a court does grant injunctive relief under any of the safe harbors, it must first give the service provider notice and an opportunity to appear. The only exception is for orders ensuring preservation of evidence or other orders that have no material adverse effect on the operation of the provider's network.

§ 12.3 Anti–Circumvention Provisions

The DMCA added new provisions to Title 17 designed to assist copyright owners in the use of technological measures to prevent unauthorized access to, and copying of, digitized copyrighted works.

These provisions are codified at 17 U.S.C. §§ 1201–05.

A. Causes of Action Under § 1201

Section 1201 creates three new causes of action designed to prevent the circumvention of technological measures that are used to control access to copyrighted works or to prevent infringement of the exclusive rights of copyright owners:

Circumvention. Section 1201(a)(1) creates a cause of action for circumventing technological measures that control access to copyrighted works.

Technology to Circumvent Access Protection. Section 1201(a)(2) creates a separate cause of action for making, offering to the public, or otherwise trafficking in any technology (whether it be a product or a service, or any component thereof) that:

(1) is primarily designed to enable circumvention of technological measures that control access to copyrighted works;

(2) has limited commercially significant uses other than such circumvention; or

(3) is marketed for use in such circumvention.

Technology to Circumvent Copyright Protection. Section 1201(b) creates a cause of action for making, offering to the public, or otherwise trafficking in any technology (whether it be a product or service, or any component thereof) that:

(1) is primarily designed to circumvent technological measures that protect any right of a copyright owner;

(2) has limited commercially significant uses other than such circumvention; or

(3) is marketed for use in such circumvention.

B. Exempt Activities

Certain activities are exempt from one or all of the causes of action recognized in § 1201. One set of exemptions has been established by the Library of Congress, pursuant to a congressional mandate in § 1201(a)(1)(C). The other exemptions are set forth in the statute itself.

1. *Exemptions by Regulation*

Under § 1201(a)(1)(C), the prohibition against circumventing access protection measures under § 1201(a)(1)(A) does not apply when it would adversely affect users of particular classes of copyrighted works in their ability to make noninfringing uses of those works. However, this exemption applies only to specific classes of works which have been identified in Library of Congress regulations.

Specifically, section 1201(a)(1)(C) requires the Librarian of Congress to promulgate regulations every three years identifying entire classes of copyrighted works with respect to which noninfringing uses are likely to be adversely affected by the § 1201(a)(1)(A) circumvention prohibition, and exempting such uses from the prohibition. The standard for exempting a class of works is that the application of the anti-circumvention rule to prevent access to these works would adversely affect users' ability to make noninfringing uses of this class of works. In applying this standard, the Librarian must consider the following factors: the general availability of the copyrighted works, their availability for nonprofit archival, preservation, and educational uses, the impact of the anti-circumvention provision on criticism, comment, news reporting, teaching, scholarship, or research, and the effect of circumvention on the value of the works. The Librarian may consider any other appropriate factors as well.

The most recent regulation promulgated pursuant to this rulemaking authority exempts non-infringing uses of the following six classes of works:

(1) audiovisual works in the library of a college film or media studies department, when circumvention is for the purpose of making compilations of portions of those works for classroom use by professors;

(2) computer programs and video games in obsolete formats, when circumvention is for the purpose of preservation or archival reproduction of published digital works by a library or archive;

(3) computer programs protected by dongles (*i.e.*, hardware devices that connect to computers to authenticate software) which prevent access due to malfunction or damage and which cannot reasonably be replaced or repaired;

(4) literary works in ebook format, when all existing ebook editions of the work contain access controls that prevent enablement of the

read-aloud function or of screen readers that convert the text into a specialized format for persons with disabilities;

(5) computer programs in the form of firmware that enables wireless handsets to connect to a wireless telephone network, when circumvention is for the sole purpose of lawfully connecting to a wireless telephone network; and

(6) sound recordings, and audiovisual works associated with them, distributed on CDs and protected by technological measures that control access to lawfully purchased works and create or exploit security flaws that compromise the security of personal computers, when circumvention is for the sole purpose of good faith testing, investigating, or correcting such flaws.

37 C.F.R. § 201.40 (Nov. 27, 2006).

2. *Statutory Exemptions*

Section 1201 itself sets forth a number of exemptions which apply to one or more of the three causes of action arising under the statute:

Nonprofit Libraries, Archives, and Educational Institutions. Under § 1201(d), no cause of action for unlawful circumvention of access protection under § 1201(a)(1)(A) will arise if a nonprofit library, archive, or educational institution gains access to a commercially exploited copyrighted work solely to make a good faith determination of whether to acquire a copy of that work for uses permitted by copyright law. This exemption applies only if an identical copy of the work is not reasonably available in another form, and only if the copy which was accessed is retained no longer than necessary to make the good faith determination, and is used for no other purpose. To qualify for the exemption, a library or archive must be either open to the public or available to all persons doing research in a specialized field. This exemption does not apply to trafficking claims—that is, claims arising under § 1201(a)(2) or (b).

Law enforcement, Intelligence, and Other Government Activities. None of the § 1201 causes of action applies to government employees or government contractors engaged in lawfully authorized investigative, protective, information security, or intelligence activities. 17 U.S.C. § 1201(e).

Reverse engineering. No cause of action arises under § 1201(a)(1) (circumvention of access protection) if the defendant has lawfully obtained the right to use a copy of a computer program, and circumvents access protection for a particular portion of that program for the sole purpose of lawfully reverse engineering the program in order to make it interoperable with an independently created computer program. Likewise, no cause of action arises for trafficking under § 1201(a)(2) or (b) if the defendant develops or employs a means of circumvention for purposes of such reverse engineering. To a limited extent, the information obtained, or means of circumvention employed, under these exceptions may be shared with others engaged in such reverse engineering. The reverse engineering exceptions do not apply, however, if the defendant's actions constitute copyright infringement. 17 U.S.C. § 1201(f)(1).

Encryption research. This exemption applies to activities necessary to study flaws in encryption technologies applied to copyrighted works, for the purpose of advancing encryption technology (defined as the scrambling and unscrambling of information using mathematical formulas). 17 U.S.C. § 1201(g).

In the case of published works, this exemption allows circumvention of access protection where necessary to conduct good faith encryption research, if the person lawfully obtained the encrypted material and made a good faith effort to obtain authorization before the circumvention, provided that the circumvention is not infringing or otherwise unlawful.

The exemption also allows a person to develop and employ the means to carry out circumvention for the sole purpose of good faith encryption research, and to share the means of circumvention with another person with whom he or she is collaborating in such research.

Exceptions regarding minors. This exemption provides that, in applying the § 1201(a) prohibition against making or trafficking in a component or part of an access circumvention technology, courts may consider the necessity for its incorporation (actual or intended) in a technology designed solely to prevent minors from accessing material on the Internet. 17 U.S.C. § 1201(h).

Protection of personally identifying information. This exemption permits circumvention of an access protection measure when all of the following conditions are met:

(1) the measure, or the work it protects, is capable of collecting or disseminating identifying information about the online activities of a person seeking to access the protected work;

(2) the measure, or the work it protects, collects or disseminates identifying information about the person seeking to access the protected work, without providing that person with conspicuous notice and the opportunity to prevent or restrict this collection or dissemination;

(3) the act of circumvention has the sole effect of identifying and disabling this ability to collect and disseminate such identifying information, and does not otherwise affect a person's ability to access any work; and

(4) the act of circumvention has the sole purpose of preventing the collection or dissemination of such identifying information, and is not otherwise unlawful.

Security Testing. Section 1201(j)(2) permits circumvention to access a computer, computer system, or computer network, with the consent of its owner or operator, solely for good faith testing, investigation, or correction of security flaws or vulnerabilities. Section 1201(j)(3) lists factors to be considered in determining whether a particular person qualifies for this exemption. Section 1201(j)(4) permits development, distribution, and use of circumvention technology for use in such security testing.

C. Analog Copy Protection Technology

Section 1201(k) prohibits the manufacture, importation, or distribution of analog videocassette recording devices that fail to integrate automatic gain control copy control technology, a copy control system that applies to analog video signals.

D. Case Law Interpreting § 1201

The trafficking prohibitions in §§ 1201(a)(2) and (b) have proven controversial, as they can prevent parties from making available the tools necessary to access and use protected works even for purposes that are lawful, non-infringing, and in the public interest. In an early decision, *Universal City Studios, Inc. v. Reimerdes,* 111 F. Supp.2d 294 (S.D.N.Y. 2000), the defendant developed a program to circumvent the CSS protection technology which the plaintiffs used to control access to their motion picture DVDs, and posted the executable code on the Internet. When the plaintiffs brought § 1201(a) claims based on trafficking, the district court held that it was immaterial whether the defendant's purpose was to facilitate copyright infringement or to engage in non-infringing activities (such as developing a Linux DVD player), because the conduct did not fall within one of § 1201's narrow statutory exceptions. The court also held that, notwithstanding the reference to fair use in § 1201(c), it was no defense that the defendant's technology could be used by persons seeking to make fair use of CSS-protected works: "Congress elected to leave technologically unsophisticated persons who wish to make fair use of encrypted copyrighted works without the technical means of doing so." *Id.* at 324. On appeal, the Second Circuit agreed:

> [Section 1201(c)] simply clarifies that the DMCA targets the *circumvention* of digital walls guarding copyrighted material (and trafficking in circumvention tools), but does not concern itself with the *use* of those materials after circumvention has occurred. Subsection 1201(c)(1) ensures that the DMCA is not read to prohibit the "fair use" of information just because that information was obtained in a manner made illegal by the DMCA.

Universal City Studios, Inc. v. Corley, 273 F.3d 429, 443 (2d Cir. 2001); *see also id.* at 459 ("Fair use has never been held to be a guarantee of access to copyrighted material in order to copy it by the fair user's preferred technique or in the format of the original.")

Some courts have expressed concern that § 1201 might be used to limit the rights which copyright law gives to consumers who purchase electronic goods containing copyrighted material. For example, in *Chamberlain Group, Inc. v . Skylink Techs., Inc.,* 381 F.3d 1178 (Fed. Cir. 2004), the defendant sold a universal garage door remote transmitter that a homeowner could program to operate garage door openers purchased from the plaintiff. The defendant's transmitter circumvented the plaintiff's access protection software in order to be interoperable with the copyrighted software in the plaintiff's opener. In rejecting the plaintiff's trafficking claim, the Federal Circuit noted that if these facts rendered the defendant liable for trafficking, then they also rendered the homeowners liable for circumvention. The court rejected such a construction of the statute as "absurd and disastrous," noting that it would allow the manufacturer to restrict a consumer's right to use its product in conjunction with competing goods, a restriction the court viewed as copyright misuse. *Id.* at 1201. The court concluded that § 1201 "prohibits only forms of access that bear a reasonable relationship to the protections that the Copyright Act otherwise affords copyright owners." *Id.* at 1202. The court then laid out what it considered the necessary elements for a § 1201(a) trafficking claim:

A plaintiff alleging a violation of § 1201(a)(2) must prove: (1) ownership of a valid copyright on a work, (2) effectively controlled by a technological measure, which has been circumvented, (3) that third parties can now access (4) without authorization, in a manner that (5) infringes or facilitates infringing a right protected by the Copyright Act, because of a product that (6) the defendant either (i) designed or produced primarily for circumvention; (ii) made available despite only limited commercial significance other than circumvention; or (iii) marketed for use in circumvention of the controlling technological measure. A plaintiff incapable of establishing any one of elements (1) through (5) will have failed to prove a prima facie case. A plaintiff capable of proving elements (1) through (5) need prove only one of (6)(i), (ii), or (iii) to shift the burden back to the defendant. At that point, the various affirmative defenses enumerated throughout § 1201 become relevant.

Id. at 1203. Here, the plaintiff failed to make the necessary showing under elements (4) and (5), because its sale of garage door openers carried with it an implied license permitting its customers to use the openers, and because copyright law did not give the plaintiff a right to prevent its customers from using their openers in conjunction with competing products.

Other courts have cautioned that similar abuse could occur where a merchant incorporates a minor software component in an otherwise uncopyrightable product in order to control consumers' ability to use the product in conjunction with competing aftermarket goods, such as replacement parts. For example, in *Lexmark International, Inc. v. Static Control Components, Inc.,* 387 F.3d 522 (6th Cir. 2004), the defendant supplied a microchip that circumvented the authentication technology used by the plaintiff to prevent customers from refilling and reusing its toner cartridges. Because the cartridges also contained additional copyrighted software, the plaintiff argued that the defendant was trafficking in a circumvention device under § 1201(a)(2). However, the Sixth Circuit rejected that claim, finding that the plaintiff's authentication technology did not in fact block access to the copyrighted software contained in its cartridges. *Id.* at 547–49. Thus, the defendant's microchip did not circumvent any technology that was actually being used to control access to a copyrighted work.

In contrast to *Lexmark*, the Eighth Circuit found violations of both § 1201(a)(1) (circumvention of access control) and § 1201(a)(2) (trafficking in access control circumvention device) in *Davidson & Assocs. v. Jung*, 422 F.3d 630 (8th Cir. 2005), where online gamers found a way to make the plaintiff's copyrighted video games available to multiple players online while bypassing the technological measures used by the plaintiff to verify that each player in the multiplayer environment had an authorized copy of the game. Unlike the software in *Lexmark*, the copyrighted games in *Davidson* were in fact protected by the plaintiff's access controls. Accordingly, the Eighth Circuit held that the defendants were liable for both circumvention and trafficking.

Unlike § 1201(a), § 1201(b) prohibits trafficking in devices that circumvent copy protection, but it does not prohibit the circumvention itself. Thus, a person who lawfully gains access to a copy-protected copyrighted work may circumvent that protection for a lawful purpose, such as making fair use of the work. However, anyone who provides the technology necessary to accomplish this circumvention faces liability for trafficking. Thus, it appears that

§ 1202(b) permits circumvention of copy protection, but does not allow anyone to provide the means by which that circumvention may be accomplished. This issue was explored in *United States v. Elcom*, 203 F. Supp.2d 1111 (N.D.Cal. 2002), where the government brought criminal charges against a defendant for supplying a device that allowed ebook readers to circumvent the publisher's restrictions on, *inter alia*, making a copy of the ebook. The district court held that while Congress chose to permit circumvention of copy protection in order to make sure that § 1201 would not preclude fair use of a work, fair use was irrelevant to the trafficking charge, because the most common use of circumvention devices would be for infringing copying rather than fair use copying.

Section 1201 has survived several First Amendment challenges. For example, when *Reimerdes* was appealed, the Second Circuit held that § 1201 liability for trafficking could arise from merely linking to websites that posted the circumvention code, and that such liability did not run afoul of the First Amendment, because the trafficking prohibition was a content-neutral regulation that did not burden substantially more speech than necessary to further the government's legitimate interests. *Universal City Studios, Inc. v. Corley*, 273 F.3d 429, 455 (2d Cir. 2001).

§ 12.4   Copyright Management Information

Section 1202, also added by the DMCA, creates two causes of action designed to prevent the falsification or the unauthorized alteration or removal of copyright management information attached to or accompanying a copyrighted work.

As defined in § 1202(c), "copyright management information" consists of certain information conveyed in connection with copies, phonorecords, performances, or displays of a work, including in digital form. The definition encompasses any of the following types of information (but does not include any personally identifying information about a user):

(1) the title and other information identifying the work, including the information contained in a notice of copyright;

(2) the name of, and other identifying information about, the work's author;

(3) the name of, and other identifying information about, the work's copyright owner, including the information contained in a notice of copyright;

(4) the name of, and other identifying information about, a performer whose performance is fixed in a work other than an audiovisual work (except that this category does not apply to public performances by radio and television broadcast stations);

(5) in the case of an audiovisual work, the name of, and other identifying information about, a writer, performer, or director who is credited in the audiovisual work (except that this category does not apply to public performances by radio and television broadcast stations);

(6) terms and conditions for use of the work;

(7) identifying numbers or symbols referring to such information or links to such information; or

(8) such other information as the Register of Copyrights provides by regulation.

Section 1202(a) creates a cause of action against any person that knowingly, and with the intent to induce, enable, facilitate or conceal infringement, provides, distributes, or imports for distribution any false copyright management information.

In addition, under § 1202(b), liability may arise from undertaking any of the following actions without the authority of the copyright owner or any other legal authorization:

(1) intentionally removing or altering copyright management information;

(2) distributing, or importing for distribution, copyright management information which the defendant knows has been removed or altered without the authority of the copyright owner or any other legal authorization; or

(3) distributing, importing for distribution, or publicly performing works, copies, or phonorecords, knowing that copyright management information has been removed or altered without the authority of the copyright owner or any other legal authorization.

Civil liability under § 1202 arises only if the defendant that undertakes any of these actions either knew or had reasonable grounds to know that it would induce, enable, facilitate, or conceal an infringement of any right under Title 17. Criminal penalties apply only if the defendant had actual knowledge that its actions would have such consequences.

Section 1202(b) does not apply to government employees or government contractors engaged in lawfully authorized investigative, protective, information security, or intelligence activities. 17 U.S.C. § 1202(d).

Section 1202(e) creates two additional exceptions to liability under § 1202(b). In the case of analog transmissions, § 1202(b) does not apply to broadcast stations or cable systems making analog transmissions, or to those who provide programming for such a station or system, if:

(1) avoiding a violation of § 1202(b) would not be technically feasible or would create an undue financial hardship, *and*

(2) the defendant did not intend to induce, enable, facilitate or conceal infringement of a right under Title 17.

In the case of digital transmissions, § 1202(b) does not apply to a situation in which all of the following conditions are satisfied:

(1) the category of works in question is the subject of a digital transmission standard (established through a voluntary consensus standard-setting process that meets the requirements of § 1202(e)(2)(A)) for the placement of copyright management information;

    (2) a person (other than the defendant) failed to adhere to that standard in placing the copyright management information in question; and

    (3) the defendant did not intend to induce, enable, facilitate or conceal an infringement.

If no digital transmission standard has yet been established for placement of copyright management information with respect to the category of works in question, then § 1202(b) will not apply if the defendant did not intend to induce, enable, facilitate or conceal an infringement, and either:

    (1) transmission of the copyright management information would degrade the digital signal; or

    (2) transmission of the information would conflict with a government regulation or an industry-wide standard (meeting certain statutory requirements).

§ 12.5 Civil Remedies and Criminal Penalties

Civil remedies for violations of §§ 1201 and 1202 include temporary and permanent injunctions, impounding of the circumvention product (while the action is pending), damages, costs and reasonable attorney's fees (at the court's discretion), and destruction or remedial modification of the circumvention product (upon rendering of a final judgment or decree finding a violation).

Damages may include actual damages arising from the violation, as well as the defendant's profits therefrom, to the extent that these are not duplicative. In the alternative, at any time before the final judgment is entered, the plaintiff may elect to recover statutory damages. For violations of § 1201, the court may award statutory damages of $200–$2500 per act of circumvention, product, component, offer, or performance of service. For violations of § 1202, the court may award statutory damages of $2500–$25,000 per violation. Where a defendant has committed a second violation within three years after being found liable under § 1201 or § 1202, the court may increase any damages awarded, up to triple the amount that would otherwise be awarded.

A court may reduce or remit damages if the defendant was not aware, and had no reason to believe, that its actions violated § 1201 or § 1202. In such a case, the court is *required* to remit damages if the defendant is also a nonprofit library, archive, educational institution, or public broadcasting entity.

A violation of § 1201 or § 1202 gives rise to criminal penalties if the violation is willful and for purposes of commercial advantage or private financial gain. Criminal penalties include a fine of up to $1,000,000 ($500,000 for a first offense), and/or up to ten years imprisonment (five years for a first offense). These criminal penalties do not apply to nonprofit libraries, archives, educational institutions, and public broadcasting entities.

CHAPTER 13
PREEMPTION

§ 13.1 Introduction

Federal copyright law preempts enforcement of state statutes or common law in a number of situations. There are two types of copyright preemption: (1) *statutory* preemption, under § 301 of the Copyright Act, which applies when a state law provides protection *equivalent* to federal copyright law; and (2) *conflict* preemption, which applies when a state law interferes with the purposes and objectives of federal copyright or patent law. Both types of preemption are grounded in the Supremacy Clause of the Constitution. In analyzing a preemption question, it is important to consider both types of preemption, because a state law that is not preempted by § 301 may nonetheless be preempted due to conflict with the overall federal scheme of copyright or patent law.

§ 13.2 Statutory Preemption

The origins of statutory preemption under § 301 lie in the 1976 Copyright Act, under which, for the first time, federal copyright protection was extended to all works of authorship beginning at the moment of tangible fixation, regardless of whether the work was published. The 1909 Act, in contrast, denied federal copyright protection to most unpublished works, relegating them to the protection of common law copyright under state law. When unpublished works were brought within the scope of federal copyright protection in the 1976 Act, Congress enacted § 301 to establish that, on and after January 1, 1978, works of authorship fixed in a tangible medium of expression would be protected exclusively by federal copyright law.

Preemption under § 301 applies only to state laws; no federal laws are subject to statutory preemption.

Under § 301, the analysis of whether preemption applies depends initially on whether the state law in question creates rights similar to § 106 or to § 106A. The analysis is somewhat different, depending on which copyright statute is implicated. Section 301(a) addresses preemption with respect to § 106, and § 301(f) addresses preemption with respect to § 106A.

A. Preemption Under § 301(a)

Legal or equitable rights afforded by state law are preempted under § 301(a) only if both of the following conditions are satisfied:

(1) the legal or equitable right is "equivalent to any of the exclusive rights within the general scope of copyright as specified by section 106"; and

(2) the legal or equitable right applies to "works of authorship that are fixed in a tangible

medium of expression and come within the subject matter of copyright''.

Rights equivalent to rights within the general scope of copyright under § 106. Statutory preemption applies only to state laws establishing legal or equitable rights that are equivalent to rights within the general scope of § 106. Courts interpret this restriction to mean that preemption applies to a state law right if that right would be abridged by an act which, in and of itself, would infringe one of the § 106 rights. In contrast, if the state law requires proof of an "extra element" instead of or in addition to the acts of reproduction, performance, distribution, adaptation, or display, § 301 does not preempt it. The extra element must be one that makes the nature of the action qualitatively different from a copyright claim. In addition, the extra element must be something other than the defendant's state of mind. Thus, for example, § 301 would preempt a state law providing a cause of action for "intentional" copying or distribution of a copyrightable work.

If the state law concerns conduct broader than that which is prohibited by § 106—for example, a state law prohibiting all performances of a work, rather than just public performances—preemption will apply. The result is likely to be the same in many instances where the state law applies to a quantitatively narrower range of conduct—for example, only public performances for audiences of 1000 or more. However, if the narrower range of conduct is defined not by a difference in scope but by a difference in the qualitative nature of the conduct (other than mental state), the "extra element" test is likely to be satisfied, and preemption will not apply. It is less clear whether statutory preemption would apply where state law protects a right not encompassed by § 106—for example, where state law recognizes an exclusive right in private, but not public, performances. (In this example, even if statutory preemption does not apply, a court is likely to find conflict preemption on the ground that Congress intended to insulate private performances from interference by the copyright owner.)

State law causes of action which typically involve an "extra element" insulating them from § 301 preemption include:

Cause of Action	*Extra Element*
Breach of contract	Promise and breach
Trademark infringement	Likelihood of confusion
Unfair competition	Likelihood of confusion
Breach of confidence	Promise and breach
Breach of fiduciary duty	Fiduciary duty and breach
Trade secret misappropriation	Secret obtained by improper means
Invasion of privacy	Privacy interest

Even with respect to these categories, however, the preemption question requires an analysis of the particular state law in question to determine whether in fact an extra element is required. Thus, for example, § 301 would likely preempt a state unfair competition law which prohibits copying another's protected expression without evidence that the expression serves as a trademark and that the copying creates a likelihood of confusion as to source. In contrast, a claim of "passing off" is unlikely to be preempted, even where the defendant has passed off his own copyrightable expression as that of another (for example, if a defendant published a novel under John Grisham's name when it was authored by another), because passing off involves the extra element of likelihood of deceit or confusion as to source. While a likelihood of deceit or confusion as to source is also an element of "reverse passing off"—for example, where a publisher removes an author's name from a manuscript and publishes it under another name—it has been suggested that courts will be more inclined to find preemption here, on the theory that the extra element of source confusion is a relatively minor component of a claim that is based largely on unauthorized reproduction and distribution. In a case involving a film that had already entered the public domain, the Supreme Court held that recognizing a claim for reverse passing off would create an unacceptable "mutant" species of copyright law. *Dastar Corp. v. Twentieth Century Fox Film Corp.*, 539 U.S. 23 (2003). Although in this case the reverse passing off claim was grounded in federal law (§ 43(a) of the Lanham Act), the Court's reasoning strongly suggests that it would have found the claim preempted had it been brought under state law.

Outside of the context of trade secrets, courts have generally held that § 301 preempts state law claims based on misappropriation of uncopyrightable information. Some of these courts have engaged in fine hair-splitting in an effort to distinguish the Supreme Court's decision in *International News Service v. Associated Press*, 248 U.S. 215 (1918), which upheld an injunction preventing one news service from copying information from a competitor's news bulletins and newspapers. Although no copyrightable expression was taken, the Court recognized a limited, temporary, quasi-property interest in information constituting "hot news," and held that this interest was protectible under unfair competition law. There is considerable doubt whether *INS* remains good law, and subsequent case law makes clear that whatever validity it retains today is limited to its specific facts. Because *INS* was decided long before enactment of § 301, it is questionable whether, on the same facts, the Court would hold that a similar state law survives statutory preemption today. Nonetheless, the legislative history of § 301 specifically mentions *INS*, and states Congress's intent not to preempt this type of claim. Therefore, courts continue to try to distinguish *INS* even while holding, for example, that § 301 *does* preempt state law protection of real-time information gleaned from copyrighted broadcasts. Many of these distinctions are simply unpersuasive. *See, e.g., National Basketball Ass'n v. Motorola, Inc.,* 105 F.3d 841 (2d Cir. 1997) (suggesting that the "extra element" in *INS* was the fact that the defendant's activity threatened the very existence of the plaintiff's business).

While most breach of contract claims contain the "extra element" necessary to avoid preemption, courts and commentators have been careful to distinguish claims based on "quasi-contract" (also known as "contracts implied in law") from claims based on express contracts or contracts implied in fact. While the latter two categories are true contract claims which involve an exchange of promises, claims based on quasi-contract are not. Quasi-contract claims are based on the unauthorized use of the plaintiff's property, and the duty to compensate the plaintiff is imposed by law in order to avoid unjust enrichment. Thus, it has been held that a quasi-contract claim for the unauthorized copying, distribution, performance, adaptation, or display of a fixed work of authorship is preempted because it does not involve an "extra element" to distinguish it from a § 106 claim.

Courts have had particular difficulty applying statutory preemption analysis to right of publicity claims and claims for breach of "shrinkwrap" licensing agreements.

A shrinkwrap license is non-negotiated agreement that accompanies the purchase of a copy of a copyrighted work—typically, computer software. The copyright owner purports to license (rather than sell) to the purchaser the copyrighted content embodied in the tangible good, and imposes a series of conditions and restrictions on the use of the copy and/or the copyrighted content. These conditions and restrictions typically purport to limit or negate the rights which copyright law ordinarily grants to the purchaser of a lawfully made copy, such as the § 109 first sale privilege, fair use under § 107, or the § 117 copying privilege for software.

Some courts have held that shrinkwrap license claims are not preempted by § 301 because the existence of a contract provides the necessary extra element. One court, however, has held that such claims are preempted where the contract requires the licensee to waive an important statutory privilege otherwise granted by copyright law. (However, as discussed in § 13.3 below, this court relied on conflict preemption rather than § 301 preemption).

With respect to the right of publicity, the legislative history states that such a claim would not be preempted if it contains an "extra element" such as an invasion of personal rights, a breach of confidentiality, or a likelihood of confusion. While right of privacy claims clearly involve an invasion of personal rights, right of publicity claims are based on an injury to the commercial value of property. Some courts and commentators have also suggested a broader argument against preempting the right of publicity, arguing that a person's voice, likeness, and identity are not copyrightable subject matter. However, where the plaintiff has already consented to the commercial use of his or her likeness in a copyrighted work (such as a photograph or motion picture) some courts have held that the right of publicity is preempted with respect to that particular work. Alternatively, where a person's "identity" is conjured up by using a copyrighted work that is closely associated with that person (typically music), some courts have applied preemption. Where the right of publicity is based on imitation of a musician's sound recording, several courts have held that there is no preemption, because § 114(b) provides that imitating a sound recording is not copyright infringement, no matter how close the imitation. (See § 8.7 above.)

Works of authorship fixed in a tangible medium of expression which fall within the subject matter of copyright. This restriction establishes that § 301 does not preempt state laws protecting subject matter that is categorically ineligible for federal copyright protection. For example, state law may protect works that are not fixed in a tangible medium of expression, such as impromptu speeches, conversations, live sporting events, and other improvisational performances. (Most states, however, do not have a well-developed body of law regarding protection for such events.)

Sound recordings that were fixed in the United States before February 15, 1972 are an important category of works of authorship that are excluded from the subject matter of copyright—so important, in fact, that § 301(c) addresses them specifically, stating that § 301 will not preempt rights or remedies provided by state law with respect to such works until February 15, 2067. Due to the commercial significance of these works, states are rapidly developing a body of law addressing their protection. Beginning on February 15, 2067, however, § 301(c) provides that these early recordings will be protected neither by state nor federal law. Any state law protecting these recordings after that date will be subject to preemption under the terms of § 301(a).

If a work fits within one of the general copyrightable subject matter categories under § 102 and
§ 103, but is unprotected by federal copyright because it is unoriginal, then § 301 will preempt any
state law that provides copyright-like protection to
the work. For example, if a poem is ineligible for
federal copyright because it was copied in its entirety, § 301 preemption will apply. Section 301 also
preempts application of state misappropriation laws
which prohibit the copying of uncopyrightable information from copyrighted works (such as information contained in a copyrighted biography, data
reproduced from copyrightable software, or real-
time scores and other information obtained from a
copyrighted broadcast of a basketball game). Although in these cases the information itself is not
copyrightable, this is because it lacks originality;
therefore, state law protection is preempted by
§ 301. The same result applies to any copyrightable
work that has entered the public domain.

B. Preemption Under § 301(f)

With the enactment of the Visual Artists Rights
Act (VARA) in 1990, Congress added § 301(f) to
indicate the circumstances in which state laws
would be preempted by the new moral rights provisions of §§ 106A and 113(d), effective June 1, 1991.
(The general provisions of VARA are discussed in
§ 7.8 above.) This provision, like § 301(a), applies
only to state laws, and thus has no preemptive
effect on any federal statutes.

In general, a state law is preempted by VARA if:

    (1) it provides legal or equitable rights that are equivalent to any of the rights provided by § 106A; and

    (2) the state law rights apply to "works of visual art," as defined in VARA.

Notwithstanding these general provisions, VARA preemption does not apply to:

    (1) a cause of action arising from undertakings commenced before June 1, 1991;

    (2) activities violating a legal or equitable right that is not equivalent to any of the rights conferred by § 106A with respect to works of visual art; or

    (3) activities violating legal or equitable rights "which extend beyond the life of the author."

While these provisions make clear that preemption would apply to a state law granting a right of attribution or a right of integrity to the author of a work of visual art during the creator's lifetime, the scope of VARA preemption is not always clear. For example, while it is clear that VARA's preemptive effect ends at the author's death, it is not clear whether VARA preempts a state moral rights law *during* the author's lifetime if the state law *also* applies postmortem. Also, because VARA has no postmortem preemptive effect, and because VARA protection for certain pre-VARA works applies postmortem, some works will enjoy postmortem protection under *both* state law and VARA.

Because § 301(f) preempts state laws only with respect to "works of visual art," a category that is narrowly defined in § 101, it does not preclude states from granting moral rights protection to other categories of works, such as music, sound recordings, literary works, and motion pictures. However, it has been suggested that at least some state laws of this nature might be preempted under § 301(a). For example, a state law granting a right of integrity to the author of a literary work could be seen as granting a right "equivalent" to the exclusive right to create derivative works under § 106(2); however, if the state's integrity right is unassignable (like the integrity right under VARA), it could be argued that the state-created right is not the "equivalent" of the § 106(2) right, which is assignable. Of course, there remains the possibility that conflict preemption would apply, since the author's retention of the unassignable integrity right could interfere with the exclusive rights of the copyright assignee under § 106.

C. No Preemption by § 1101

The anti-bootlegging statute codified at 17 U.S.C. § 1101, which offers limited protection against copying, distribution, or transmission of live musical performances. (see § 7.9 above), expressly states that it does not preempt any rights or remedies available under state laws. Thus, for example, states are free to apply their right of publicity laws to live musical performances. While there is no statutory preemption under § 1101, conflict preemption is still a possibility.

§ 13.3   Conflict Preemption

Even before enactment of statutory copyright preemption in 1976, it was well settled that, under the Supremacy Clause of the Constitution, states could not enact laws which interfered with the purposes of federal copyright or patent laws. Such interference may occur, for example, where a state extends protection to a work that Congress intended to place in the public domain (as in *Sears/Compco*, below), or where a state impedes the enforcement of a copyright owner's exclusive rights. This principle applies even after enactment of § 301, and can result in preemption of state laws that survive § 301 scrutiny. The purpose of conflict preemption in the fields of copyright and patent law is to promote national uniformity in the regulation of these forms of intellectual property. With respect to any subject matter, Congress must be free to decide what is protected by patent or copyright, and what belongs in the public domain, and no state may interfere with the balance struck by Congress.

The principle that state laws must not impede the goals of federal copyright and patent laws was established in the paired cases of *Sears, Roebuck & Co. v. Stiffel Co.*, 376 U.S. 225 (1964) and *Compco Corp. v. Day–Brite Lighting, Inc.* 376 U.S. 234 (1964), collectively known as *Sears/Compco*. Both cases involved the application of state unfair competition laws to prohibit the unauthorized copying of product designs that were neither copyrighted nor patented, where the finding of a likelihood of confusion was based only on the facts of copying and similarity. The Court refused to enforce the state law because it conflicted with the objectives of federal patent law, holding that, while a state could take appropriate steps, where necessary, to prevent consumer confusion as to the source of a product, "a State may not, when the article is unpatented and uncopyrighted, prohibit the copying of the article itself or award damages for such copying." *Sears*, 376 U.S. at 232–33. To allow a state to forbid copying in these circumstances "would interfere with the federal policy, found in Art. 1, § 8, cl. 8. of the Constitution and in the implementing federal statutes, of allowing free access to copy whatever the federal patent and copyright laws leave in the public domain." *Compco*, 376 U.S. at 237.

The fact that subject matter clearly falls within the scope of federal patent and/or copyright laws does not mean that states are automatically precluded from regulating that subject matter. For example, in *Kewanee Oil Co. v. Bicron Corp.*, 416 U.S. 470 (1974), the Court held that state regulation of trade secrets was not preempted; even though the ideas protected under state law were potentially patentable subject matter, the availability of trade secret protection as an alternative to patent protection did not, in the Court's view, frustrate the objectives of federal patent law. Thus, conflict preemption does not automatically apply to every state law that regulates subject matter within the general scope of subject matter addressed in the federal patent or copyright regimes.

The Court clarified and reaffirmed the principles of *Sears/Compco* and *Kewanee Oil* in *Bonito Boats, Inc. v. Thunder Craft Boats, Inc.*, 489 U.S. 141 (1989), by noting that states may place limited restrictions on the copying of unpatented trade dress (that is, elements of the design of a product or its packaging which function as trademarks) in order to prevent confusion as to source, even though trade dress may also be the subject of design patent protection (and, while not mentioned by the Court, copyright protection as well). However, the Court held that a state law prohibiting a specific method of copying the unpatented design of a boat hull (an uncopyrightable "useful article") was preempted under the Supremacy Clause, because Congress intended to permit the public to copy designs that do meet the requirements for patent or copyright protection. In 1998, Congress addressed boat hull designs in the Vessel Hull Design Protection Act, codified in Chapter 13 of Title 17, providing a ten-year term of limited federal protection for registered designs. (See § 7.10 above.)

Where Congress has clearly indicated its intent to protect a class of works, or to relegate a class of works to the public domain, the Supremacy Clause prevents states from overriding that decision, because Congress has the exclusive right to regulate with respect to those works. However, in *Goldstein v. California*, 412 U.S. 546 (1973), the Court recognized that there can be situations in which Congress has not established any policy with respect to a particular class of works. In such cases, uniformity is not required, and the states are free to act. In *Goldstein*, the Court reached this conclusion with respect to a California criminal law that prohibited the unauthorized copying of uncopyrighted musical recordings. Although the Sound Recording Act of 1971 extended federal copyright protection to sound recordings, it applied only to sound recordings that were fixed on or after February 15, 1972. Today, § 301(c) explicitly defines the extent to which states may protect sound recordings fixed before that date, but during the years between the Sound Recording Act of 1971 and the 1976 Copyright Act, the copyright statutes were silent on the power of states to protect these early, uncopyrighted recordings. Addressing this statutory void in 1973, the *Goldstein* Court held that Congress had indicated no intention either to protect these recordings or to relegate them to the public domain, and thus California was free to craft its own scheme of protection. In distinguishing the state laws that were preempted in *Sears/Compco*, the Court observed:

> The application of state law in these cases to prevent the copying of articles which did not meet the requirements for federal protection disturbed the careful balance which Congress had drawn and thereby necessarily gave way under the Supremacy Clause of the Constitution. No comparable conflict between state law and federal law arises in the case of recordings of musical performances. In regard to this category of "Writ-

ings," Congress has drawn no balance; rather, it has left the area unattended, and no reason exists why the State should not be free to act.

412 U.S. at 570. Three years after the *Goldstein* decision, in § 301(c), Congress clearly expressed its intent to preempt state protection for sound recordings fixed before February 15, 1972, but also indicated that this statutory preemption would not take effect until February 15, 2047 (now extended to February 15, 2067 by the CTEA). With respect to any undertakings commenced before that date, state laws continue to be enforceable.

Lower courts have applied conflict preemption on many occasions to determine whether enforcement of a state law would impermissibly interfere with the goals of federal copyright law. Yet courts and commentators often disagree as to the proper outcome on similar facts. Although several courts have held that shrinkwrap licenses used in connection with selling a copy of computer software are enforceable under state contract laws and are not preempted, one court held that a state law enforcing a shrinkwrap license was preempted because (1) the licensing terms conflicted with the purchaser's rights under § 117, (2) the duration of the license could outlast the copyright term, and (3) the state law applied to all software, regardless of whether the software was copyrightable as an original work of authorship. *See Vault Corp. v. Quaid Software Ltd.*, 847 F.2d 255 (5th Cir. 1988).

In a widely criticized decision, the Ninth Circuit held that a state law allowing contracts of unspecified duration to be terminated at will was preempted by § 203 of the 1976 Act (which allows grantors to terminate copyright grants after 35 years, even if the grant specifies a longer term). *Rano v. Sipa Press, Inc.*, 987 F.2d 580 (1993). Other circuits have squarely rejected *Rano,* finding no conflict preemption, because § 203 does not *require* copyright grants to last for a minimum 35–year term. *Walthal v. Rusk*, 172 F.3d 481 (7th Cir. 1999); *Korman v. HBC Florida, Inc.,* 182 F.3d 1291 (11th Cir. 1999). The purpose of § 203 is to protect authors from being locked into unfavorable longterm contracts, and state law termination-at-will provisions support rather than conflict with that goal. In contrast, a state law that *prohibited* early terminations of copyright grants would be preempted by § 203 to the extent that it prevented grantors from terminating their contracts at the end of 35 years.

INDEX

Where there are multiple references, page numbers in **bold** indicate primary references.

†